ARNHEM
1944

WILLIAM F. BUCKINGHAM

Battles & Campaigns

A series of illustrated battlefield accounts covering the classical period through to the end of the twentieth century, drawing on the latest research and integrating the experience of combat with intelligence, logistics and strategy.

Series Editor

Hew Strachan, Chichele Professor of the History of War
at the University of Oxford

Published

Ross Anderson, *The Battle of Tanga 1914*
'An excellent book' *Peter Hart, author of Jutland 1916*

Ross Anderson, *The Forgotten Front. The East African Campaign 1914–1918*
'Excellent... fills a yawning gap in the historical record' *Gary Sheffield, Times Literary Supplement*

William Buckingham, *Arnhem 1944*
'Startling... reveals the real reason why the daring attack failed' *The Daily Express*

Brian Farrell, *The Defence & Fall of Singapore 1941–1942*
'An original and provocative new history of the battle that marked the end of the British empire' *Hew Strachan*

David M. Glantz, *Before Stalingrad*
'Another fine addition to Hew Strachan's excellent Battles and Campaigns series' *BBC History Magazine*

Michael K. Jones, *Bosworth 1485*
'Insightful and rich study of the battle... no longer need Richard play the villain' *Times Literary Supplement*

Martin Kitchen, *The German Offensives of 1918*
'Comprehensive and authoritative... first class' *Professor Holger H. Herwig, War in History*

M.K. Lawson, *The Battle of Hastings 1066*
A *BBC History Magazine* Book of the Year 2003

Marc Milner, *Battle of the Atlantic*
'The most comprehensive short survey of the U-boat battles' *Sir John Keegan*

A.J. Smithers, *The Tangier Campaign*
'The fullest account of the British Army's first major expedition abroad' *Professor Hew Strachan*

Tim Travers, *Gallipoli 1915*
'A book of the highest importance... masterly' *John Lee, The Journal of Military History*

Matthew C. Ward, *The Battle for Quebec 1759: Britain's Conquest of Canada*

Commissioned

Stephen Conway, *The Battle of Bunker Hill 1775*
Martin Kitchen, *El Alamein 1942–1943*
John Andreas Olsen, *Operation Desert Storm*
Michael Penman, *Bannockburn 1314*

ARNHEM
1944

WILLIAM F. BUCKINGHAM

The
History
Press

For everyone who helped this work to happen, to those who were there, and especially those who did not come back

Front Cover Illustration: The first lift into Wolfheze: Paratroopers from 1st Parachute Brigade drop onto DZ X, with LZ Z and unloaded Horsa gliders in the foreground. That the Horsas carried jeeps or artillery pieces of some kind is evident from their detached tail sections. National Archive USA. Courtesy of Tempus Archive.

Back Cover Illustration: Operation Garden: a British-manned M10 crosses a Bailey Bridge over the Meuse-Escaut Canal during the build-up to Market Garden. This was the type of bridge erected by the Guards Armoured Division over the Wilhelmina Canal at Son. National Archive USA.

First published in 2002 by Tempus Publishing Limited
This edition first published 2004

Reprinted 2015 by
The History Press
The Mill, Brimscombe Port
Stroud, Gloucestershire GL5 2QG
www.thehistorypress.co.uk

© William F. Buckingham, 2002, 2004, 2015

The right of William F. Buckingham to be identified as the Author
of this work has been asserted in accordance with the
Copyright, Designs and Patents Act 1988.

British Library Cataloguing in Publication Data.
A catalogue record for this book is available from the British Library.

ISBN 978 0 7524 3187 1

Typesetting and origination by Tempus Publishing Limited
Printed and bound in Great Britain

CONTENTS

INTRODUCTION

On Sunday 17 September 1944, 2,023 transport aircraft and 478 gliders lifted off from airfields across southern and eastern England. They were carrying troops from the US 82nd and 101st Airborne Divisions and the British 1st Airborne Division, and comprised the first wave of the largest airborne operation in history – Operation Market. The operational aim of Market was to open a sixty-mile corridor across five major water obstacles for Allied ground forces, codenamed Garden, running from the Belgian border to the Dutch town of Arnhem on the Lower Rhine. The strategic objective of Market Garden, to give the operation its full name, was to capitalise upon the German defeat in Normandy and bring the war to a close by the end of 1944 by opening a way into the North German Plain. The deepest penetration into German-held territory, to seize the road and rail bridges over the Lower Rhine at Arnhem, was entrusted to the British 1st Airborne Division, which was confidently informed to expect relief by friendly ground forces within forty-eight hours.

Nine days later, the remnants of the British 1st Airborne Division were evacuated from a precarious foothold on the north bank of the Lower Rhine three miles west of Arnhem. Only a little over the equivalent of a battalion succeeded in seizing the north end of the road bridge in Arnhem, where they were cut off and overrun after fighting for three days and four nights against overwhelming odds. The remainder of the Division was all but destroyed, first in futile attempts to reach their embattled colleagues at the bridge, and then holding the Oosterbeek pocket. Relieving ground forces from British 30 Corps took six days rather than the promised maximum forty-eight hours to reach the south bank of the Lower Rhine west of Arnhem. When they did arrive, they wasted two days deciding their next move, by which time it was too late to do anything other than assist in evacuating what was left of 1st Airborne across the river. A few figures illustrate the scale of 1st Airborne's defeat. Including the attached Polish 1st Independent Parachute Brigade, the Division took 11,920 men into Arnhem, of which 3,910 remained fit enough for evacuation. Of the rest, 1,485 were killed, and the remaining 6,525 were captured, the majority of them wounded.[1]

Thus what was claimed to be the premier British airborne formation was virtually destroyed, as was the attached 1st Polish Independent Parachute Brigade, and the British ground forces involved also suffered heavy losses they could ill afford by that stage of the war. Nor was the cost restricted to the British. The US 82nd and 101st Airborne Divisions suffered heavy losses, less in seizing their objectives, and more in keeping the corridor south of Arnhem open after British 30 Corps had relieved them. The fact that both US Divisions remained in the front-line in Holland for several weeks after 1st Airborne was withdrawn is frequently overlooked. The 82nd Airborne was not withdrawn until 11 November 1944, after fifty-six days in continuous action, during which it suffered a total of 3,400 casualties; the 101st Airborne was not withdrawn until almost the end of November, and suffered 3,792 casualties.[2]

Examination of what happened at Arnhem began virtually as soon as 1st Airborne's survivors had been evacuated across the Lower Rhine. In the fifty-eight years since then, over twenty books, two feature films and several television documentaries dealing specifically with the battle have appeared. As one would expect with this degree of coverage, the course of events that led up to Market Garden and during the fighting at Arnhem and Oosterbeek have been pretty firmly established, and the main factors that contributed to the failure of the operation have been at least identified. However, this near exhaustive coverage has been confined almost exclusively to recounting the battle and events immediately preceding it. Such an approach is valid, but it has two main problems. First, the root of many of the drawbacks that contributed to the failure of Market Garden pre-dated September 1944 by a considerable period, and the narrow focus thus misses some of the context vital for a full understanding. Second, this preference for narrative at the expense of analysis has led to an over-concentration on detailing a relatively small corner of the canvas, to the detriment of the bigger picture. It also means that many well known factors have received far less comment than they in fact merit.

For example, the most salient reason for the 1st Airborne Division's failure at Arnhem was the distance between the landing zones and the bridges that were the Division's objective. Most accounts acknowledge the fact that these zones were chosen by the RAF planners, and that their choice was allowed to stand despite the misgivings and, in some cases outright objection from the airborne soldiers involved. However, this was not, as some accounts imply, an isolated occurrence arising from specific circumstances. Taking the long view clearly shows that this was in fact official policy that dated back to the very beginning of the British airborne force, when the Air Ministry secured untrammelled control over the air side of airborne operations as the price for its co-operation in the project. The result was an airborne planning machine totally controlled by the RAF, in which the planners formulated their schemes totally divorced from any operational considerations but their own, and with no requirement to act upon, or even acknowledge, those of the airborne soldiers tasked to carry them out.

Taking the long view also highlights the very significant part British army politics played in the failure of Operation Market. Brigadier Frederick 'Boy' Browning, the so-called 'Father of British Airborne Forces', was appointed commander of the 1st Airborne Division when the formation was created as a non-operational titular headquarters for the British airborne effort in November 1941. By September 1944 he had risen to Major-General and as deputy-commander of the 1st Allied Airborne Army, was the most senior soldier in the Allied airborne hierarchy. However, this spectacular progress was based purely on political aptitude and ruthless ambition, for despite received wisdom and his own pretensions Browning had no operational airborne experience at all. It is therefore significant that, having decided to accompany the Market force to Holland, Browning was one of the main drivers behind the operation, and that he approved the Arnhem air plan even though it flew in the face of all airborne experience to date. Browning's political machinations also impacted directly on the 1st Airborne Division, for he was responsible for dispatching it to Arnhem commanded by an officer with even less airborne experience than himself. Major-General Robert Elliot Urquhart was given the command at the beginning of 1944 purely as a favour to Montgomery. The crux of this particular problem was the British army's tendency to value personal recommendation over specialist expertise or operational experience.

These are not necessarily new revelations, although they and other elements that played a part in the outcome at Arnhem have not until now received the detailed analysis they warrant. In addition, this work examines three factors that have received little, if any, attention previously. First, there is the condition of the British 1st Airborne Division. Despite its crucial role in events, there has been an unquestioning acceptance that the Division was the longest established and most highly experienced British airborne formation. However, an examination of 1st Airborne's development from its establishment as an operational entity at the beginning of 1942 casts serious doubt on this received wisdom. In practical terms the Division had existed for only fourteen months when it embarked on Operation Market, only the first five of which were operational, and it contained a high proportion of inexperienced personnel drafted in to replace losses sustained in the Mediterranean. Arguably more seriously, the Division made less than effective use of the available training time in the first half of 1944 and, apart from a single week-long training exercise, it had never functioned as a complete operational entity until it arrived on the ground near Arnhem.

Second, there is the matter of the 1st Polish Independent Parachute Brigade, commanded by Major-General Stanislaw Sosabowski, which was attached to the 1st Airborne Division for Market Garden.

Most accounts of the battle do little more than detail the Poles' courageous but futile attempts to cross the Lower Rhine, although at least one recent work mentions the post-battle attempt by Browning and others to blame the Poles, and Sosabowski in particular, for the failure of Market Garden.[3] This shameful episode can only be put into its proper context by taking the long view. In fact, the Poles made a series of major but unacknowledged contributions to British airborne development while building their parachute brigade, which became operational in September 1941. Sosabowski earned Browning's enmity by repeatedly frustrating attempts to subsume the Polish formation into the British airborne force, which began as soon as the latter assumed command of 1st Airborne Division HQ. When Browning finally got his way, Sosabowski compounded his original error by publicly questioning the wisdom of Operations Comet and Market, and then by criticising the senior British officers involved in the latter, including Browning. There was thus much more to the selection of the hapless Pole as a scapegoat and the slandering of his men's courage than the fact that they were available.

Finally, there is the matter of the battle narrative. As stated above, the course of events at Arnhem between 17 and 25 September 1944 has been pretty firmly established, although almost exclusively from the British side. The same can be said for events in the airborne corridor, which is contained primarily in US accounts. In recent years, however, material dealing with the German side has also become available, and this new information casts a significantly different light on some aspects. This work is therefore an attempt to weave together all three perspectives.

In closing I should like to extend my thanks to the following individuals: Mr William J. Stone, formerly of the 321st Field Artillery, 101st Airborne Division, for allowing me to quote from his personal account; Ms Mary Wilkinson, of the Imperial War Museum's Department of Printed Books, for her kind permission to reproduce maps from Otway's *Airborne Forces*; Hew Strachan, for providing me with this opportunity and valuable guidance and advice; and my son Chris, for acting as sounding board, unpaid research assistant and putting up with all the inconvenience.

FROM PARACHUTE RAIDERS TO AN ARM OF SERVICE

THE ESTABLISHMENT OF THE BRITISH AIRBORNE FORCE AND THE
1ST AIRBORNE DIVISION, JUNE 1940–DECEMBER 1943

Virtually all accounts of, and references to, the battle of Arnhem adhere to two constants. The first is largely to ignore prior developments apart from those in the immediate run up to the battle. Such a narrow focus is, of course, perfectly valid, but it misses some of the underlying reasons for what happened at Arnhem. This restricted context leads into the second constant, which is an unquestioning acceptance of the received wisdom that the British 1st Airborne Division was a long established and highly experienced British airborne formation. We shall therefore begin with a brief examination of the development of the British airborne force for two reasons. First, in order to establish the accuracy of received wisdom regarding the 1st Airborne Division, and second to detail the involvement in that process of the man who bears the single greatest responsibility for what happened at Arnhem: Frederick 'Boy' Browning.

Although the British had been leading exponents of transporting troops and materiel by air in the empire through the inter-war period, the catalyst for the establishing of a parachute and glider force at home was the German airborne assault on the Low Countries in May 1940. As the RAF was an independent service, the project of raising a force of 5,000 parachutists had to be a joint venture with the army. The price of securing the Air Ministry's overt co-operation was agreement with the principle that the RAF maintained sole control over all planning, including the selection of landing areas, until the troops were on the ground. This seemingly innocuous arrangement was marginally acceptable for small-scale raiding operations, but it was to be directly responsible for the most serious flaw in the Arnhem portion of the Market Garden plan. The War Office merged the parachute effort into the Commando raiding force for administrative convenience, the RAF set up the beginnings of a training infrastructure, and No.2 Commando commenced training at RAF Ringway at the beginning of July 1940. Officially, the upshot was both services successfully co-operating under difficult circumstances, albeit with a little friction. This cosy picture belies the reality. The army, while favourably disposed to the new project, initially minimised its involvement while making good the losses suffered at Dunkirk and preparing for seemingly imminent German invasion. The RAF, while pretending enthusiasm, privately viewed the whole project as an irrelevant distraction and a pointless diversion of resources, and came very close to strangling the new force at the outset by covertly acting against the wishes of the Prime Minister, Winston Churchill. This included unilaterally scaling back the size of the new force to 500, promoting the use of non-existent gliders as an alternative to the parachute, concealing possession of a number of suitable transport aircraft, and providing a handful of dangerously unsuitable obsolete bombers instead. The latter ploy, which initially cost the lives of some of the army parachute volunteers, was a recurring and deliberate feature of RAF aircraft provision even after the US began to provide numbers of Douglas C-47 transports from late 1943.

Consequently the new parachute force, which was rechristened No.11 Special Air Service (SAS) Battalion in November 1940, still numbered less than 500 basically trained parachutists by the end of April 1941.[1] Churchill's dissatisfaction with this coincided with renewed army interest led by the Chief of the Imperial General Staff (CIGS), Sir John Dill. The War Office issued a notification of its intent to expand the parachute force on 4 July 1941, and a conference on 23 July worked out the details for a parachute brigade of four battalions. A dedicated Airborne Forces Depot was to be set up at Hardwick Hall in Derbyshire, along with a brigade HQ and an 'Air Troop' from the Royal Engineers (RE). Two new parachute battalions were to be raised and trained by 1 March 1942, with a third to follow. Brigadier Richard Gale MC, a tough, uncompromising and operationally oriented officer, was chosen to command the 1st Parachute Brigade. The officer Gale selected to lead the new 3rd Parachute Battalion, Gerald Lathbury, was to command the brigade in Sicily and at Arnhem.

Gale's most immediate problem was the 11 SAS Battalion, which had gained a not totally undeserved reputation for poor discipline. The War Office recommended disbandment and dispersing any retained personnel across the brigade, but this failed to take into account the changes wrought by Lieutenant Colonel E.E. 'Eric' Down. Down merely laughed when greeted with boos and foot stamping on assuming command of 11 SAS Battalion in June 1941, and his uncompromising attitude resulted in him being labelled 'Dracula'. However, Down led by example in everything and in a short space of time became extremely popular with his men, gaining the more affectionate label 'Charlie Orange', the phonetic abbreviation for commanding officer. Gale was so impressed he merely re-named Down's unit the 1st Parachute Battalion. Down's tenure marked the point where the British airborne force changed from freebooting raiders to highly trained light infantry that merely used a novel method of transport to reach the battlefield.

The new parachute battalions began to form at Hardwick Hall in September 1941, and became operational in January 1942. While they were training 31 Independent Brigade Group was converted into a glider, or airlanding unit in British parlance, on 10 October 1941, thereby doubling the size of the British airborne force. Even more importantly, the War Office decided that the airborne force needed an overall HQ to oversee training and development, and to fight the new force's corner in Whitehall. The new CIGS, General Sir Alan Brooke, insisted on a divisional rather than force title for the new HQ. Brooke was a keen airborne supporter; he was think-ing ahead to a larger operational role for it, and he wanted the necessary command infrastructure set up in advance. The man selected to command the new HQ was Brigadier F.A.M. Browning DSO. A Grenadier Guardsman, Browning assumed command of

HQ 1st Airborne Division with the rank of acting Major-General on 3 November 1941.

Browning is frequently credited with single-handedly expanding the British airborne force to divisional size and beyond, and is routinely referred to as the 'father of British Airborne Forces', although there is little substance for such extravagant claims. The official records clearly show that the War Office, not to mention senior officers like Dill and Alan Brooke, were working toward expanding the airborne force long before Browning became involved. There are also far better candidates for the second sobriquet, such as Richard Gale, who personally transformed the British parachute effort into an airborne force in the accepted sense and led the 6th Airborne Division into Normandy, the most vital and successful British airborne operation ever mounted. Another strong contender was Lieutenant Colonel John Rock RE, who oversaw British airborne training, research and development from the very beginning until he was killed in a glider accident in October 1942. Certainly, Browning brought no operational expertise to his new command. His major claims to fame were establishing the tradition of the Adjutant riding his horse up the steps into the Grand Entrance at the Royal Military College at Sandhurst while serving in that capacity in the 1920s, and his marriage to the novelist Daphne du Maurier. It may also be significant that Browning did not receive an operational command at the outbreak of war in 1939. He served as Commandant and Officer in Charge of Records at the Small-Arms School until mid 1940, and commanded 128 Infantry Brigade and the 24th Guards Brigade in quick succession thereafter.[2]

Browning's pre-airborne career underlines the fact that he was selected to command 1st Airborne Division HQ solely because he was a well connected Guards officer, and thus the perfect choice to fight the airborne corner in Whitehall. As Down diplomatically pointed out, all military enterprises have a political aspect, and Browning was ideally suited for such a role because he had the power of the Brigade of Guards behind him, and thus by extension the power of the Monarchy too.[3] Browning was, as one would expect from an officer from such a background, a consummately

skilled political operator. The problem was that behind the charm-
ing exterior, he was also a ruthless and manipulative empire builder,
who brooked no opposition and displayed few scruples in the
pursuit of his ambition, even if this meant interfering in operational
matters and putting men's lives at risk. Far from being the 'father of
British Airborne Forces', Browning was in fact an opportunist who
saw Airborne Forces merely as a convenient means to further his
military career.

There is ample evidence to support these charges from the beginning of Browning's involvement with the airborne forces. In January
1942 Browning personally selected C Company, 2nd Parachute
Battalion, commanded by Major John Frost, to attack the German
radar station at Bruneval and acquire parts of the apparatus. After the
selection, Browning left his liaison officer, a Grenadier named Peter
Bromley-Martin, to act in his stead. This could be construed as
admirable confidence in a subordinate; a more sceptical observer
might interpret it as a contingency measure to distance Browning
from the possible repercussions of failure. Whichever, despite drawing
up his own scheme, Frost was presented with an elaborate plan that
detailed every aspect of how he was to carry out the operation. When
Frost questioned its rigidity, Bromley-Martin bluntly informed him
that he would be replaced if he refused to accept the plan without
modification, which Frost then did.[4] When the raid was launched on
the night of 27–28 February 1942, Frost's reservations proved justified, for the RAF dropped two sticks astray. Luckily all these men
were assigned to peripheral tasks; had it been any of the other designated groups, the imposed plan would have been unworkable.

In the event, the Bruneval raid was an outstanding success, and
the German apparatus seized gave Bomber Command a significant
lead in the radar war. This, however, was due to a combination of
luck and initiative by the men on the ground, and in spite of the
rigid plan rather than because of it. Frost suspected the plan was
drawn up by Bromley-Martin, which may have been the case, but
Browning was ultimately responsible and it is inconceivable that he
did not fully endorse the plan or the way in which it was imposed.[5]
Browning's actions are especially important because they mirror

precisely his behaviour during Market Garden. As we shall see, on both occasions he oversaw the imposition of unsuitable plans with no regard for the opinions of those tasked to carry them out, he interfered directly in operational matters despite his total lack of experience, and he also distanced himself from possible repercussions. Apart from the scale, the only significant difference was that in September 1944 Browning's behaviour had infinitely more serious consequences.

Browning's ambition and political skill are clear from the speed with which he climbed the airborne ladder. By mid-1942 he was the official British adviser on airborne forces to the Commanders in Chief in all theatres of war.[6] In May 1943 he was appointed Major-General Airborne Forces, and shortly thereafter was acting as Airborne Forces Adviser to all headquarters in North Africa, including Eisenhower's Allied Force Headquarters in Algiers.[7] As he lacked any operational airborne experience, quite what advice Browning was able to offer is open to question, not least because US airborne development and experience were at least equal to that of the British, and in advance in some instances. There was also the fact that the British were almost totally reliant on USAAF transport aircraft. This, however, did not prevent Browning acting in an extremely high-handed and arrogant manner toward his American allies.

Shortly after the commander of the US 82nd Airborne Division, Major-General Matthew B. Ridgeway, arrived in North Africa, Browning turned up unannounced at his HQ. Although they were nominally equal in rank, Browning demanded to see the American's plan for the up-coming Sicily operation, and left him in no doubt that he (Browning) was in charge. Browning reinforced the impression that he viewed the US airborne force as part of his personal fiefdom a few days later, when he cavalierly decided to inspect the US 509th Parachute Infantry Battalion without reference to Ridgeway or anyone else in the US chain of command. He then added insult to injury by attempting to have the 509th made honorary members of British Airborne Forces, complete with maroon berets. Some of this was undoubtedly down to a clash of personalities. Even without the arrogance, Browning the

Guardsman was a privileged stereotype guaranteed to upset American egalitarian sensibilities, and the fact that Ridgeway was a rather pompous individual convinced he was destined for greatness did not make him any easier to work with.

Ridgeway's enmity for Browning was reciprocated. In November 1943, Colonel James M. Gavin, commanding the US 505th Parachute Infantry Regiment, was posted temporarily to the Chief-of-Staff Supreme Allied Command (COSSAC) in London. While British Lieutenant-General Frederick Morgan was welcoming Gavin, Browning entered Morgan's office and in the ensuing conversation snidely criticised Ridgeway for not parachuting into Sicily with his Division the previous July.[8] This was extremely ill-mannered for a supposed military diplomat and rather hypocritical given that Browning lacked operational experience or any formal parachute qualification; Browning made only two training jumps and injured himself both times.[9] Admittedly, he did then train as a glider pilot, but it should be noted that he qualified on the General Aircraft Hotspur, which was little more than a glorified sport glider, and therefore nothing like the heavier and more demanding types flown into combat by the Glider Pilot Regiment. Incidentally, Ridgeway made a voluntary parachute jump at Fort Benning in mid-August 1942, even though as a divisional staffer he was not required to do so.[10] While he did not jump into Sicily, he did command his Division for the remainder of that campaign, and he jumped into Normandy with it on 6 June 1944, despite lacking formal parachute training.

In fact, Browning's extraordinary outburst to Gavin reveals the true reason for his antipathy toward Ridgeway. This was quite simply that the American was more qualified for the overall airborne command Browning coveted, and therefore posed an intolerable threat to his overweening ambition. In the event, Browning stayed ahead of his American rival and succeeded in reaching the second highest rung on the airborne ladder, but Ridgeway remained a constant threat to his supremacy.

As we have seen, 1st Airborne Division was established as an administrative HQ in November 1941. It was re-designated an operational formation in January 1942, although it was a considerable time before this goal was achieved. This was partly due to a lack of dedicated leadership. The re-designation meant that Browning was being expected to carry out two jobs simultaneously, and he naturally gravitated toward the Whitehall side. To be fair, the real blame for this lay with the CIGS, Alan Brooke, and the War Office, who saddled the airborne force with an unworkable compromise by failing to delineate clearly between research and development on the one hand and operational matters on the other. The situation was not properly rectified until the separate posts of Major-General Airborne Forces and Commander Airborne Establishments were created in May 1943, and 1st Airborne Division was given a full-time divisional commander. There were also organisational problems, not least of which was that the Division's paper War Establishment was not finalised until the second half of 1942. A lack of suitable volunteers retarded the raising of a second parachute brigade, leading to the scrapping of the voluntary principle and the practice of re-designating existing infantry battalions as parachute units from the middle of 1942. In addition, a near total lack of troop-carrying gliders prevented the 1st Airlanding Brigade from attaining operational status until well into 1943. Finally, 1st Airborne's plight was exacerbated yet further by the despatch of the 1st Parachute Brigade to North Africa for Operation Torch. This was done at Browning's instigation, and meant that the Division's other units, and especially the still forming 2nd Parachute Brigade, had to be stripped of parachute-qualified personnel to bring the 1st Parachute Brigade up to strength.[11]

There was no real justification for sending 1st Parachute Brigade to North Africa, and little was achieved apart from the virtual destruction of the brigade for no discernible return. All three of 1st Parachute Brigade's battalions carried out separate drops at Bône, Souk el Arba and Depienne on 12, 16 and 29 November 1942 respectively. The second two drops were carried out at the behest of the British 1st Army, commanded by General Sir Kenneth Anderson. Anderson seems to have disliked paratroops on principle, and revelled in his ignorance of the most basic requirements and realities of airborne employment. At one point he forbade the

1st Parachute Battalion to return if cloud obscured its drop zone; instead the battalion was to carry out an impromptu drop as near as possible to the enemy. Worse, the 2nd Parachute Battalion's drop at Depienne went ahead even though the ground attack it was supposed to spearhead was cancelled. Unfortunately no-one told Frost, and the 2nd Battalion was then obliged to carry out a three-day fighting withdrawal to friendly territory, losing almost half its strength: killed, wounded or missing in the process. It seems that 1st Army considered the 1st Parachute Brigade to be an expendable reconnaissance asset, and committed its constituent battalions merely because they were available. It therefore comes as no surprise that Anderson employed the brigade in the conventional infantry role in the severe fighting in Tunisia through the winter of 1942–43. The 1st Parachute Brigade spent almost five continuous months in the line, and suffered 1,700 casualties.

The 1st Airborne Division finally became an operational formation at the end of May 1943, when it concentrated in North Africa in preparation for the invasion of Sicily. By July it consisted of the rebuilt 1st, 2nd and 4th Parachute Brigades, the latter having been formed in the Middle East, and the 1st Airlanding Brigade. The Division was commanded by Browning's chosen successor Major-General George Hopkinson, former commander of the airlanding brigade. Hopkinson was a curious choice, because he lacked experience due to the continuing shortage of gliders. Browning may have thought this would make him easier to control, but if so he was sadly mistaken, for Hopkinson immediately went over Browning's head to Montgomery as part of a personal crusade to raise the profile of glider troops. This led to 1st Airlanding Brigade being assigned the vital task of seizing the Ponte Grande Bridge at Syracuse just ahead of the Sicilian invasion, even though the brigade was only partially trained and there were only a handful of gliders available.

Hopkinson ingeniously got around the latter handicap by obtaining 136 US Waco CG 4 gliders, but these were still in their packing crates, and the men from the Glider Pilot Regiment who were to fly them had never seen the type before, disassembled or otherwise. Neither were they trained in night flying, although the landing was to take place in darkness, and the chosen landing zone was criss-crossed with rocky outcrops and stone walls. When the glider pilot's commander, Lieutenant Colonel George Chatterton, attempted to point out the risks Hopkinson gave him the blunt choice of compliance or resignation. Like Frost the previous year, Chatterton complied for the sake of his men, and noted that Hopkinson was so delighted he behaved like a small boy.[12] One scathing assessment has likened Hopkinson to an overgrown Boy Scout, who presented a bigger danger to the men under his command than the enemy, and let his enthusiasm override his common sense.[13]

Unsurprisingly the landing on the night of 9–10 July 1943 was a fiasco, partly due to high winds, alert anti-aircraft defences and a light mist over the landing area. The rest was directly attributable to Hopkinson's insistence on committing men to battle with insufficient training and practice. 1st Airlanding Brigade dispatched 144 gliders to Sicily. Seventy-eight came down in the sea after their inexperienced tug pilots released them too early, two machines fetched up in Malta and Tunisia as a result of drastic navigation errors, ten combinations aborted and returned safely to North Africa, and forty-two were scattered along a twenty-five-mile stretch of the Sicilian coast. Only twelve landed on or near the designated landing area. A party of around 100 men managed to seize the Ponte Grande, and defended it until overrun on the afternoon of 10 July. Ironically, it was recaptured by troops advancing from the landing beaches just over an hour later, who appear to have been unaware of the Ponte Grande operation, but who nonetheless also liberated some of the erstwhile defenders from their Italian captors. The 1st Airlanding Brigade and the Glider Pilot Regiment paid a high price for Hopkinson's childish enthusiasm and personal ambition. The former formation lost 313 killed, including 225 drowned in ditched gliders; the total casualty ratio was one in four. This was exceeded by the Glider Pilot Regiment, which lost a total of 101 killed, wounded and missing from the 272 pilots involved, a casualty ratio of over one in three.

While the shattered glider unit licked its wounds, 1st Airborne Division's second operation in Sicily was carried out by the reconstituted 1st Parachute Brigade. This was the seizure of the Ponte Primasole over the River Simeto between Augusta and Catania. The plan was for the 1st Parachute Battalion to seize the bridge simultaneously from both ends, while the 2nd and 3rd Battalion occupied high ground to the south and attacked an anti-aircraft position to the north respectively. The gliders carrying the brigade's heavy equipment were to land south of the bridge. This scheme was not only overly complicated, but dispersed the brigade's combat power on peripheral tasks rather than concentrating it on the primary mission of seizing the bridge. As we shall see, this tendency was also to handicap the brigade's effort at Arnhem. Neither was this the only prophetic similarity. Lathbury was assured that friendly ground forces would relieve the airborne troops within twelve hours; in fact it took forty-eight. 1st Parachute Brigade also experienced severe difficulties in establishing and maintaining radio contact with the relieving forces, although they were able to talk to ships providing gunfire support without difficulty.

116 US C-47 transports and nineteen gliders lifted the 1st Parachute Brigade's 1,900 men on the night of 13–14 July 1943.[14] They were fired on by Allied ships and the intensity of the enemy flak off the coast caused some of the inexperienced and inadequately trained US aircrew to panic. The crew of the aircraft carrying Lieutenant Colonel Alastair Pearson, commanding the 1st Parachute Battalion, insisted on flying parallel with the coast until Pearson threatened them with his pistol.[15] Eleven aircraft were shot down, three with their passengers still on board. Only thirty-nine C-47s dropped their troops on or near the drop zone. The remaining forty-eight delivered their loads up to twenty miles wide, and at least one stick was dropped onto Mount Etna; some of these men may have fallen into the volcano's crater. Only 295 men and four gliders landed where they were supposed to. As the official history dryly points out, the ground operations of 1st Parachute Brigade could not proceed according to plan.

Despite this, the bridge was secured before dawn on 14 July by a scratch force numbering 292, led by a wounded Brigadier Lathbury. Holding it, however, was another matter, for the German

troops in the area reacted with greater speed and aggression than
the Italians at the Ponte Grande. Ironically, many of these were
the 1st Parachute Brigade's opposite numbers from the 1st
Fallschirmjäger Division, which had jumped onto some of the same
drop zones only hours before the British arrived. By the late afternoon Lathbury's men were forced to retire to the south end of the
bridge, and this position too became untenable after German
troops crossed the river to the east. Lathbury thus ordered his men
to break out in small groups after dark, aiming for the high ground
held by the 2nd Parachute Battalion to the south, which then
became the focus of 1st Parachute brigade's defence. Tanks from the
British 4th Armoured Brigade relieved the paratroopers at
midnight on 15 July, and the bridge was re-taken six hours later
with the assistance of Lieutenant Colonel Pearson, who acted as a
guide for the attackers. The fight for the bridge cost the 1st
Parachute Brigade 115 killed, wounded and missing.

The Primasole Bridge drop was the last airborne operation
carried out by 1st Airborne Division in the Mediterranean.
However, Division HQ and the 2nd and 4th Parachute Brigades
were dispatched by warship to secure the Italian naval base at
Taranto and airfields in the surrounding area. Taranto was taken
without a fight on 9 September 1943, although 130 men from the
6th Parachute Battalion were drowned when the ship carrying
them struck a mine. The next nine days were spent seizing airfields,
accepting Italian surrenders and harassing German rearguards, using
a variety of commandeered local transport, including bicycles,
buses, a steamroller and trailer and a complete railway train. The
most significant event was the death of Major-General Hopkinson
during a fight between the 10th Parachute Battalion and a German
rearguard at Castanelleta, twenty-five miles north west of Taranto.
Hopkinson thus achieved the dubious honour of becoming the
only British airborne general to be killed by enemy action. The
details are sketchy, but given what we have seen it is highly likely
that Hopkinson had once again allowed his schoolboy enthusiasm
to override common sense, this time with fatal consequences.
Down succeeded Hopkinson as commander of 1st Airborne

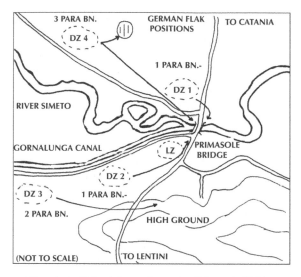

1st Parachute Brigade's attack on the Primasole Bridge, 14-15 July 1943.

Division, and the Division was recalled to the UK in October 1943, in preparation for the invasion of France. The 2nd Parachute Brigade was to remain in the Mediterranean, reducing 1st Airborne Division's line-up to the one it would take into Arnhem the following September: the 1st and 4th Parachute Brigades and the 1st Airlanding Brigade, plus divisional troops.

This catalogue of inadequate and incompetent leadership and inappropriate and poorly thought out employment clearly shows that received wisdom about the 1st Airborne Division requires some revision. While the Division had existed on paper for two years and nine months when it flew into Arnhem, in practical and operational terms it had only been in existence for fourteen months. Neither was the Division operating as an operational entity throughout the latter period, quite the opposite. At the top, HQ 1st Airborne only exerted command in an operational capacity once, for just over a week when it accompanied the 2nd and 4th Parachute Brigades into southern Italy in September 1943. Indeed, as we shall see the Division only ever operated once as a complete entity before Arnhem, again for a week, in training Exercise Rags in mid-May 1944. Given this, and that the divisional HQ merely served in an administrative capacity for the remainder of the time, it is difficult to see how the 1st Airborne Division could be described as an experienced formation.

The same verdict applies generally to the Division's three brigades. The 1st Parachute Brigade saw a good deal of action during its deployment in the Mediterranean. However, the virtual destruction of the brigade in the winter of 1942–43 reduced the number of experienced personnel to a cadre at best, and the confused and scattered nature of the fighting at the Ponte Primasole did little to add to this. The 1st Airlanding Brigade's combat debut at the Ponte Grande arguably achieved little more than providing a costly example of how not to carry out an airborne operation. This verdict also applies to the 1st Parachute Brigade's drops at Souk el Arba and Depienne and, at least to an extent, to the Ponte Primasole too. Finally, the 4th Parachute Brigade's operational activity was restricted almost exclusively to a handful of small-scale parachute drops carried out by one of its battalions in the Aegean and Adriatic before it joined 1st Airborne, and the skirmishing that followed the sea-landing in southern Italy.

This is not intended as a criticism of the airborne soldiers at the sharp end, whose courage and professionalism rescued the majority of the British airborne operations carried out in the Mediterranean from becoming even bigger disasters. However, this does not alter the fact that the 1st Airborne Division left the Mediterranean in October 1943 in much the same state as that in which it had arrived five months earlier. In practical terms it remained an administrative headquarters loosely linked to its constituent formations, and largely divorced from their operational activities, despite spending six months in the field with them. The sole reason for optimism was the elevation of the highly capable Down as a replacement for Hopkinson, which gave the 1st Airborne Division its first competent and qualified commander. If anyone was capable of turning the Division into a properly functioning and battleworthy instrument in time for the cross-Channel invasion, it was Eric Down.

THE 1ST AIRBORNE DIVISION, PATRONAGE AND ONE-SIZE-FITS-ALL COMMAND PHILOSOPHY

ENTER MAJOR–GENERAL ROBERT ELLIOT URQUHART

The British 1st Airborne Division arrived in the UK in December 1943. Division headquarters was set up at Fulbeck Manor in Lincolnshire and its sub-formations and divisional troops were located nearby at various places across the East Midlands. 1st Parachute Brigade was based around Grantham in Lincolnshire, 4th Parachute Brigade around Uppingham in Leicestershire, and 1st Airlanding Brigade was located in the region of Woodhall Spa in Rutland and south Lincolnshire. On arrival at their billets, the troops were granted some well-earned leave. The 1st Parachute Brigade, for example, had been on active service in the Mediterranean since November 1942. 1st Airborne Division's arrival in the UK completed the line-up of the three Allied airborne divisions that would carry out Operation Market Garden in September 1944. First to arrive was the US 101st Airborne Division, which arrived from the United States in October 1943. The other was the US 82nd Airborne Division, which had served in the Mediterranean alongside 1st Airborne and reached the UK in February and April 1944.

1st Airborne Division had barely disembarked from its voyage from the Mediterranean when it suffered arguably its most serious and far-reaching setback, the repercussions of which were to have a direct bearing on events at Arnhem. This was the strange, if not perverse, decision to replace Down as commander of the Division with an officer with no airborne or divisional command experience whatsoever. The officer chosen was newly promoted

Major-General Robert Elliot 'Roy' Urquhart who, after commanding the British 231 Infantry Brigade Group in Sicily and Italy until September 1943, was serving as Brigadier-General Staff to the British 12th Corps in south-east England. If his biography is to be believed, Urquhart had no inkling of his imminent elevation to General rank before he received a War Office signal informing him of his new appointment. Following a short interview with Browning, Urquhart had a hand-over meeting with a less than enthusiastic Down at the Naval and Military Club, and officially assumed command on 10 January 1944.

Despite the clearly controversial nature of Down's sidelining, it has received remarkably little attention. The official history makes no mention of it whatever, and other published works almost invariably infer that the position of 1st Airborne commander became vacant after Down was urgently dispatched to India to oversee the formation of what was to become the 44th Indian Airborne Division. Responsibility for selecting a non-airborne replacement is routinely shifted onto the War Office, which is claimed to have suggested this course to Browning. The latter is alleged to have acquiesced with the proviso that the selected candidate should be 'hot from the battle'.[1] Aside from the fact that it can hardly have been common practice for divisional hand-overs to be conducted over hastily arranged lunches at the Naval and Military Club, this cosy and convenient picture is at variance with the facts on a number of counts.

First, while Down did end up in command of the Indian Airborne Division, there was no great hurry for him to get to India. The decision to raise such a Division was only taken in September 1943, during an Indian conference attended by Browning that tentatively scheduled the Division to be operational by the winter of 1944–45. In fact, the Supreme Allied Commander South East Asia, Admiral Louis Mountbatten, did not officially sanction the establishment of the 44th Indian Airborne Division until October 1944. While the official history does not state precisely when Down arrived in India, it cannot have been before August 1944. According to Major-General Stanislaw Sosabowski, commander of the 1st Polish Independent Parachute Brigade, Down was instrumental in the relocation of Sosabowski's Brigade from its base at Leven in Scotland to Peterborough at the beginning of July 1944, and attended exercises with the Poles at the end of that month. This shows that Down was kicking his heels in a temporary staff appointment throughout the period 1st Airborne Division was training to become fully operational. It also suggests that there may have been an ulterior motive for Down's sidelining, given that there appears to have been no pressing need for Down's services in India.

Similarly, there was more to the decision to replace Down with a non-airborne officer. The War Office's role appears to have been strictly administrative. Urquhart's biographer, John Baynes, refers to Browning discussing the matter of Down's successor with Montgomery, and claims it was the latter who suggested a non-airborne replacement. Browning agreed with his oft-quoted bit about the candidate being 'hot from the battle', and Montgomery immediately suggested Urquhart. This is a far more likely explanation than passing responsibility to some faceless War Office bureaucrat, because Urquhart was a long-standing Montgomery protégé, having come to his notice after taking up a staff appointment with the British 3rd Infantry Division in October 1940. Urquhart was promoted to Lieutenant Colonel within two months, and assumed command of the 2nd Battalion, The Duke of Cornwall's Light Infantry in March 1941.

This was all at Montgomery's instigation and it is highly likely that he had a hand in Urquhart's relatively rapid rise thereafter. In March 1942 Urquhart was posted as General Staff Officer Grade One (GSO1) to the 51st Highland Division, which arrived in Egypt as Montgomery took command of the British Eighth Army. Exactly a year later he assumed command of 231 Infantry Brigade Group, which he led in the invasion of Sicily and then into Italy. The linkage with Montgomery was overtly renewed in mid-September 1943, when Urquhart rested for a week at British 8th Army headquarters at Montgomery's invitation. All this suggests that Urquhart's recall to the UK to serve as Brigadier-General Staff to the British 12th Corps and subsequent elevation to command 1st Airborne was perhaps less of a surprise than he implies.[2]

Montgomery's motivation was relatively straightforward, being a standard example of British Regular Army patronage; it was the norm for senior officers to assist the careers of officers they considered promising. Montgomery took things further than most by going out of his way to locate and cultivate such individuals, as illustrated by his habit of surrounding himself with hand-picked officers on whose loyalty he could absolutely rely. This process was complemented by one of Montgomery's other habits, that of making it his business to familiarise himself with all units under his command, or that were likely to be so. This goes some way to explaining why he was discussing airborne matters, and specifically the issue of who was to command 1st Airborne, with Browning. It should be remembered that the British 6th Airborne Division had been earmarked to operate under the aegis of Montgomery's 21st Army Group for the Normandy invasion, and 1st Airborne Division was slated to assist in the expansion of the initial beachhead if, and when, necessary. This was sufficient justification for Montgomery to take an interest.

Montgomery had developed a more than passing interest in airborne matters when Hopkinson brought the existence of the force to his attention in North Africa and presented him with a maroon Airborne Forces beret. After taking command of 21st Army Group, Montgomery visited many of 6th Airborne's subformations and units, down to battalion level in some instances. In March 1944 he inspected the 1st Polish Independent Parachute Brigade at Leven in Scotland, although at that time Sosabowski's unit did not come under British command at all.[3] Despite all this contact with airborne units, however, it does not appear to have occurred to Montgomery that airborne command might require specialist training and aptitudes that were not necessarily inherent in service with line infantry units. This one-size-fits-all approach was not uncommon in the British army before or since, and during peace as well as in wartime. At the time of writing, for example, the commander of the British 16th Air Assault Brigade was not, as one might expect, drawn from the Parachute Regiment or the Army Air Corps, but from the Household Cavalry. This time-honoured practice appears to explain why Montgomery thought it appropriate to nominate an officer with no airborne experience whatsoever to command an airborne Division.

Montgomery's motivation can thus be put down to patronage, but this does not explain why Browning acquiesced. It is highly likely that professional considerations played a part. Montgomery was clearly on the way to the top, which is why Browning appears to have altered his plans to accommodate Montgomery's wish.

Brigadier Gerald Lathbury, then commanding 1st Parachute Brigade, had been unofficially advised, presumably by Browning that command of 1st Airborne Division would be his on Down's departure. This suggests that Browning had already decided to get rid of Down, and merely substituted Montgomery's *protégé* because it was more profitable from a career perspective. That Down had previously been sidelined for divisional command in favour of the far less qualified Hopkinson shows that Browning considered Down unsuitable, and given what we have seen of Browning so far, it is not difficult to ascertain why. The fact that Down had vastly more airborne experience than Browning can only have exacerbated the latter's sense of inferiority, and Down compounded his error by being an operationally rather than career oriented soldier, and thus far more likely to rock the boat. It is highly unlikely that Down would have accepted the Arnhem plan that Browning foisted on his successor.[4]

From Browning's perspective therefore, Down clearly had to go, and replacing him with Urquhart rather than promoting someone else from within the airborne establishment was the better option for several reasons. Because Montgomery's string pulling had taken place behind the scenes, Urquhart was beholden to Browning for his premature elevation to divisional command, a reliance exacerbated by Urquhart's lack of airborne experience. From Browning's perspective, this made it easier to control Urquhart, and reduced the likelihood of him causing embarrassment by ploughing his own unauthorised furrow as Hopkinson had done. There may also have been an element of divide and rule involved. Some, Urquhart included, were of the opinion that 1st Airborne had returned from the Mediterranean with a rather inflated idea of its operational experience and importance in the airborne scheme of things.[5]

Such tendencies cannot have been viewed with other than disfavour by Browning, not least because of his recent experience with Hopkinson. Placing a tame outsider in command of 1st Airborne Division thus allowed him to send a clear message as to where the power lay.

All this may have been convenient for Browning, but it complicated Urquhart's life considerably. Not only did he have to assert himself as an unqualified outsider, but also as one who had been imposed over two insiders with much more airborne experience, one of whom remained as a senior subordinate. As if this were not enough, he also had to overcome the rather cocky and self-assured self-image with which the Division had returned from the Mediterranean. This perception was doubtless prompted in part by resentment at the airborne forces' tendency to regard themselves as an exclusive and superior brotherhood in comparison with the remainder of the army. However, the evidence suggests there may have been a little more to it. Lieutenant Colonel Mark Henniker RE, who had commanded 1st Airborne's Royal Engineer contingent in the Mediterranean, thought that many within the Division surrounded themselves with a mystique that was not entirely justified by experience. Urquhart himself noted that while the Division's constituent brigades and units were vitally in need of formation-level training, there was some reluctance to accept that any additional training was necessary.[6] Major Philip Tower, who joined 1st Airborne after its return to the UK, put things more bluntly. Tower recognised the quality of his new airborne comrades, but felt they overestimated their abilities. In particular, he noted an unwillingness to acknowledge that any worthwhile experience was to be had outside the airborne fold.[7] Such arrogance would have been ill-advised even if reality matched self-image. The reality was that 1st Airborne Division had little reason for such complacency on arrival in the UK, for it was far from adequately trained at any level.

At the lower level, 1st Parachute Brigade and 1st Airlanding Brigade needed to absorb and train up the large number of inexperienced replacements for the losses suffered in Sicily. This process in itself took time. According to the operational records, all three of 1st Airborne's brigades were not fully mobilised until 10 February 1944.[8] While 4th Parachute Brigade had less need for replacements, it had yet to operate in its primary parachute role as a whole, and needed to reintegrate the 11th Parachute Battalion, which had been operating independently in the eastern Mediterranean until shortly before its parent Brigade returned to the UK. This tied in with Urquhart's own observations, in which he identified the Division's most serious deficiencies as formation-level training and experience. This was especially critical, given that 1st Airborne had never operated as a Division even in training, and that operating as a divisional entity was the very role it was assigned to fulfil after the initial Normandy landings.

Urquhart began well, by visiting the headquarters of his three teeth brigades even before he officially assumed command on 10 January 1944. According to the operational records, he visited 1st Parachute Brigade on 5 January, 4th Parachute Brigade on 6 January, and 1st Airlanding Brigade on 7 January. Thereafter he worked his way around virtually every unit in 1st Airborne Division, beginning with the parachute and glider infantry battalions. Eye-witnesses invariably refer to Urquhart's straightforward and low-key manner, which sometimes bordered on diffidence, creating a good impression with all he met.[9] Major Ian Toler from the Glider Pilot Regiment, for example, was mid-way through talking what he described as a rather unassuming general through the intricacies of the Horsa glider before he realised he was addressing his new divisional commander.[10]

The problem was that, when Urquhart assumed command, 1st Airborne Division required more than the creation of good impressions among subordinates. It needed a shake up, and not merely to imprint Urquhart's authority and to dispel any sense of self-importance. The Normandy invasion was time-tabled for late May to early June 1944, and 1st Airborne Division was slated to be ready for operations immediately the sea-landings commenced. Time was therefore of the essence if the Division was to be a properly integrated, fully functioning and combat-ready instrument at the time required. Urquhart thus had, at best, less than five months before he might have to lead 1st Airborne Division against the cream of the German army and *Waffen* SS in northern France. The likelihood is that Urquhart fully intended to embark on just such a course. Certainly, that is precisely how he approached the matter on assuming command of 231 Infantry Brigade in May 1943. Once he had familiarised himself with his new command, Urquhart immediately took it away from practising beach landings in preparation for Sicily for a four-day hard-living exercise in the desert, codenamed 'Nomad'.[11] Unfortunately, for a variety of reasons it was to be four months before Urquhart got to lead 1st Airborne Division in its entirety on exercise in the field.

Not least of these reasons were the allied matters of scale and geographical distance. As we have seen, 1st Airborne Division was widely scattered across the East Midlands, and much of it was a long way from Urquhart's headquarters at Fulbeck in Lincolnshire. This meant any contact with 1st Airborne outside the precincts of Divisional headquarters at Fulbeck required a good deal of travelling. Moreover, 1st Airborne's formations and units were frequently away from their base locations undergoing exercises or specialist training. Being a conscientious individual, Urquhart doubtlessly lengthened the process by attempting to familiarise himself with the technical aspects of his units and their equipment, as Major Toler found out. The RAF did provide him with a pilot and personal Airspeed Oxford aircraft, complete with Airborne maroon nose and Pegasus formation sign. However, its utility was limited because it was only useful in clear weather, because many of 1st Airborne's units were a long way from the nearest RAF airfield, and because Urquhart disliked flying and was frequently airsick.

The situation was exacerbated yet further by the fact that Urquhart's responsibilities ran sideways and up, as well as down. He was obliged to work personally with the USAAF's 9th Troop Carrier Command and the RAF's No.38 and 46 Groups, whose aircraft would carry 1st Airborne into battle. He was also obliged to attend high-level meetings and operational planning sessions relating to the upcoming invasion, most of which were held in or near London. These increased manifold in the run up to and after the Normandy landings, and often required Urquhart to stay in a caravan in the grounds of Browning's Airborne Corps Headquarters at Moor Park, just north of London, and commute to Fulbeck by road or air depending on the weather. Urquhart's schedule was thus clearly a punishing one, and stress was probably a major factor in the severe attack of malaria that hospitalised him for three precious weeks from mid-April 1944. By the time Urquhart was fit to return to duty in May 1944, 1st Airborne Division's training window was virtually gone.

All this obviously limited Urquhart's contact with his command, as the operational records clearly show. Unit war diaries make only a handful of references to him explicitly, almost all of which are connected to his initial introductory visits to units and higher headquarters. Occasions where he could have been present, such as exercise briefings, are only marginally more plentiful. There are a number of implications arising from this, not least that such limited exposure to airborne theory and practice must have limited Urquhart's ability to judge the feasibility of proposed operations. More importantly, it must also have inhibited his ability to impress his authority on 1st Airborne, because he had so little opportunity to monitor the doings of his subordinate commanders and their units. In particular, Urquhart was unable to rectify the deficiency he noted as the most pressing, that of formation-level training, although he began to address it on the sole occasion he was able to assume operational command of 1st Airborne Division in its entirety. This was Exercise 'Rags', which commenced on 10 May 1944 and ranged from north Nottinghamshire into Yorkshire. Its overall aim was to practise the Division in the rapid follow-up role on a broad front, and within this to enhance co-operation between the Division's headquarters, constituent brigades and light artillery regiment. Laudable and necessary as this was, the realism of the exercise was compromised because the initial deployment was by road rather than from the air.

Of course, it can be argued that Urquhart had a divisional staff to rely on when it came to judging the feasibility of prospective operations. It can also be argued that Urquhart's task was simplified by his previous command of 231 Infantry Brigade Group. In addition to three infantry battalions, this formation contained a squadron of tanks, an organic engineer element, anti-tank and anti-aircraft units, and a variety of other administrative and logistic elements. It therefore resembled a miniature Division, and thus required the same co-ordination and delegation skills required for successful divisional command. There is some merit in this, but it overlooks the most crucial points of all, which were that 1st Airborne Division was an airborne formation, and not a conventional infantry unit, and that it was not a fully integrated and functioning organisation.

By 1944, the maxim that airborne soldiers were normal troops who merely used unusual methods of transport to get to the battle-field had gained wide currency within the British army. It dated from the expansion of the British airborne force from a small-scale raiding force in mid-1941. Then Brigadier Richard Gale used the idea to draw a line between his new parachute brigade and what had gone before, and it formed the cornerstone of Down's parallel reformation of 11 SAS Battalion into the 1st Parachute Battalion. However, while there was thus a grain of underlying truth it was inaccurate, not to say disingenuous, to apply the same maxim to airborne forces as they subsequently developed. The popularity of the maxim was probably based in part on resentment generated by the superior attitudes routinely displayed by the airborne fraternity to the non-airborne, and by the fact it fitted neatly with the British army's one-size-fits-all attitude to higher command appointments. Doubtless it was used to soothe any doubts Urquhart may have had over his lack of airborne experience. The fact remains, however, that the realities of airborne operations, even ones of divisional or multi-divisional size, differed significantly from those of their earthbound counterparts.

This difference was reflected in a variety of ways. At the very lowest tactical level, the War Establishment of airborne infantry units contained a higher proportion of sub-machine guns than comparable infantry units, to generate more short-range firepower for assault operations. Parachute infantry companies employed sergeants rather than corporals as section commanders, an expan-

sion of the normal senior NCO ratio intended to offset the consequences of scattered drops or casualties incurred during the
landing phase. There was also some recognition that commanding
airborne units required a special approach, at least from within the
airborne establishment. Frost, who by early 1944 was one of the
most experienced airborne commanders in the British army, noted
that airborne operations required a specific physical and mental
approach to overcome the unaccustomed handicap of fighting
without the resources routinely available in regular ground operations. Interestingly, Frost was talking with specific reference to the
imposition of non-airborne commanders, although it is unclear
whether he was doing so with the benefit of hindsight. Neither
Montgomery nor Browning appears to have been fully aware of
this fundamental point, or, if they were, they seem to have been
quite happy to ignore it. The evidence also suggests that Urquhart
did not fully appreciate the difference either, given his behaviour
once on the ground at Arnhem.

The upshot of all this is clear. By June 1944, 1st Airborne
Division was set to be committed to battle by men whose grasp of
the realities of airborne operations was less than complete, and the
same applied to the Division's commander. In addition, circumstances conspired to prevent Urquhart absorbing the intricacies of
his new command in the time available, as they did to prevent 1st
Airborne Division making good its lack of experience operating as
a cohesive entity. There was, however, one area that might have
helped offset these deficiencies. Even allowing for the need for 1st
Parachute and 1st Airlanding Brigades to absorb replacement
personnel, there was still sufficient time to implement an intensive
training regime to bring all 1st Airborne's teeth formations to the
highest pitch of combat readiness. Had this been done, it would
have gone at least some way to offset Urquhart and 1st Airborne
Division's other deficiencies. In the event, circumstances were to
conspire against this too.

ARROGANT, HINDERED BY PARACHUTE MACHISMO AND AT THE BACK OF THE QUEUE FOR RESOURCES

IST AIRBORNE DIVISION, JANUARY TO JUNE 1944

As we have seen, on its return from the Mediterranean 1st Airborne Division generated a perception of reluctance to accept the need for additional training, and of overestimating its capabilities. However, whatever impression it may have created among outsiders and newcomers, some within 1st Airborne's brigades and battalions were aware of its deficiencies. The clearest evidence of this comes from 1st Parachute Brigade, which put together a detailed internal memo on 9 January 1944.[1] This stressed the need for intensive fitness training, synthetic parachute training to introduce the troops to the latest parachute techniques, and to familiarise them with the Armstrong Whitworth Albemarle, a type the Brigade had little experience with. The memo also contained details of a parachute exercise, codenamed 'Travesty Novelty', which was intended to include the entire Brigade. Scheduled to run from 27–29 January, 'Travesty Novelty' was to employ thirty Albemarles and seven Handley Page Halifax bombers. An attached appendix listed the planned allocation of aircraft for Brigade training up to the middle of February. Ten Albemarles were requested for familiarisation parachute training on 25 January 1944, and between thirty-five and fifty unspecified aircraft were required in four increments between 26 January and 18 February.[2]

Unfortunately, things did not turn out like that. The parachute training scheduled for 25 January was postponed for twenty-four hours and then indefinitely, and Exercise 'Travesty Novelty' was similarly postponed and then cancelled on 28 January. While the operational records do not give a reason for these cancellations, it is highly likely that they were due to a shortage of resources. The British 6th and US 82nd and 101st Airborne Divisions were undergoing intensive preparation for their spearhead role in the Normandy invasion at that time, which obviously put 1st Airborne at the back of the queue, good intentions not withstanding.

As it turned out, 1st Parachute Brigade commenced parachute training only slightly later than it had originally intended, albeit on a much reduced scale. Beginning at the end of January, the Brigade's three parachute battalions were rotated individually through a refresher parachute course at Stoney Cross on the edge of Salisbury Plain, a process that took until the end of February to complete. Thereafter, two company-size jumps were carried out by 120 men from the 3rd Parachute Battalion and 100 men from the 1st Parachute Battalion on 23 and 30 March respectively, the latter including elements of the 6th Airborne Division at Netheravon in Wiltshire. Brigade HQ, the 2nd Parachute Battalion and 16 Parachute Field Ambulance performed a mass drop at Repsley Heath the next day, and the full Brigade dropped from US C-47 transports for Exercise 'Tony' on 11 April. This was the only Brigade jump performed by 1st Parachute Brigade before Arnhem, although poor aircrew skills reduced the value of the exercise considerably. Despite perfect conditions, the drop was widely scattered and some aircraft returned with their paratroopers on board because they were unable to locate the drop zone. As far as 1st Parachute Brigade was concerned, the performance of the US aircrew showed no improvement since the fiasco at the Ponte Primasole the previous July. Lathbury made his views known in no uncertain terms to the US 52nd Troop Carrier Wing and its superior, US 9th Troop Carrier Command. The only other parachute training undertaken by the Brigade was a small-scale drop for a signals exercise on 1 June 1944, which involved five aircraft.

It is unclear whether the 4th Parachute Brigade had less opportunity for parachute training, or merely considered it a lower priority. Like 1st Parachute Brigade, 4th Parachute Brigade spent the whole of February undergoing parachute training, in this instance at the Parachute Training Squadron (PTS) at RAF Ringway, in increments of 400. This was to acquaint the Brigade with the latest training techniques and equipment, which were not available in India or the Middle East where 4th Parachute Brigade's personnel had done their basic parachute training.[3] Some elements, presumably the Brigade signals section, also parachuted in for a Brigade navigation exercise linked to a signals exercise codenamed 'Stroller' on 18 February. 4th Parachute Brigade's last parachute descent was Exercise 'Dorothy', a two-day exercise using US aircraft that began on 8 April 1944, and which involved the 10th and 11th Parachute Battalions, Brigade HQ and support units. Like 1st Parachute Brigade, 4th Parachute Brigade were less than impressed with their US hosts, although on this occasion the dissatisfaction lay largely with pre-jump ground arrangements. British battalion commanders complained of poor liaison and latrine arrangements, insufficient sheltered accommodation, inadequate canteen provision, and that some aircrew was late in reporting to their aircraft. Other complaints stemmed from US ignorance of British operating procedures, including claims that the US air commander had no knowledge of the signals for cancelling the drop, and that the C-47 crews were ignorant of British Standing Orders for parachuting.[4] As no complaints were recorded regarding the drop itself, it can be assumed to have been a success.

The amount of parachute training carried out by 1st Airborne Division's two parachute brigades was not exactly abundant. Despite its relative paucity, however, it appears to have been adequate, at least in individual training terms. All ranks received at least a refresher parachute course, most had the opportunity to carry out at least one additional jump under tactical conditions, and personnel unfamiliar with the Albemarle and/or C-47 were able to make at least one descent from those machines. However, the benefits were largely offset by a series of connected drawbacks. In particular, limitations in the parachute training infrastructure and aircraft availability drew out the time required to complete a relatively modest amount of training, as well as causing a good deal of associated disruption. Stoney Cross, for example, lay over 150 miles from 1st Parachute Brigade's billets around Grantham, and the 4th Parachute Brigade's personnel had to travel almost 100 miles to Ringway, considerable distances under winter and wartime conditions. Disruption was exacerbated by Ringway's practice of accepting trainees only in increments of 400, which did not fit with the standard parachute battalion establishment of around 600 men. Each of 4th Parachute Brigade's battalions thus had to rotate through the course in two separate and unequal parts. Even though the course only took around six days, including travelling time, this had obvious implications for other training, and was probably the rationale for expanding Signals Exercise 'Stroller' into a Brigade navigation exercise on 18 February 1944.

Parachute training also obliged both brigades to spend a good deal of time in preparatory work of one kind or another in addition to time actually spent jumping. Personnel had to be prepared, possibly with synthetic parachute training, parachutes had to be collected, issued and fitted, weapons had to be broken down, and kit-bags and containers packed. The bulk of 1st Parachute Brigade was thus engaged for almost all the last week of March in preparation for the jump at Repsley Heath on 31 March 1944. Exercise 'Tony' presumably required at least a similar amount of preparation, and the same must have applied to 4th Parachute Brigade in the run up to Exercise Dorothy. On the other hand, the airfields used by the US 52nd Troop Carrier Wing were located in Lincolnshire, and thus near both brigades' billets. This cut down the amount of pre-jump travel and other administrative arrangements considerably, and the use of local drop zones may have helped too.

Therefore, parachute training took up a good deal of training time from the total available. A variety of more mundane activities used up more time and exerted their own varying degrees of disruption between March and the end of May 1944. During their refresher training in February 1944, for example, almost half of 4th Parachute Brigade's units were obliged to change locations, and the 1st Parachute Brigade undertook a reorganisation of its

support units at the end of March. The commanders of both parachute brigades and all their battalion commanders were away from
their commands for the first week in March, attending a course by
the School of Infantry's Battle School at Barnard Castle in North
Yorkshire. 1st Parachute Brigade lost its commander again in the
middle of April, when Lathbury took over as acting divisional
commander for the three weeks it took Urquhart to get over his
malaria attack.

On 14 March 1944 Montgomery inspected both brigades in his
capacity as commander of 21st Army Group, followed by His
Majesty King George VI two days later. These inspections may
have been brief, but, the British army being the British army, it
would be extremely surprising if they were not preceded by an
inordinate amount of preparation, even allowing for the operational orientation of Airborne Forces. There were also more useful
diversions. The 11th Parachute Battalion spent nine days from 19
March at Newtown in Wales on unspecified training. This may
have been for field firing, as the operational records show that 156
Parachute Battalion and 10th Parachute Battalion spent two-week
stints field firing at Midhope near Sheffield beginning on 2 April
and 2 May 1944 respectively. Weapon training appears to have been
a priority in 4th Parachute Brigade, given that all three of the
Brigade's parachute battalions spent two days in turn field firing at
Strensall, just north of York, between 22 and 28 May 1944.

This brings us to the most important aspect of 1st Airborne's
activities in the run up to the Normandy invasion, that of tactical
training, and particularly at battalion and brigade level. Although
no details appear in the Brigade War Diary, 1st Parachute Brigade's
training summary for February 1944 claims company and battalion
exercises were carried out at some point during that month.
However, given that the Brigade was involved in its refresher parachute training at that time, and that the summary goes into detail
on parachute-related matters and mentions the 'exercises' only in
passing, it is possible that this merely referred to routine company
and battalion training. 1st Parachute Brigade carried out two tactical exercises, codenamed 'Johnny' and 'William', during March

1944. Intended to practise night-attack skills, the former commenced on 8 March, and the latter on 15 March 1944. Both appear to have been company-sized, two or three-day affairs, given that the Brigade Training Summary for March records that the Brigade had carried out platoon and company training for the whole of the month. Johnny was complete in time for Montgomery's inspection on 14 March, and William was completed on 17 March, including an interruption for the King's inspection the previous day.

Things moved up a step the following month. The whole of the 1st Parachute Brigade parachuted in for Exercise Tony on 11 April 1944, to practise night reorganisation. Ten days later, the full Brigade participated in Exercise 'Mush', which ran from 21–23 April 1944, and involved the whole of 1st Airborne Division acting as enemy for 6th Airborne Division. 1st Parachute Brigade deployed by road for Mush, as it did for Exercise Rags, 1st Airborne's one and only formal divisional exercise. Rags ran from 8–14 May 1944, and was intended to practice co-operation between the Division's constituent formations in the rapid exploitation role. 4th Parachute Brigade appears to have spent less time in the field than its sister formation. The former's first tactical exercise was a two-day affair codenamed 'Silk', held between 24–25 March 1944. The exercise involved the entire Brigade, which deployed by vehicle for a seize-and-hold operation in the vicinity of Newark in Nottinghamshire. The whole Brigade, minus 156 Parachute Battalion, also took part in Exercise Dorothy, which ran from 8–9 April 1944. The objective of Dorothy was presumably the same as that of 1st Parachute Brigade's subsequent Exercise Tony, which was to practice reorganisation after a night drop. Thereafter, 4th Parachute Brigade participated in Exercise Mush and Exercise Rags, alongside the rest of 1st Airborne Division.

This shows that, as was the case with parachute training, the amount of tactical field training carried out by 1st Airborne's two parachute brigades was not abundant either. The average member of 1st Parachute Brigade spent fourteen days on battalion and brigade-level tactical exercises, and his counterpart in 4th

Parachute Brigade spent twelve days similarly engaged. If the time spent on individual parachute training is added in, the totals become twenty-six and nineteen days respectively. In effect, this means that both parachute brigades spent less than one-fifth of the total time available engaged in parachute and field training. Even allowing for the additional activities cited above, this is an inordinately small proportion, which begs the question of what they were doing for the remainder.

If the operational records are accurate, they appear to have spent the bulk of it engaged in routine platoon and company training. The usual focus of such training was to teach and practise basic skills, such as weapon handling, camouflage and concealment, fitness, section and platoon battle drills and so on. James Sims, for example, who joined the 2nd Parachute Battalion's Support Company during this period and fought at the Arnhem road bridge, recalled endlessly practising three-inch mortar drills aimed at maximising speed and accuracy, and regularly completing 'long carries'. This was a term for route marches carrying the barrel, bipod or baseplate of the stripped-down mortar or an equivalent load of ammunition in addition to full battle order and personal weapon.[5] According to Frost, the official yardstick for all personnel was the ability to cover thirty miles per day carrying sixty pounds. Company and platoon training also assisted in the process of assimilating replacements into their platoons, and bringing them up to the required standards. However, while there can be no doubt that such training was both necessary and beneficial, it is difficult to see how dedicating four-fifths of the available training time can have been justified or necessary. This suggests there must have been more to it, and this was certainly the case, at least with regard to the 1st Parachute Brigade.

When 1st Airborne Division returned to the UK in December 1943, some of its officers were posted to units in 6th Airborne Division to give the latter the benefit of their battle experience. The officer selected from 1st Parachute Brigade was the commander of 1st Parachute Battalion, Lieutenant Colonel Alastair Pearson. The commander of the 1st Battalion's Support

Company, Major P. Cleasby-Thompson, himself a veteran of the
Battalion's adventures in North Africa, was promoted in Pearson's
place. Cleasby-Thompson was from a Guards background, and
promptly embarked on a programme to infuse his new command
with Guards-style discipline, assisted by a Guards RSM. This,
predictably, did not go down well, especially with those who had
served in the Mediterranean. The result was what Frost
euphemistically described as unrest and what one more recent
writer bluntly called mutiny.[6] The fact that Lathbury posted
Cleasby-Thompson and his RSM after listening to the men's
grievances suggests there must have been some justification for
their behaviour. Major David Dobie from the 3rd Parachute
Battalion was promoted to replace Cleasby-Thompson, and
commanded the 1st Battalion at Arnhem.

The 3rd Parachute Battalion also had problems, albeit ones that
stemmed from the top rather than the rank-and-file. Lieutenant
Colonel E.C. Yelland was obliged to step down when the battalion
was unable to march on a test exercise.[7] He was replaced by
Lieutenant Colonel John Fitch, who had joined 1st Parachute
Brigade as Brigade-Major in January 1944. The 2nd Parachute
Battalion does not appear to have suffered anything as serious,
although Frost's biography suggests that it did suffer from low-level
indiscipline, which was probably endemic across 1st Parachute
Brigade, and possibly even further. Frost refers specifically to the
problem of 'hard cases', disinclined to toe the line, and widespread
absenteeism, particularly after weekend passes, which interfered
with training, weakened discipline and caused rifts between those
who shirked and those who did not.

There is no obvious evidence to suggest that the 4th Parachute
Brigade suffered from the same kind of disciplinary problems. This
may have been because the 4th Parachute Brigade's constituent
battalions contained a high proportion of pre-war regular soldiers,
and because the Brigade had returned virtually intact from the
Mediterranean. On the other hand, it could merely be that
whoever was responsible for maintaining the official records
neglected to include them, and it may be significant that Urquhart

referred to the Brigade as a difficult command.[8] All the evidence regarding the 1st Parachute Brigade's disciplinary problems was gleaned from published secondary sources, and the official records do not contain even a hint that anything was amiss.

The 4th Parachute Brigade carried out even less training than the 1st Parachute Brigade. The impression is not one of formations training hard against the clock. Rather, it is of formations very much running on a business-as-usual basis. Saunders' semi-official history devotes almost as much space to describing the recreational activities of both parachute brigades as it does to detailing their training. Similarly, Frost refers to local hospitality and regular weekend leaves to London and, significantly, a widespread inclination to take advantage of every recreational opportunity available. In the 2nd Parachute Battalion at least, training usually ended at around four in the afternoon, after which the troops were left to their own devices unless a night exercise of some kind had been scheduled.[9] 1st Parachute Brigade HQ did decree at the end of February 1944 that all units were to devote two nights per week to night training. A regular format for such training was to drop small parties from sealed trucks equipped with maps and compasses at random locations around Lincolnshire, and leave them to find their own way back to camp. Predictably, many found that the best way to minimise the disruption to their sleep was to waylay a civilian, usually on the way home from a local hostelry, and demand directions.[10] Whilst undoubtedly a good demonstration of 'ABI', or Airborne Initiative, such corner-cutting undermined the point of the training and provides a clear example of the low-level disciplinary problems mentioned by Frost.

All in all, it is therefore not hard to see how 1st Airborne Division gained a reputation in some quarters for overestimating its capabilities to the point of arrogance. It is also clear that such attitudes were based largely on wishful thinking, at least as far as the Division's two parachute brigades were concerned. The evidence shows that neither the 1st Parachute Brigade nor the 4th Parachute Brigade made best use of the time available for training between January and May 1944. In some instances, such as parachute training, this was largely due to factors beyond their control. Nonetheless, the fact remains that neither brigade trained as hard as it could have, or should have, and proof of this verdict can be seen by looking no further than 1st Airborne's third infantry formation, the 1st Airlanding Brigade.

If their respective War Diaries are accurate, both parachute brigades frittered away the month of January dealing with administrative matters. In the same period 1st Airlanding Brigade had arranged for the 7th Battalion, the King's Own Scottish Borderers (7th KOSB) to provide live load duty for glider pilot training at RAF Brize Norton, rotating one company per week, and carried out its first large-scale exercise. Exercise 'Pioneer' commenced on 31 January 1944, and involved Brigade HQ, the 2nd Battalion, The South Staffordshire Regiment (2nd South Staffs) in its entirety and a proportion of 7th KOSB and 1st Battalion, The Border Regiment (1st Border). By the end of May 1944, 1st Airlanding Brigade had carried out no less than eight tactical exercises, seven of which involved most or all of the brigade, and at least two of which used large numbers of gliders.

Exercise 'Dreme' took place on 4–5 April 1944, and used 140 Horsa gliders from RAF Keevil. Eighteen of these crashed, and 7th KOSB lost twenty-five men killed. 1st Airlanding Brigade also deployed by glider for Exercise Mush, employing 235 machines; the Brigade War Diary makes no mention of casualties. Of the ground exercises, in addition to Exercise Rags, the 2nd South Staffs and 7th KOSB carried out Exercise 'Goshawk' on 20–21 March, and 2nd South Staffs also acted as enemy for 4th Parachute Brigade's Exercise Silk toward the end of the same month. Exercise 'Damper', which took place on 8–9 April, involved all three of 1st Airlanding's infantry battalions in practising the occupation and organisation of defensive positions, and liaison between them and 1st Airborne's organic artillery. The exercise included live artillery fire controlled by Forward Observation Officers from the 1st Airlanding Light Regiment RA. Exercise 'Contact', a two-day affair that began on 17 March, was particularly imaginative. Involving a single company from each of the brigade's infantry battalions, the exercise was a competition that pitted each company in turn against a typical German defensive position. Unfortunately, the operational records do not reveal which company put in the most praiseworthy performance.

In between this, 1st Airlanding Brigade's infantry battalions reorganised their support companies, which involved retraining personnel previously equipped with lightweight Polsten 20mm cannons on the Vickers medium machine-gun,[11] and coped with a visit from Montgomery on 14 March. Personnel from the Brigade carried out several demonstrations and exchanges of varying sizes with other units including the US 82nd Airborne Division and the British 11th Armoured Division, and the 7th KOSB found time to practise street-fighting drills in Hull. In addition, the Brigade was twice obliged to relocate in its entirety, moving from Rutland to Bulford in Wiltshire at the end of March 1944, and then returning to Lincolnshire in mid-May, after the conclusion of Exercise Rags. The move to Bulford was presumably to place the Brigade closer to the airfields used by the Glider Pilot Regiment. If so, it must have avoided much of the disruption incurred by the parachute battalions in commuting for their refresher parachute training.

All this clearly shows what could been achieved in the time available. At twenty days, the average member of the 1st Airlanding Brigade spent almost twice as much time engaged in tactical training as his parachute counterparts, and participated in twice as many separate exercises. More importantly, six out of the eight exercises carried out by 1st Airlanding Brigade involved all or most of the brigade, which meant that respective battalion and Brigade headquarters had more opportunities to train as a single operational entity. 1st Airlanding Brigade thus went further than any other in 1st Airborne Division to rectifying the shortfall in formation-level training identified by Urquhart when he assumed command. This is rendered all the more laudable by the fact that, like the 1st Parachute Brigade, two of 1st Airlanding's constituent battalions were also engaged in absorbing replacements at the same time.

The only obvious difference between 1st Airlanding Brigade and its parachute equivalents appears to have been more of a willingness to apply itself vigorously to the task in hand, although the fact that it was a gliderborne formation may have had some bearing on the matter. Parachute units almost invariably surround themselves with a carefully crafted and jealously guarded air of macho glamour, and there is no evidence to suggest that 1st Airborne Division's parachute battalions were an exception to the rule. This attitude undoubtedly contributed greatly to the general perception of 1st Airborne as arrogant and overconfident. By contrast, glider units did not labour under such a glamorous image, being commonly classified as less dashing than parachute troops but more so than normal infantry.

However, there is no obvious evidence to support this view, apart from fifty years of parachute propaganda following the disbandment of the Glider Pilot Regiment in the 1950s. There was little to choose between the performance of the 1st Airlanding Brigade and 1st Parachute Brigade once on the ground in Sicily. The first Allied troops to land in Normandy on D-Day were glider troops from D Company, the 2nd Battalion, The Oxfordshire and Buckinghamshire Light Infantry (2nd Ox & Bucks) from the 6th Airborne Division. These men, commanded by Major John Howard, did not lack *élan* in seizing and holding the bridges over the River Orne and the Orne Canal. The same can be said of the 2nd Ox & Bucks's sister battalion in 6th Airlanding Brigade, the 12th Battalion, The Devonshire Regiment, more popularly known as the 'Red Devons'. The 12th Battalion's D Company suffered heavy casualties, including the company commander and second-in-command, in an attack that involved a bayonet charge during the Battle of Breville on 13 June 1944.[12] While the glider may have attracted a less glamorous image than the parachute, there is no doubt that it was a manifestly more dangerous mode of transport to the battlefield, not least because a glider landing was merely a controlled crash even under ideal conditions. Consequently, glider operations routinely involved a far higher level of injuries and fatalities than parachuting. Glider troops deserve rather more credit than they are routinely accorded in the popular mind. Events at Arnhem were to show that, generally speaking, parachute machismo was a poor substitute for the systematic training undertaken by 1st Airlanding Brigade.

The relative hazards of the glider and the parachute aside, there is now sufficient evidence to assess the condition of the 1st Airborne Division when its training window closed at the beginning of June 1944. Although the situation varied between units, low-level training within the Division, that is up to battalion level, was adequate at the very least. Even allowing for the disciplinary problems in the 1st and 3rd Parachute Battalions, both parachute brigades devoted more than sufficient time to platoon and company training to bring individual, section, platoon and company training and battle drills to a high pitch. The same can be said for 1st Airlanding Brigade, and the larger number of training exercises carried out by the latter provided additional opportunity for practice under realistic conditions. Matters were assisted by the fact that the battalion was the British army's basic administrative building block, which meant that battalion staffs were able to practise their responsibilities even while their constituent companies were undertaking 'independent' training.

Surprisingly, Urquhart does not appear to have shared this view in his account of the opening stages of the battle. Instead, he makes much of the fact that this was a baptism of fire for many of 1st Parachute Brigade's personnel, and that others had not been under fire for a considerable time, as an explanation for slow progress in the face of relatively light German opposition at Arnhem.[13] The logical extension of Urquhart's repeated special pleading on this point is that he considered his men to be insufficiently trained, but this is not borne out by the performance of the airborne troops in the ferocious fighting at the Arnhem road bridge and in the Oosterbeek perimeter, which clearly shows that there was little wrong with 1st Airborne's basic raw material and its individual training. Street-fighting remains the most difficult of all infantry operations, which in this case was largely carried out by NCOs and men operating on their own initiative. This would have been impossible had a significant proportion of those men not had a thorough grounding in basic infantry skills.

The position was less straightforward at battalion and brigade level. The evidence shows that the 1st Airlanding Brigade was the best trained of 1st Airborne's three infantry brigades. By rights, the second best trained should have been 1st Parachute Brigade, and not solely because it spent marginally more time training in the field as a complete brigade than the 4th Parachute Brigade. While 1st Parachute Brigade had suffered heavy losses in its ill-starred operations in North Africa and more especially Sicily, it retained a leavening of officers and men with battle experience. By the time the Brigade left for Arnhem, this category included all three of the Brigade's battalion commanders and, arguably most importantly, the Brigade commander himself. Brigadier Lathbury, it will be remembered, had commanded the portion of the 1st Parachute Brigade delivered in the right place through the chaos at the Ponte Primasole, and therefore had first-hand experience of the reality of live airborne operations. However, as we have seen, this generated little if any urgency in the 1st Parachute Brigade's training regime, a short-coming that may have been directly attributable to this leavening overestimating the value of its experience and capabilities. Neither did it prevent the disciplinary problems suffered by 1st and 3rd Parachute Battalions, which appear to have arisen from the same source.

Consequently, the training gap between the 1st and 4th Parachute Brigades may have been more apparent than real. The 4th Parachute Brigade was not totally without combat experience, because the 11th Parachute Battalion had carried out several small-scale parachute operations in the Aegean and Adriatic. The Brigade also contained a high proportion of regular soldiers and its commander, Brigadier John Hackett, was a highly intelligent and forthright regular cavalry officer who did not tolerate indiscipline or low standards. The bulk of the 1st Parachute Brigade did not perform especially well in the first vital hours after jumping in to Arnhem, and certainly did not display the *élan* routinely attributed to parachute troops. Whether the 4th Parachute brigade would have performed any better in the same specific circumstances can only be speculated upon, for it was dismembered on arrival at Arnhem and fed piecemeal into a rapidly deteriorating situation.

Generally speaking, apart from the fact that their personnel losses had been made good, the condition of 1st Airborne Division's constituent infantry formations by June 1944 remained much the same as when they arrived in the UK in December 1943. More seriously, this also applied to the 1st Airborne Division itself. During its entire sojourn in the Mediterranean, 1st Airborne Division had never operated in its entirety in its primary role. In the nine months between returning to the UK and being dispatched to Arnhem, the Division spent precisely six days in the field as an operational entity, and even then was largely deployed by truck rather than parachute or glider. In practical terms therefore, 1st Airborne Division remained a loosely linked collection of formations rather than the properly integrated and cohesive operational instrument it should and could have been, had the six-month training period been properly utilised.

In fact, in at least one respect 1st Airborne Division's situation was considerably worse than it had been previously, and that was over the matter of command. On its return from the Mediterranean, it will be remembered, the Division was commanded by the highly experienced Down, who was the perfect man for the job of knitting together 1st Airborne's constituent parts. However, Down was sidelined in favour of Urquhart. This switch was one of the main roots of all that subsequently befell the 1st Airborne Division. Urquhart's ignorance of the requirements and realities of airborne operations rendered him unable to shape his Division's training, even had other circumstances not conspired against him. As we shall see, this ignorance was also clearly apparent in the planning for Operation Market, and in his behaviour once on the ground in Holland. It is highly unlikely that Down would have permitted the six-month training window to be squandered in the way it largely was, and there is every possibility that he would have refused to accept the plan under which Urquhart led 1st Airborne to Arnhem. In fairness, it has to be said that much of this was not Urquhart's fault. There is no evidence that he actively sought the command, and he questioned his suitability to Browning, who brushed his doubts aside. The cavalier manner in which Browning administered his airborne fiefdom was to claim a heavy price from the officers and men of the 1st Airborne Division, who had a right to expect better.

This, then, was the reality behind the received wisdom that the 1st Airborne Division was the premier and most experienced British airborne formation when it was dispatched to Arnhem. 1st Airborne was premier only in the numerical sense. Its experience was a widely spread and thin leavening at best, only its lower-level personnel were trained to anything approaching a uniformly adequate standard, and it was commanded by a man with no airborne experience whatsoever. It may be overstating the case to say that 1st Airborne was not battle worthy, but by how much is a matter of opinion.

PLAGIARISED, BULLIED
AND HIJACKED

THE 1ST POLISH INDEPENDENT PARACHUTE BRIGADE,
SEPTEMBER 1941–AUGUST 1944

Polish interest in parachuting, albeit as a sport rather than a military skill, dated back to the late 1930s. The activities of the Polish LOPP (League for National Air Defence) mirrored that of the Soviet *Komsomol* and *Oasviakhim*, by promoting sport parachuting and gliding and providing public facilities. The first Polish public parachuting tower was erected in Warsaw in 1936, and by 1939 seventeen more had been erected across the country. Polish Boy Scouts gave a parachuting demonstration at the 5th International Scouting Jamboree in August 1937.[1] The Polish military initially used parachuting as a character-building exercise for trainee officers, with voluntary training courses being offered to cadets in their final year of training; other options included sport gliding, rock climbing and hill walking. Military parachute towers were constructed at officer cadet schools at Bydgoszcz and Legionovo, and at the infantry school at Komorovo. Volunteers underwent a four-week course, which incorporated pre-jump ground training, two or three jumps from a captive balloon, and three jumps from an aircraft. They were also taught parachute packing, and were responsible for packing their own equipment. On completion of the course, successful candidates were awarded a small enamelled parachute badge which, though unofficial, was permitted on military uniform.[2]

In September 1937 the Poles formed a parachute sabotage and diversion force, and established a Military Parachuting Centre at Bydgoszcz in May 1939. Entry was open to volunteers of all ranks, and the Centre was also tasked with research and development work. The first course of trainees graduated in June 1939, but the German invasion on 1 September 1939 caused the second course to be cut short. The Centre was destroyed in the fighting, and the graduates and staff were dispersed. This proved fortuitous for the establishment of a British airborne force, for at least some of these men and their invaluable expertise eventually wound up in Britain after the débâcles in France and Norway.[3]

In mid-1941 the exiled Polish General Staff in London passed a paper containing the distilled essence of their own airborne experience and operational theorising to the War Office. Whilst largely unacknowledged by the British, this paper was nonetheless heavily plagiarised, and provided a significant and much-needed boost to the British airborne effort, which had hitherto concentrated overwhelmingly on administration and training.[4] More practical assistance was also provided, and at least three Polish officers served at Ringway. A Lieutenant Bleicher had been an instructor at the Polish State Gliding School, and Lieutenants Julian Gebolys and Jerzy Gorecki had been similarly employed at the Polish parachute training centre at Bydgoszcz. The latter pair proved especially useful when large numbers of Polish trainees began to pass through the Parachute Training Squadron (PTS) at Ringway. In addition, Gebolys was responsible for introducing the British and the Americans to the idea of manipulating the rigging lines to spill air from the canopy during the descent. This allowed the parachutist to exert a limited degree of directional control, and was christened the 'Polish Method' in Gebolys's honour.

Parallel with this, the Poles were raising their own airborne units in Britain. The first was raised in September 1940 by the Polish General Staff's Sixth or Special Bureau, the Polish equivalent of the British Special Operations Executive, which was responsible for liaison with the underground Home Army in Poland.[5] Christened the *Cichociemni*, Polish for 'Silent and Unseen', the unit was intended for covert operations, and was drawn largely from Polish officers evacuated from France in June 1940. The first contingent of twenty volunteers, drawn from the Polish 4th Cadre Rifle Brigade, commenced training at the Special Training Centre

(STC) at Lochailort near Fort William in Scotland, and moved to RAF Ringway for parachute training in October.

The *Cichociemni* were followed by a more conventional airborne effort. This was the transformation of the entire 4th Cadre Rifle Brigade, raised and commanded by Colonel Stanislaw Sosabowski, into a parachute unit. Sosabowski had escaped from Poland in 1939, and served with the reconstituted Polish army in France in 1940. He escaped again to Britain via Dunkirk, and ended up in Glasgow with a large number of other Poles. Sosabowski's efficiency in organising a holding camp at Biggar led to him being given command of the Canadian Officers Cadre Brigade in July 1940. This unit was intended to provide officers for an abortive scheme to raise units in Canada from Polish *émigrés*. The brigade was renamed the 4th Cadre Rifle Brigade in mid-August 1940, and was assigned a coastal defence role in Fife in eastern Scotland in October 1940, occupying billets around Leven.[6] The conversion of the 4th Cadre Rifle Brigade into a parachute unit was conceived jointly by Sosabowski and the Polish General Staff. The rationale was that an airborne operation was likely to be the quickest way to get liberating troops onto Polish soil; hence the Brigade's motto, 'By The Shortest Way'. This explains why, unlike other Polish units raised in Britain, Sosabowski's unit remained under the direct control of the Polish government, in exile, at least until June 1944.

The Poles established a preliminary parachute training centre in the grounds of Largo House, an eighteenth-century mansion near Leven, in February 1941.[7] Although done without reference to the British airborne training infrastructure, it was configured to match British practices and equipment. For example, open-ended barrels were mounted in the loft of one of Largo House's stable block, to mimic the aperture exit of the Armstrong Whitworth Whitley. Dropping through the barrels onto PT mats and sawdust allowed trainees to practise exit drills. The Poles also erected a sixty-foot parachuting tower, similar in design to those used for sport para-chuting in Poland in the 1930s. The Polish General Staff contributed a grant of £500 to cover the cost of construction, and the tower was ceremonially opened on 20 July 1941. It used a cable attached to a parachute, which was kept open by a metal hoop. The cable feed was controlled by compressed air, which allowed the instructor to control the rate of descent and to coach the trainee throughout the descent. British visitors to Leven were so impressed with the idea that a similar structure was in regular use at Ringway by mid-1943. The effectiveness of the tower is clear from the fact that Sosabowski's men suffered virtually no injuries when they began to rotate through Ringway in late 1941. Interestingly, Sosabowski considered tower training alone to be sufficient to maintain parachuting skills after the qualifying course. In his view, aircraft training jumps were superfluous and a source of needless injuries. Given the disruption parachute training caused 1st Airborne Division's parachute brigades, it is interesting to speculate whether a similar regime might have been beneficial for them.

The Leven tower was not the only Polish airborne innovation the British copied. The 'Monkey Grove' set up in the grounds of Largo House was a large assault course equipped with a variety of obstacles and facilities for more conventional PT. The purpose of the course was to prepare trainees physically and psychologically for live parachute training.[8] The essential features of the Monkey Grove, and indeed the entire Polish preliminary training effort, were subsequently incorporated into what became the Airborne Depot at Hardwick Hall. Like Largo House, the Depot was intended to toughen prospective parachute training candidates for the rigours of the PTS, and included a series of tests to ensure their physical and mental suitability. Incidentally, this principle remains a feature in British airborne selection to the present day, with candidates being physically tested through the physical rigours of 'P' Company, and mentally on the 'Trainazium' confidence course, before being allowed to pass on to parachute training.

Another Polish practice subsequently adopted by the British concerned the selection of personnel for parachute service. Sosabowski rejected the voluntary principle, and members of the 4th Cadre Rifle Brigade were not given a choice about becoming paratroopers. Only those who failed to pass a medical board using criteria employed at Ringway were released for service with Polish units elsewhere. According to Sosabowski, this policy was adopted to ensure equality of sacrifice, although he may have also had an ulterior motive.[9] The supply of Polish recruits to maintain Polish units in Britain was beginning to run short by 1941, and competition was fierce for those available. This largely explains the substantial diplomatic effort to secure the repatriation of Polish POWs from the Soviet Union at this time. Had he adhered to the voluntary principle therefore, Sosabowski might have had little chance of finding replacements. Sosabowski's unit achieved operational status on 23 September 1941, following a mock parachute assault on a British coastal battery at Kincraig Point for the benefit of the Polish Commander-in-Chief, General Sikorski. Sikorski was most impressed, and issued specially commissioned Polish parachute qualification wings at the end of the exercise. He also authorised renaming the 4th Cadre Rifle Brigade the 1st Polish Independent Parachute Brigade, a change confirmed by the Polish General Staff on 4 October 1941.

Up to this point, relations between Sosabowski's unit and the British airborne establishment had been cordial. The British gained a great deal from the Poles generally, and reciprocated with advice, equipment and some practical assistance, such as providing parachute training for the entire Polish Brigade at Ringway, or allowing Sosabowski to 'borrow' the twelve RAF aircraft used in the demonstration for Sikorski. However, this began to change after the 1st Polish Independent Parachute Brigade completed its basic training in September 1941. It appears that the existence of a fully formed parachute brigade outside the British airborne fold whetted Browning's empire-building appetite, for he took a keen interest in the Polish Brigade from the outset. His first visit to the Polish unit was on 21 November 1941, only three weeks after he assumed command of the 1st Airborne Division, and the presentation he made to the Poles was highly symbolic. It was a pennant, bearing a Pegasus on one side and a Polish Eagle on the other, inscribed with the words '1st British Airborne Division to the 1st Polish Parachute Brigade'. Missing the word 'Independent' from the Polish unit's title may or may not have been accidental.

The independence of Sosabowski's unit, and the principle that it was to be used only for the liberation of Poland, had been guaranteed by an agreement between Sikorski and the British CIGS, Alan Brooke, in 1942. This, however, did not prevent Browning from turning on the charm in an effort to woo Sosabowski. In November 1941 he broached the idea of using the Polish Brigade to foment revolt in the large Polish expatriate community in Northern France. This highly unlikely scenario must have been a gambit to assess Sosabowski's attitude. In September 1942 Browning tried another unlikely device, suggesting Sosabowski take command of an airborne Division incorporating all British and Polish airborne units. Sosabowski diplomatically referred Browning to his political masters on both occasions, and informed them of his suspicion that Browning was intent on gaining control of his brigade. In March 1943 Browning increased the pressure, with a government-level request for control of the Polish Brigade. Two months later he visited Sosabowski's HQ and bluntly informed him that he was attempting to get the agreement between Sikorski and Alan Brooke annulled, in order to employ the Polish Brigade in Europe. He also made a request to the Polish General Staff for control of the brigade, and when that was refused, tried to have the Poles moved south to Salisbury Plain. Sosabowski correctly saw through this attempt to take control of his brigade by the back door, but his refusal to comply led to a whole series of problems in obtaining aircraft and other equipment for training from Ringway.

Matters took a turn for the worse after Sikorski died in an air crash at Gibraltar on 4 July 1943. Within the year the high-level pressure brought to bear on the Polish government by Alan Brooke and Montgomery, among others, proved decisive. Thus in March 1944 the Polish Cabinet agreed to allow Sosabowski's Brigade to be employed on the European mainland, providing a series of pre-conditions were met. Montgomery rejected the very idea of pre-conditions out of hand, however, and on 6 June 1944 the Polish Cabinet caved in and handed control of the Brigade to the British. Thus, after two years and nine months, Browning finally gained control over Sosabowski and his command. The

Brigade moved from Leven to Peterborough, on the edge of 1st Airborne Division's concentration area, at the beginning of July 1944. There it embarked on a series of working up exercises, leading up to a three-day brigade exercise beginning on 30 July. It is interesting to note that the working up exercises carried out by Sosabowski's unit ran from individual training through company and battalion and up to the full brigade, all in the space of a single month, and including at least one aircraft parachute jump. This performance casts an even more critical light on the activities of the British 1st and 4th Parachute Brigades in the period January to June 1944, and shows what could have been achieved with a little more thought, organisation and application. The 1st Polish Independent Parachute Brigade was considered to be fully operational with effect from 1 August 1944, and it came under command of the 1st Airborne Division on 10 August.

The British justification for their Machiavellian railroading of the Poles can be summed up as follows. Browning was favourably disposed toward the Poles, but he became increasingly exasperated with Sosabowski's refusal to see sense and acknowledge that his brigade could be most efficiently employed under British command. Sosabowski was merely stalling when he complained that his formation was understrength and insufficiently trained, because he was determined to keep his unit back for a private war with the Germans. Sosabowski's behaviour was thus selfish and counter to the common Allied good, and displayed extreme ingratitude for all the assistance unstintingly provided by their British hosts.[10]

The problem with this is, of course, that it takes no account of the fact that the Poles achieved most of what they did without British assistance, or with a minimal amount at best. Tales of Browning's largesse toward the Poles have been much exaggerated. More importantly, the British view totally ignores the scale and importance of the Polish input into the British airborne effort. The 1941 Polish General Staff paper provided the British with a major short-cut in their doctrinal development, as did adopting the Polish training practices employed at Leven, and the fact that these were blatantly plagiarised by the British added insult to injury. It can therefore be strongly argued that the Poles were more sinned against than sinning. In addition, there were some very pertinent reasons why Sosabowski would not have wanted his men placed under British command. Given his close contact with the British airborne establishment, Sosabowski must have been aware of the misuse and incompetent handling of the British airborne units in the Mediterranean. Add to this the not unjustified British reputation for being somewhat cavalier with the lives of non-British forces under their command, as exemplified by their handling of Australian and Canadian forces in both world wars, and Sosabowski's reluctance becomes very understandable. As we shall see, Sosabowski's fears proved to be fully justified, although it is doubtful if he anticipated the extent to which the British were to mistreat him and his brigade, even in his worst nightmare.

CHANGE AT THE TOP, HURRY UP AND WAIT AT THE BOTTOM

THE FORMATION OF THE 1ST ALLIED AIRBORNE ARMY AND 1ST AIRBORNE DIVISION, JUNE–SEPTEMBER 1944

Whatever its actual condition, 1st Airborne Division was designated operational on the eve of the Allied invasion of Normandy as scheduled, and immediately went on standby for operations in support of the landings. In fact, 1st Airborne, or parts thereof, were committed for two prospective operations before the invasion commenced. Hackett's 4th Parachute Brigade was placed on four-hour standby for a reinforcing drop wherever needed in the beachhead, codenamed 'Tuxedo'. Operation 'Wastage' was basically Tuxedo expanded to include the whole Division, and was intended as a stop-gap measure in case poor weather disrupted the disembarkation of follow-on forces. In the event, both operations were cancelled. However, while 1st Airborne was preparing for Tuxedo and Wastage, the US 82nd and 101st and British 6th Airborne Divisions were making ready to spearhead the sea-landings, in the largest airborne effort in history to date.

At the same time the British 6th and US 82nd and 101st Airborne Divisions were engaged in Normandy, a new level of command was being formed over them in the UK. The need for additional integration within the Allied airborne effort had increased steadily from the first large-scale Allied airborne operations in the Mediterranean in 1943. At the most basic level, it was necessary to regularise equipment, practices and procedures, particularly as co-operation between the British and US airborne and air forces became more widespread. For example, the Americans adopted the British practice of equipping paratroopers with kit bags for extraneous kit and the RAF's 'Eureka/Rebecca' radar homing devices to assist its pathfinder units in setting up drop zones,[1] while the British airborne force became increasingly reliant upon the USAAF for transport. The latter brought its own complications, as shown by the complaints levelled at their US carriers by 1st and 4th Parachute Brigades following Exercises Tony and Dorothy in April 1944.[2] Consequently, Eisenhower's Supreme Headquarters Allied Expeditionary Force (SHAEF) issued its Standard Operating Procedure for Airborne and Troop Carrier Units in March 1944. This was intended to regularise training and operational procedures between all four airborne and air forces, and to delineate their respective responsibilities.

Developments at the higher level were less straightforward and more controversial. The idea of establishing an overarching airborne command level, to control airborne formations and the air transport units that carried them into battle, appears to have originated with Eisenhower in May 1944. He was strongly supported by his superior Marshall and the USAAF Chief, Major-General Henry 'Hap' Arnold, and, it is interesting to note given his close and developing relationship with Browning, by Montgomery too. Embarking on such a course made a certain amount of sense, if only because of the huge expansion of the Allied airborne force. When the British airborne force made its large-scale combat debut in November 1942 its total operational strength was a single parachute brigade. Eighteen months later, on the eve of the Normandy invasion, the British airborne force in the UK had expanded into the 1st British Airborne Corps, which was responsible for the 1st and 6th Airborne Divisions, the 1st Special Air Service Brigade and the 1st Polish Independent Parachute Brigade. Similarly, US 82nd Airborne had been joined by the 101st and 17th Airborne Divisions, which were grouped together under the aegis of US XVIII Airborne Corps. An additional level of command could be expected not only to enhance co-ordination between the US and British airborne forces, but more importantly to allow the most efficient allocation of their respective air transport resources.

However, Eisenhower's idea was strongly opposed by a number of senior US officers, including Lieutenant-General Omar Bradley, the commander of the US 1st Army, and airborne generals Ridgeway and Gavin, who felt such a development would be an unnecessary bureaucratic encumbrance. Their preference was to retain the US airborne force for the support of US ground formations. In addition, they were particularly worried by the possibility of a joint command coming under British control. Browning's empire-building tendencies and lack of operational airborne experience, it seems, had not gone unnoticed. Eisenhower, however, remained undaunted. On 2 June 1944 SHAEF issued a proposal for what was to become the 1st Allied Airborne Army, which Eisenhower approved in his capacity as Allied Supreme Commander on 20 June. USAAF Lieutenant-General Lewis H. Brereton, then commander of the US 9th Air Force, was selected to command the 1st Allied Airborne Army on 17 July 1944, and the formation was formally established on 2 August 1944.[3] Browning was given the post of Deputy Commander.

In the event, 1st Allied Airborne Army was a compromise that pleased no-one except possibly Eisenhower. Brereton did not want the appointment which, as an airpower zealot, he considered to be a demotion, and Browning was dissatisfied because he felt the command should have been his. This was compounded by the fact that the two men did not get on. By any standard, Brereton was an odd choice, given his total lack of airborne experience, and it is highly likely that Bradley was behind it. Bradley was highly dissatisfied with Brereton's performance with the US 9th Air Force and was apparently delighted to see him removed. Such a compromise would have been typical of Eisenhower's conciliatory style of command.[4] Even though they failed to stymie the establishment of the 1st Allied Airborne Army therefore, Bradley's faction came out best because they ensured that an American commanded the new formation, and because it firmly placed the British in second place. Overall then, the resulting arrangement was the worst of both worlds, but it was nonetheless the one under which Operation Market Garden was launched.

While all this was going on at the top, 1st Airborne Division was busy standing by for a host of aborted operations. The first, unnamed, operation after Tuxedo and Wastage tasked 1st Airborne to reinforce the US 82nd Airborne Division between 7–10 June 1944, but the operation was abandoned after it became apparent that the planned landing zones were unsuitable for the Horsa glider. Operation 'Wild Oats' proposed dropping 1st Airborne near Carpiquet airfield near Caen, in order to block the advance of German reinforcements toward the British invasion beaches. As this was the operational area of the 12 SS *Panzer* Division, it is perhaps fortunate that the Canadian ground advance rendered Wild Oats unnecessary. The same can be said of an unnamed scheme concocted in mid-July to drop 1st Airborne mid-way between Caen and Falaise, given that the German defenders included two SS and one *Heer Panzer* divisions that had repeatedly mauled British and Canadian armoured units.

The period 22 June–3 July was spent preparing for 'Beneficiary', a joint British-US operation in support of a US landing to seize St Malo in Brittany. Next came Operation 'Swordhilt', which ran 20 July–4 August, and was intended to cut off Brest by destroying the Morlaix Viaduct. Operation 'Hands-Up' was scheduled to take place in the same area between 15 July–15 August, in support of the US 3rd Army. Hands-Up was overtaken by Operation 'Transfigure', which tasked 1st Airborne and the 101st Airborne to seize landing strips near Rambouillet for the British 52nd (Lowland) Division. The 52nd was originally a mountain warfare unit, but was re-designated an 'Airportable' formation and attached to 1st British Airborne Corps in the summer of 1944. The object of Transfigure was to block the German line of retreat toward Paris. When it was cancelled, both Divisions remained in their marshalling area on standby for Operation 'Boxer', the seizure of the heavily fortified port of Boulogne; it was finally cancelled on 26 August.

The missions up to and including Boxer were connected to enlarging the beachhead and the initial breakout after the German defeat at Falaise, and were instigated by SHAEF. Responsibility shifted to the 1st Allied Airborne Army once the latter headquarters became operational on 2 August, however, and the focus of projected missions switched to supporting Montgomery's 21st Army Group in its dash across northern France and into the Low Countries. The first two missions ran parallel and overlapped with Boxer. Operation 'Axehead' was intended to seize crossings over the River Seine, using 1st Airborne and the 1st Polish Independent Parachute Brigade. Operation 'Linnet' was a larger affair involving the 82nd and 101st Airborne Divisions and the British 52nd (Lowland) Division, as well as 1st Airborne and the Poles.

Linnet was scheduled for 3 September 1944, and was intended to block the German withdrawal from Normandy by seizing bridges across the River Escaut and other terrain in the area of Tournai and Lille in north-eastern France; again, it was overtaken by the rapid British and Canadian ground advance. A derivative, codenamed 'Linnet II', proposed shifting the operation east to the area of Maastricht on the German border, but both operations were cancelled on 5 September. At the same time as the Linnets were cancelled, 1st Allied Airborne Army was placed directly at the disposal of British 21st Army Group. This was to assist 21st Army Group in crossing the Lower Rhine, although one other mission was briefly considered. Operation 'Infatuate' proposed an airborne landing on the fortified island of Walcheren, which blocked the mouth of the River Scheldt and thus access to the much-needed port of Antwerp. Infatuate never moved beyond the feasibility study stage, due to the lack of suitable landing zones. Walcheren was a relatively small target for parachute insertion, and was unsuitable for glider landings because almost the entire island lay below sea level, and was criss-crossed by dykes and flooded areas.

Between D-Day and 5 September 1944, therefore, fourteen airborne operations were carried forward to differing stages of readiness before being cancelled. According to Urquhart, this was a major factor in reducing 1st Airborne Division's combat readiness, and was thus partly responsible for the Division's poor perform-ance in the initial stages of the advance on Arnhem.[5] Leaving aside the fact that there was already a good deal wrong with 1st Airborne's combat readiness, this received wisdom has been

repeated in virtually every work on Arnhem, although the number
of cancelled operations differs between accounts. Urquhart specifically claims that 1st Airborne prepared for sixteen cancelled operations, Middlebrook cites fifteen, and Powell refers to eighteen.[6]
Otway's official history, however, lists fifteen operations planned
and cancelled before Operation Market Garden, although the last
was subsumed into the latter; hence the fourteen operations cited
above. Otway provides dates for launch and cancellation, and was
writing relatively soon after the event with access to the operational records. He is thus unlikely to have missed any proposed
operations, and it is anyway unclear where any additional proposed
missions could have fitted into the time available.

The impression invariably given is that 1st Airborne went
through the whole preparation process, with planning and briefings at all levels, packing and attaching parachute containers and
loading, glider loading and so forth, for all fourteen operations.
This is a little misleading. Wild Oats was cancelled after a planning
team from 1st Airborne spent twenty-four hours in Normandy,
Swordhilt was cancelled after a warning order had been issued, and
Infatuate never proceeded beyond the feasibility study stage. The
only people in 1st Airborne to deal with these three missions
would therefore have been the divisional signal clerks and possibly
some officers on the planning staff. Otway's official account
strongly suggests that the unnamed plan to reinforce the 82nd
Airborne in the period immediately after D-Day, as well as that to
land 1st Airborne mid-way between Caen and Falaise, did not
advance much further, if at all.

Of the remaining nine cancelled operations, preparations for
Tuxedo clearly ran the full gamut, given that 4th Parachute
Brigade was placed on four-hour standby from D-Day, and similar
conditions presumably applied to the whole of 1st Airborne when
Tuxedo was subsumed into Wastage. This was also the case with
Beneficiary, which raised the novel prospect of landing the whole
of the 1st Airlanding Brigade on a beach, Hands-Up and
Transfigure. While the remaining four operations – Boxer,
Axehead, Linnet and Linnet II – also involved full preparation, it

should be noted that they were all proposed and cancelled in turn during a single, albeit extended, period of standby. This must have lowered the amount of logistic preparation, for the operations were running concurrently at times, which makes it highly unlikely that the aircraft, gliders and containers were unpacked and repacked at every cancellation. The troops would therefore only have had to put up with a surfeit of briefing and planning sessions. Interestingly, the typed confirmation orders issued for Market by 1st Airborne on 12 September cited the aircraft allotment to be the same as for Operation Linnet.[7]

All in all, therefore, this examination shows that actually 1st Airborne was fully prepared for only just over half the operations it is routinely credited with in the run up to Arnhem. That is not to suggest that the round of briefings and cancellations did not have a negative effect on 1st Airborne's morale. Had that been the case, it is unlikely that some of the troops would have begun to refer to their formation as the '1st Stillborn Division'. In part, this was the fault of 1st Allied Airborne Army HQ, which at times passed details of prospective operations to 1st Airborne before they had been approved or even assessed by the senior ground commands involved. This wasted much time and effort on the part of 1st Airborne's planners at the very least.[8] Nonetheless, the fact remains that the number of operations 1st Airborne prepared for, and the degree of preparation undertaken, was significantly less than implied by Urquhart and many others.

The warning order for 1st Airborne Division's fifteenth prospective operation, codenamed 'Comet', went out at the beginning of September 1944. Comet formed the blueprint for Operation Market, complete with potentially fatal flaws.

FROM COMET TO MARKET

THE EVOLUTION OF THE ARNHEM PLAN

As with the previous five operations 1st Airborne had been warned about, Comet was to assist the ground advance of Montgomery's 21st Army Group, and included the 1st Polish Independent Parachute Brigade. By the beginning of September, the lead elements of 21st Army Group had outrun the proposed airhead around Tournai (Operation Linnet), and were well into Belgium heading for Brussels and the Dutch border. Eisenhower authorised Comet as a means to get them over the three major water obstacles in Holland. According to Otway, Comet tasked the 4th Parachute Brigade to seize the crossing over the River Maas near Grave; 1st Airborne HQ, 1st Airlanding Brigade and the Poles those over the River Waal at Nijmegen; and 1st Parachute Brigade those over the Lower Rhine at Arnhem. Interestingly, Sosabowski's account differs from the official history, and adamantly claims that the Poles were to support Hackett's 4th Parachute Brigade at Grave. Comet was originally envisaged as a night operation with *coup-de-main* landings to seize the bridges, although at some point – precisely when is unclear – this was changed to a daylight landing. The reason was presumably a lack of moonlight, which is why Market was launched in daylight, although it is routinely ascribed to an American reluctance to go in at night.

Comet was scheduled for 8 September, but was postponed for two days. It is not clear when the warning order reached 1st Airborne. Sosabowski claims it was 2 September, and was originally code-named 'Fifteen', being changed to Comet three days later. Urquhart gave a detailed briefing at RAF Cottesmore on 6 September. This included two serious interlinked errors, which played the major part in the disaster that later occurred at Arnhem. These were the distance from the landing zones to the objectives,[1] and that the plan took no account of likely German reactions. Urquhart justified this by citing intelligence reports indicating that there were no German forces in the area. Nonetheless, Hackett considered Comet to be a potential disaster, and laid the blame firmly on the inexperience and naivety of the high-level RAF airborne planners. He likened these to cooks producing superb dishes requiring garnish to taste, the dish being the plan to get the airborne troops on the ground, and the enemy being the garnish added as an afterthought, if at all.[2]

How vociferous Hackett was is unclear, but Urquhart was left in no doubt of Sosabowski's opinion. The latter interrupted the Cottesmore briefing several times, culminating in his oft-quoted line 'But the Germans, general, the Germans!'.[3] Sosabowski felt so strongly that he asked Urquhart to confirm his orders in writing on 8 September. To his credit, Urquhart flew him to Browning's HQ the same day. Browning made light of the matter, with an off-hand comment that together the Polish and British airborne force could achieve anything. When Sosabowski refused to be mollified, Browning asked for his solution, which was that Comet required three airborne divisions rather than three brigades. In the event, Comet was cancelled, four hours short of H-Hour, on 10 September, and was modified rather than discarded.

Comet was cancelled because 21st Army Group had outrun its supplies, and because of unexpectedly stiff German resistance in the areas selected for the ground jump-off. There were two reasons for the supply shortfall. Instead of securing a major port in Normandy, two temporary harbours codenamed 'Mulberries', were constructed at Omaha Beach (Mulberry A) and Gold Beach (Mulberry B), which allowed personnel and materiel to be unloaded directly over the beach. This was only intended as a temporary expedient until Cherbourg could be secured, but the German garrison comprehensively demolished the docks there. Other Channel ports were tenaciously defended after Hitler declared them 'Festungen' (fortresses) to be defended to the death; some held out to the end of the war. The Allies were thus obliged to rely on the Mulberries, and Mulberry A was destroyed in a severe storm on 19–22 June 1944.

The second reason was the speed and scale of the Allied breakout from Normandy. The Allies had expected a costly step-by-step battle across France, but the destruction of *Heeresgruppe* B near Falaise on 21 August 1944, with an estimated loss of 10,000 killed, 50,000 prisoners and nearly 400 armoured vehicles, led to a virtual German collapse. Patton's 3rd Army and Montgomery's 21st Army Group crossed the River Seine on 26 and 29 August respectively. By 30 August Patton's troops were closing on Metz and Nancy in Lorraine, while Montgomery's men liberated Brussels on 3 September and reached the Belgian-Dutch border shortly thereafter. No-one had envisaged such a rapid and spectacular advance, and especially one largely dependent on a relatively small temporary port that required everything to be hauled across the breadth of France and Belgium. Two divergent axes running north and south of the Ardennes thus replaced Eisenhower's planned broad front, and the position was exacerbated by Montgomery and Patton each demanding exclusive access to what supplies were available. Eisenhower met Montgomery at Brussels on 10 September 1944 and, despite Eisenhower having to remind him who was in charge at one point, Montgomery persuaded the Supreme Commander to allow him to implement a narrow thrust into Holland to Arnhem. For this he was assigned all three of 1st Allied Airborne Army's airborne divisions and the attached 52nd (Lowland) Division. Thus was Operation Market Garden born from Operation Comet.

Eisenhower's decision was both fair-minded and courageous. Montgomery was still smarting from being forced to hand over supreme control in Europe to Eisenhower on 1 September, and made no secret of his dissatisfaction with Eisenhower's handling of matters. While Patton and certain sections of the US press were its most vociferous propagators, the view that Eisenhower was overly sympathetic to the British was widely shared in the US leadership in Europe.[4] Eisenhower's decision appears to have been purely pragmatic, however. Patton's 3rd Army may have been across the

Meuse and into Lorraine, but that region contained a number of fortified areas, the legacy of the series of shifts in the Franco-German border from the second half of the nineteenth century, backed by the modern defences of the Siegfried Line. Patton was convinced the latter was an empty shell, and that his army was capable of rapidly pushing on and over the Rhine into Germany proper. However, the fixed defences at Metz gave Patton's men their first serious pause since the breakout from Normandy, and subsequent events in the Hürtgen Forest and in the Reichswald suggest Patton was being rather optimistic.

Given this, Eisenhower was correct to back an advance into Holland, which faced no permanent fortifications and offered the prospect of outflanking the Siegfried Line altogether. Montgomery, predictably, took Eisenhower's assent as the signal to start planning a subsequent deep thrust into Germany, as shown by the directive issued on 14 September warning the British 2nd Army to pre-pare for an advance toward Hamm in order to cut off the Ruhr. However, Eisenhower claimed to have made it clear to Montgomery that clearing the approaches to the port of Antwerp to relieve the supply situation was his first priority, and that estab-lishing a bridgehead over the Lower Rhine was as far as he was willing to go at that time. Eisenhower's reaction to Montgomery's directive was therefore a memo merely stating that it met the basic concept as agreed at the 10 September meeting, which was not the same as granting permission for the larger scheme.[5] Be that as it may, the important point is that Montgomery had secured permis-sion to implement his narrow thrust, along with the lion's share of available resources. This set in train the chain of events that was to culminate in the destruction of the 1st Airborne Division over the nine days between 17–26 September 1944.

There is one further aspect to consider before moving on to examine the Market Garden plan. This is Montgomery's approach to the Comet concept, because it has become fashionable to place all the responsibility upon him for the Arnhem debacle.[6] Montgomery's reputation was firmly based on methodical execu-tion of carefully prepared plans, which endeavoured to minimise friendly casualties; the latter was a legacy of Montgomery's service on the Western Front during the First World War. This pattern began with the battle of El Alamein, and continued after Market Garden with the operations to clear the Reichswald and the subsequent crossing of the Rhine at Wesel. Indeed, the German commander of the reconstituted *Heeresgruppe* B in Holland, *Feldmarschall* Walther Model, and his chief-of-staff, General Hans Krebs, discounted the possibility of an Allied airborne operation in Holland precisely because Montgomery was in charge.[7] Embarking on a risky venture like Comet/Market Garden was thus out of character for Montgomery, and raises the question of why he acted as he did.

Montgomery may have been prompted by a desire to capitalise on the Germans' disorganisation after their defeat at Falaise. This was apparent in Holland, where the locals dubbed the peak of the panicked and disorganised German flight on 5 September 'Mad Tuesday'.[8] On this basis, striking rapidly to retain the initiative made perfect operational sense. Montgomery was also under political pressure from London to launch Comet/Market Garden in order to neutralise German V2 missile launching sites in western Holland. The first of these missiles struck the British capital on 8 September, and Montgomery showed Eisenhower the communication urging haste on 10 September. However, neither of these factors appears sufficient to prompt a drastic switch in approach. Montgomery had been under at least as great political pressure during his repeated and unsuccessful attempts to break out of the Allied beachhead near Caen, and he did not abandon his methodical approach. Neither did he throw caution to the winds in the immediate aftermath of the destruction of the Falaise Pocket, even though the situation provided the perfect justification. Montgomery's 21st Army Group had closed up to the River Seine by 25 August, but did not cross it to commence 'the Great Swan' to Brussels and the Dutch border until 29 August.

Nor do the background circumstances appear to be the reason for Montgomery's uncharacteristic behaviour. The precarious supply situation was hardly conducive to undertaking risky operations and, more importantly, neither was the proven German ability to improvise stubborn and effective defence from the scantiest resources. The

German retreat into Holland may have peaked on 5 September, but the first steps toward reorganising the German defence started the day before. The British units laying the groundwork for Operation Garden were well aware of this. On 7 September, the Guards Armoured Division established a bridgehead over the Albert Canal at Beeringen, and over the next week succeeded in pushing a further twenty miles north and establishing two further bridgeheads over the Meuse-Escaut Canal. This progress was made in the face of fierce resistance from a variety of hastily formed units, including two battalion-size SS *Kampfgruppen* (Battle Groups) reinforced with *Jagdpanzer* IV tank destroyers and self-propelled artillery.[9]

It is therefore highly unlikely that Montgomery's uncharacteristic behaviour was prompted solely by political pressure or by a perception of continuing German disarray, which means it had to be some other factor. The fact that he had to sell Comet/Market Garden to Eisenhower shows that his change of tack was not motivated by his military superior. Admittedly, the relationship between the two commanders had grown increasingly strained since Montgomery had relinquished control of ground operations to Eisenhower on 1 September 1944. However, while pique may have been a contributing factor in his enthusiasm for Comet/Market Garden, it is unlikely to have been the sole motivation. There was another factor in the equation: the role of the deputy commander of the 1st Allied Airborne Army. The popular view of Browning's role in the run up to Arnhem is of a faithful subordinate carrying out the orders of his superior. Most accounts have him waiting at 21st Army Group's HQ on 10 September to learn what Montgomery had in mind after his meeting with Eisenhower, and flying back to the UK post haste with the details once all had been revealed.[10] At this point Montgomery is supposed to have confidently responded to Browning's assertion that 1st Airborne Division could hold the bridges at Arnhem for four days by insisting only two days would be necessary, which prompted the latter's alleged comment that the operation might be 'going a bridge too far'.[11]

All this accords perfectly with the recent tendency to view Montgomery as the villain of the piece. However, according to

Urquhart, all this took place not after Eisenhower's departure on 10 September, but on the day *before* that meeting, in Montgomery's caravan at 21st Army Group HQ. This is a far more likely scenario, because Montgomery was extremely unlikely to have tried to sell Eisenhower the Comet/Market Garden scheme without a properly drawn up plan. Indeed, the speed with which the Market plan emerged after the meeting between Eisenhower and Montgomery fully supports this suggestion. Browning was back at 1st Allied Airborne Army HQ by 14:30 on the afternoon of 10 September, and by 18:00 he was presenting a detailed briefing to senior officers from all three airborne divisions, the Polish brigade and the air transport units.[12] This was extremely fast work even allowing for the prior preparations for Comet, and means that 1st Allied Airborne Army HQ must have been working from a pre-prepared plan. It is equally likely that Montgomery was privy to the development of that planning, given the close working relationship that developed between him and Browning in the run up to D-Day, and that 1st Allied Airborne Army was tasked to support 21st Army Group after the initial breakout from Normandy. All this made Browning the logical person for Montgomery to turn to for airborne advice.

However, the cosy image of Browning as the dutiful and compliant subordinate does not sit well with the self-serving, empire-building reality, and the latter may well point to the reason for Montgomery's sudden and temporary embrace of high risk. Airborne knowledge was not Montgomery's strong point, which made him especially reliant upon Browning the airborne expert, flimsy though the latter's own credentials were. It is therefore perfectly possible that Montgomery did not fully appreciate the degree of risk involved in Comet/Market Garden either because Browning did not fully appreciate it himself, or because he deliberately minimised it for reasons of his own. There is evidence to support both these contentions. The clearest overt example of Montgomery's over-confidence is his alleged boast to Browning that his ground forces would relieve 1st Airborne Division at Arnhem within two days. Only two accounts refer to this conversation, neither author was present during the exchange, and they do not cite any eye-witnesses.[13]

It is therefore legitimate to question whether the exchange took place at all, which casts doubt on Browning's oft-quoted comment about going a 'bridge too far' as well. This was a suspiciously prescient observation with the benefit of hindsight, and faith in its veracity is further undermined by the fact that the precise wording varies, being rendered as 'I think we might be going *a* bridge too far', or 'I think we might be going *one* bridge too far'.[14] Whichever, Browning was fully aware that failure to seize any one crossing rendered the whole operation both redundant and pointless. Thus if he really did think they were going a bridge too far, he should have been arguing strenuously to persuade Montgomery not to launch the operation at all, rather than making platitudinous remarks for posterity.[15]

Montgomery's over-confidence may well have rubbed off from Browning and the higher levels of the British Airborne establishment. The latter's attitude is perfectly illustrated in Browning's dismissive response to Sosabowski's reservations over Comet, to the effect that the Red Devils could accomplish anything. Similar over-confidence was something of a constant from the earliest days of the British airborne force. The tendency and its unfortunate consequences began with the Tragino Raid of February 1941, which blithely expected the participants to cover sixty miles of mountainous terrain in forty-eight hours, and was continued by Hopkinson with his insistence that half-trained glider pilots assemble and fly unfamiliar machines into action in Sicily. Comet followed this lead by proposing the use of airborne brigades to accomplish tasks that full airborne divisions failed or were later hard pushed to accomplish, and its successor Market did not deviate from the pattern. A specific example is the delivering of 1st Airborne Division to landing zones around seven miles from their target bridges, and deliberately downplaying German strength around Arnhem, to the extent of withholding information from intelligence summaries delivered to 1st Airborne. The former example is discussed in detail below. Browning was personally responsible for the latter, which merits closer examination because it clarifies Browning's underlying motives.

On 10 September 1944, 21st Army Group issued an Intelligence Summary that referred to the presence of the 9th and 10th SS *Panzer*

Divisions in the Arnhem area. This information so concerned the
Senior Intelligence Officer at British 1 Airborne Corps HQ, Major
Brian Urquhart (no relation to the commander of 1st Airborne
Division), that he personally brought it to the attention of 1st
Airborne Corps' operations officer and Browning himself. When his
concerns were brushed aside, Major Urquhart had the area in ques-
tion photographed from the air, and when the resulting pictures
revealed the presence of German armoured vehicles near 1st
Airborne Division's proposed landing zones west of Arnhem, Major
Urquhart took them to Browning in person. Browning's reaction
was to have Urquhart examined by the senior Corps Medical
Officer, who was also Browning's personal physician, and the unfortunate major was diagnosed as suffering from nervous exhaustion
and ordered on sick leave with immediate effect. Urquhart was
offered the alternative of complying or facing a court-martial.[16] The
presence of the German armour was not included in subsequent
intelligence summaries forwarded to 1st Airborne Division.[17]

The reason for Browning's behaviour was quite straightforward.
Browning had secured the second highest rung on the Allied
airborne ladder purely on his skills as a Whitehall warrior, but by
September 1944 it was becoming increasingly apparent that his
elevated status could not be sustained solely on political acumen and
contacts. The crux of the problem was Browning's total lack of operational experience, which left him open to unfavourable comparison with senior Allied airborne officers with combat experience, of
which there was no shortage by the autumn of 1944. Foremost of
these was his arch-rival, Ridgeway, who had doubtless exacerbated
Browning's feelings of inferiority by jumping into Normandy with
his 82nd Airborne Division, and commanded the three-division US
XVIII Airborne Corps within 1st Allied Airborne Army.

Indeed, the precariousness of Browning's position *vis-à-vis*
Ridgeway was clearly demonstrated in a spat with Brereton in early
September over the Linnet II plan. The dispute is usually attributed
to Browning's concern over a lack of maps for issue to the troops,
and he put his intention to resign in writing when Brereton over-
ruled his objections. However, a more recent American account

claims that Browning was deliberately attempting to stymie Linnet II as part of Montgomery's effort to secure resources for his northern thrust plan, because Linnet II was to be launched in support of the US 1st Army rather than the British 2nd Army. Whatever the truth of the matter, and it has to be said that what we have seen of Browning would strongly support the latter, all accounts agree that Brereton responded to Browning's threat by putting Ridgeway on standby to take his place.[18] Although the cancellation of Linnet took the heat out of the situation, Browning can thus have been left in no doubt that he was expendable. Consequently, he badly needed an opportunity to shore up his increasingly threadbare reputation as an airborne commander, and the German collapse after Falaise increased the urgency of his situation by raising the unpalatable prospect of the war coming to an end before such an opportunity arose. The blunt fact is that, for Browning, Market Garden represented the final chance to consolidate his place in the airborne canon and, probably more importantly, his position in the post-war British army. The airborne assault into Holland thus had to go ahead at all costs, and withholding intelligence reports from the men at the sharp end – whose task was clearly going to be a walkover in any case – was a small price to pay for the potential reward.

Viewing matters with this in mind casts things in a somewhat different light. It certainly provides an explanation for Montgomery's curiously sudden and brief embrace of high risk with Comet and Market Garden. Browning was Montgomery's chief, and apparently sole, adviser on airborne matters. It takes no great effort of the imagination to see Browning egging Montgomery on, minimising risks and putting the best face on things in order to weave his own interests into the larger picture. It also explains the widely noted tendency toward over-confidence at the top of the Allied airborne hierarchy that so concerned the men like Sosabowski and Hackett who were charged with carrying out its plans, however unrealistic. Finally, it also explains why Browning was happy to endorse a plan for the British 1st Airborne Division that flew in the face of all airborne experience to date.

FATALLY FLAWED BY MISCONCEPTIONS, IGNORANCE AND DOGMA

THE MARKET PLAN

Things moved fast after Montgomery's 10 September meeting with Eisenhower. Authorisation for Market reached 1st Allied Airborne Army HQ at Moor Park before Browning arrived from Brussels at around 14:30 on that day. Brereton put Browning in charge of the ground side of Market with immediate effect, and by 18:00 he and Browning were delivering a preliminary briefing to thirty-four senior officers. These included Urquhart, Sosabowski, the commanders of RAF No.38 and No.46 Groups and the various Transport group commanders from US 9th Troop Carrier Command, the commander of the 101st Airborne, Maxwell D. Taylor, and Gavin, who had taken over the 82nd Airborne from Ridgeway after Normandy. The fact that the latter was summoned to Moor Park by telephone from visiting friends in London illustrates the haste with which the meeting was convened.

The briefing and following discussion laid out the basic shape of Market. The 101st Airborne was given the most southerly section of the airborne corridor, which stretched north from Eindhoven across the Wilhelmina Canal at Son and the Willemsvaart Canal at Veghel. The 82nd Airborne was assigned the central section of the corridor, which involved seizing the River Maas crossings at Grave and those over the River Waal at Nijmegen, as well as an area of high ground on the Dutch-German border south-east of Nijmegen, called the Groesbeek Heights. 1st Airborne, with the 1st Polish Independent Parachute Brigade under command, was assigned the most northerly objective, the road and rail crossings over the Lower Rhine at Arnhem, sixty-four miles from the relieving force's jumping-off positions just over the Meuse-Escaut Canal between Lommel and Neerpelt on the Dutch-Belgian border. Finally, the British 52nd (Lowland) Division was to be flown into Deelen airfield, which lay seven miles north of Arnhem, once it had been seized by 1st Airborne as one of its subsidiary missions.

Quite why 1st Airborne was allocated the most remote and hazardous objective is uncertain. Urquhart thought his formation had been given the task as a precaution to avoid the diplomatic repercussions if British ground forces failed to relieve a US airborne division marooned sixty-odd miles behind enemy lines on what was essentially a British operation.[1] Gavin, on the other hand, was of the opinion that the allocation merely reflected the location of the individual formations in the UK relative to their Dutch objectives. There are problems with both these explanations, for neither fully fits the circumstances. In the latter case, it was the location of the airfields from which they were to be lifted that counted rather than the location of the divisions themselves, and this only applied to around half of 1st Airborne's units. The Division's parachute units were lifted from US 52nd Troop Carrier Wing bases near 1st Airborne's billets in the East Midlands, but most of the British glider contingent flew from RAF bases fifty miles west of London, which were the most remote of all from Arnhem.

That said, Gavin's explanation is more logical than Urquhart's, and not merely because the latter's smacks very heavily of hindsight. Certainly, the British were not strangers to the idea of employing other people's troops as cannon fodder when the opportunity arose, as illustrated by their usage of Australian and Canadian troops in the First World War, and of the Canadians again after D-Day. It is therefore doubtful that Montgomery and Browning were overly concerned at placing US troops in harm's way in preference to their own, a position supported by the fact that the former retained and misused the two US airborne divisions in the usual British fashion after Market had failed. As these two formations had suffered heavily in Normandy, it may also be that 1st Airborne was selected because it was fresh and ready, at least on paper. It is also possible that Browning had a hand in securing the mission with most kudos for his former command. The upshot was to entrust Market's most hazardous mission to the least experienced and least battle worthy formation involved.

Brereton insisted that all the bridges had to be seized 'with thunderclap surprise'[2], and proposed that Market be launched in four days time, on Thursday 14 September. The assembled airborne commanders demurred, however, and the operation was rescheduled for seven days hence, on Sunday 17 September. As 17 September was the beginning of a no-moon period, Market had to be a daylight operation, because mass night drops were impossible without some natural illumination. The three-day postponement thus obliged a switch from previous Allied airborne practice, although it should be noted that the preference for night insertions was no more than a throwback to the prevailing air situation when the Allied, and especially British, airborne forces were established. At that time German air superiority made large-scale daylight operations hazardous in the extreme, but by September 1944 the Allies had attained a level of air superiority that would have seemed scarcely credible even a year earlier. In any event, the switch to landing in daylight was welcomed by many in the Allied airborne community. As we have seen, night landings had proved to be less than satisfactory, largely due to aircrew training deficiencies. Eisenhower was so concerned over this that he explicitly raised it with Brereton on the latter's appointment to 1st Allied Airborne Army. Landing in daylight therefore promised to avoid the widespread scattering that had dogged every large Allied airborne operation to date.

The assembled commanders reconvened their meeting at 09:00 the next day, on 11 September, at the US 9th Troop Carrier

Opposite: Operation Market Garden, route and objectives.

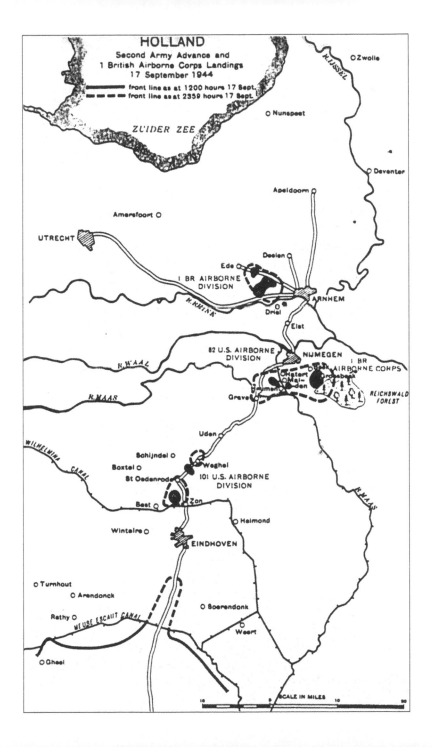

Command HQ in order to finalise the air plan and the precise allocation of transport resources. Until these issues were settled, the individual divisional commanders could not begin their detailed planning. Browning gave the 101st Airborne the largest share, followed by the 82nd Airborne, and finally 1st Airborne. That said, it should be noted that Urquhart's share still amounted to around 475 aircraft, only 110 less than the 101st Airborne, and forty less than the 82nd Airborne.[3] Quite simply, the not inconsiderable combined resources of the USAAF and RAF transport establishments in north-west Europe were still insufficient to deliver three full airborne divisions simultaneously. The logic behind the allocations was revealed when Urquhart almost immediately began to badger Browning to increase 1st Airborne's allocation. It was vital that the 101st Airborne, as the first link in the airborne chain, succeeded in securing its objectives. If it failed to do so, then the other two airborne divisions would be cut off from relief. It therefore made perfect sense to allocate the 101st Airborne the lion's share of the aircraft available for the first lift, however uncomfortable the decision might have been for the other two divisions.

The real downside of the arrangement was that 1st Airborne's bottom position in the pecking order meant its delivery would take three lifts, spread over three days. This was largely due to the decision to allow the Allied transport units to fly only one lift on the first day. The officer charged with co-ordinating the overall air plan was Major-General Paul L. Williams, commander of the US 9th Troop Carrier Command. Williams felt that there would be insufficient time between sorties to carry out maintenance and repair work, concerns doubtless based on the serious shortage of ground crew in his command, not to mention the standard of aircrew training which worried Eisenhower. Flying two lifts in a single day would have required the first to take off and form-up in darkness, a hazardous undertaking with inadequately trained aircrew. Unsurprisingly then, Brereton accepted Williams' advice, and stuck adamantly to it even in the face of special pleading from Montgomery. Brereton's support of Williams' stand was also understandable because his (Williams) Command would be providing the vast majority of the aircraft for Market. Of the 1,575 aircraft slated for the first lift, only 332 were RAF machines, all but twelve of which were deployed as glider tugs; the odd twelve were to carry 1st Airborne's pathfinders from the 21st Independent Parachute Company. Given Brereton's inflexibility, Urquhart had little option but to make the best of a bad job, but this meant that, if everything went as planned, 1st Airborne's third and final increment would arrive in Holland just in time to see 30 Corps relieving the first and second increments.

Whatever its underlying rationale, Brereton's decision to back the single lift per day idea was a bad one, that formed the first link in the chain of events that led to the failure of Market Garden. Brereton placed the needs of his arm of service ahead of the needs of the men being delivered to battle, and thus placed Urquhart and his men at a needless, avoidable and potentially fatal disadvantage by effectively preventing them from achieving the necessary concentration of effort to accomplish their mission. The one person who could, and should, have supported Urquhart in this was Browning, but support was not forthcoming from this quarter, not least because Browning had too much riding on Market going ahead. Even had he been so inclined, Browning's room for manoeuvre was severely limited by his threat to resign over Linnet II, for it is unlikely that Brereton would not have taken him up on his offer a second time, and Ridgeway was still waiting in the wings. Ironically, this might have been no bad thing, for it is highly unlikely that Ridgeway would have accepted the RAF's diktat on 1st Airborne's landing zones with the same equanimity as Browning, although quite what he would have been able to do about it is another matter.

The contention that the Americans would not have tolerated the RAF's chosen landing zones is not based on mere speculation. When Urquhart revealed his plan to the assembled Market commanders at Moor Park on 14 September, the US airborne contingent was horrified at the distance between landing zones and objectives. In Gavin's opinion the British plan resembled a peacetime exercise, and his immediate reaction was to remark to one of his senior staff officers 'My God, he can't mean it'. The

astute Gavin quickly divined that RAF intransigence lay behind
Urquhart's dispositions and also picked up on the British tendency
toward over-confidence. This was in part due to Sosabowski, who
again loudly asked 'But the Germans, how about the Germans,
what about them?', as he had at 1st Airborne's Cottesmore briefing
on 6 September.[4] Even more significantly, Taylor and his staff were
dissatisfied with the original number and location of the drop
zones assigned to the 101st Airborne by Brereton, which were
presumably carried over from the British planning for Comet.
Taylor enlisted the help of 1st Allied Airborne Army's chief-of-staff
to argue his case with Brereton, who originally insisted that the
plan be accepted as given, but then relented. Taylor and his staff
then came up with a plan that relocated and concentrated the 101st
Airborne's landing area into one large and two smaller landing
zones just north of Eindhoven.

To an extent, Brereton's poor judgement in backing the single
lift air plan can be blamed on his dearth of airborne experience.
The same excuse cannot explain the behaviour of the RAF,
however, which imposed an even more disastrous decision upon
the hapless Urquhart regarding the choice of landing zones for 1st
Airborne. Urquhart's first thought was to adapt the planning for
Comet and emulate 6th Airborne in Normandy by seizing the
Arnhem road bridge with a pre-dawn glider *coup-de-main*. He also
wanted to place at least a portion of his force as near to the bridges
as possible, and preferably on both sides of the Lower Rhine.
Unfortunately, the RAF planners led by the commander of RAF
No.38 Group, Air Vice Marshal Leslie Hollinghurst, immediately
ruled out all of these eminently sensible proposals, citing German
flak defences around the bridge and the airfield at Deelen, seven
miles to the north of Arnhem, as justification. The air plan required
1st Airborne's transports to turn north after delivering their loads,
in order to avoid aircraft moving north after delivering the 82nd
and 101st Airborne Divisions. Turning north after delivering their
loads in the vicinity of the Arnhem bridges would mean the
aircraft delivering 1st Airborne flying directly over Deelen. In any
case, it was also claimed that the open polder land to the south of

the bridge was too soft to support gliders safely, and had too many embankments and ditches for paratroops.

The immediate problem with the RAF objections was that they were based on faulty, and in some cases non-existent, intelligence. Concern over the flak defences around the Arnhem bridges appear to be based purely on hearsay evidence from RAF night bomber crews. This was a rather tenuous basis given the well-documented inability of Bomber Command crews to plot their location on the way to and from their targets – or indeed on occasion to find the latter – with any degree of accuracy. Fears over the flak defences at Deelen were even less justified, given that RAF Bomber Command had dropped over 500 tons of bombs on the airfield on 3 September, and that RAF photographic reconnaissance three days later showed that virtually all the offending flak guns had been removed. Hollinghurst's analysis also conveniently disregarded the likely effect of the not inconsiderable flak suppression effort mounted by the RAF and USAAF in support of the Market landings. In addition, the situation outlined by Hollinghurst was at variance with the intelligence disseminated to No.38 Group for Comet only a matter of days previously. This viewed Deelen as the major flak threat – which is presumably why Bomber Command targeted it – and merely issued a general warning about the possibility of running into additional mobile flak.[5] As for the polder south of Arnhem, no evidence for Hollinghurst's claims of its unsuitability have yet come to light, although conveniently unspecified Dutch resistance reports are sometimes cited. This is hardly surprising given that subsequent physical examination proved that the polder was perfectly capable of supporting large-scale glider or parachute landings. It is also interesting to note that the RAF planners designated an area just south of the Arnhem road bridge as a drop zone for use by the 1st Polish Independent Parachute Brigade in the third lift, which suggests they were well aware of its suitability. Those same planners nonetheless ignored this rather obvious contradiction and insisted that Urquhart use zones selected by them on an area of open heath and farmland around the village of Wolfheze, to the

west of Arnhem. These zones lay between seven and nine miles
from 1st Airborne's objective.

Urquhart, even with his lack of airborne experience, immediately recognised that using the zones proposed by the RAF
planners would at a stroke rob his men of surprise, their single
greatest advantage. As we shall see, his estimate was entirely
correct, for virtually every German commander in the Arnhem
area immediately deduced that the Arnhem bridges were 1st
Airborne's objective, and acted accordingly. The sole exception, at
least initially, was *Generalfeldmarschall* Walther Model, commander
of the reconstituted *Heeresgruppe* B, who decided that he was the
target and evacuated his HQ at the Tafelberg Hotel in Oosterbeek
in some haste as a result.[6] The RAF planners were unmoved by
Urquhart's objections, even when he informed them that the
troops and glider pilots were willing to take whatever risks landing
closer to the objectives entailed. They remained obdurate when
the commander of the Glider Pilot Regiment, Colonel George
Chatterton, personally supported the idea of seizing the Arnhem
road bridge by *coup-de-main*; this was rejected because it would
allegedly complicate the already complex air plan.

Appealing to Browning proved equally fruitless. When
Chatterton approached him in person about the *coup-de-main*, he
was informed that it was too late, because everything had already
been decided.[7] Given the personal stake Browning had in Market,
this reaction was predictable, although he did at least go to the
trouble of approaching the only man in the British army with the
requisite experience to render a valid judgement. This was Major-
General Richard Gale, who had planned and led the British 6th
Airborne Division's landings in Normandy. Gale's considered
opinion was that the bridge should be seized by *coup-de-main*
followed by at least a brigade landing adjacent to it. As this advice
was precisely what he did not want to hear, Browning unsurprisingly kept it to himself and asked Gale not to mention the matter
to Urquhart. This was ostensibly to avoid distracting Urquhart on
the eve of battle, but the treatment about to be handed out to the
latter's namesake, the Senior Intelligence Officer at British 1st

Airborne Corps HQ, strongly suggests that Browning's primary motive was to ensure Market went ahead. Gale later claimed that he would have resigned rather than carry out the Arnhem operation as it was foisted on Urquhart.[8]

All this raises two key questions. First, why were the RAF planners so set on riding roughshod over the needs of the airborne troops, and, second, how were they able to get away with it? The answer to the first question probably lies in Hackett's remark that likened the RAF planners to naïve cooks blithely putting together technically marvellous plans that paid no heed whatever to the subsequent realities faced by those they were transporting. This was also the view of another Market participant, Major Anthony Deane-Drummond, who was convinced that the RAF planners were drawn to the area west of Arnhem because it fitted their preconceptions of what a landing zone should look like.[9] The answer to the second question is in fact the crux of the matter, which was the total separation of responsibilities between the army and RAF.

It is important to clarify this point, not least because there are a number of assumptions and misconceptions attached to it. It is commonly assumed that it was common practice for air forces to be in total control of airborne operations until the troops were on the ground.[10] Handing total control over planning airborne operations to airmen was a purely British idiosyncrasy. The US air transport establishment viewed itself very much as the servant of the US airborne. This is why Major-General Williams' refusal to fly two lifts on the first day of Market came as such a surprise. Hitherto, the US 9th Troop Carrier Command had earned a solid reputation for conforming to the requirements of the airborne soldiers they were transporting.[11] In the British case, however, the army was allowed absolutely no input into the air planning process whatsoever. Virtually every account of events at Arnhem merely accepts this curious state of affairs with little or no comment, as Urquhart did at the time. Indeed, army resignation over the matter is well summed up by Urquhart's opinion that the RAF was unwilling to make any concessions over the Arnhem landing zones because it had already compromised by agreeing to a daylight drop.[12]

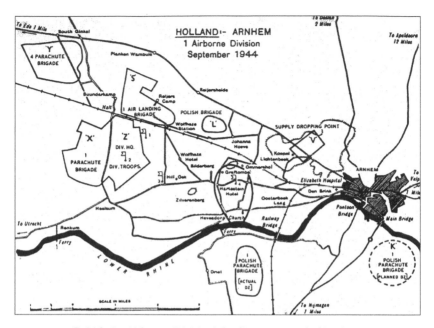

British 1st Airborne Division's landing zones and objectives.

This was a ludicrously inappropriate manner in which to carry out any inter-service enterprise, let alone one as complex as an airborne operation. It was the equivalent of allowing the Admiralty *carte blanche* to select the D-Day landing beaches purely on naval criteria, such as lack of anti-ship defences and deep-water approaches, and then forcing the land forces to adapt accordingly. In short, it was a blatant case of putting the cart before the horse. That the RAF was allowed to behave in such a manner was a direct result of the inter-service horse trading that occurred when the British airborne force was first established in June 1940, for the RAF, unlike the USAAF, was a totally independent service. Churchill and the War Office had to give the RAF total control over airborne planning in order to secure Air Ministry co-operation in the creation of a British airborne force. This, however, did not prevent the Air Ministry from initially doing everything in its power to sabotage the new force, and, when that strategy failed, it went to great lengths to keep its involvement in the airborne project to the barest minimum possible. This explains why, after four years of airborne development, the RAF were still only able to muster sufficient aircraft to move a fraction of the British airborne force, and then only by employing large numbers of obsolete bomber aircraft that were marginally suitable for the task at best.

It also explains why the RAF planners for Market felt it appropriate to deliver airborne troops to landing zones miles from their objectives. The basic problem that grew out of this needless and excessive compartmentalisation was a simple but potentially fatal conflict of priorities. The army's priority was to accomplish its assigned mission with the smallest number of casualties possible, whereas the RAF's first priority was to safeguard not its personnel but its *raison d'être*: its aircraft. There is plenty of evidence that this was the RAF's overriding preoccupation. During the run up to the Normandy invasion, for instance, Air Chief Marshal Sir Trafford Leigh-Mallory had predicted aircraft losses of between fifty and eighty per cent if the two US airborne divisions were deployed as the soldiers demanded, and Hollinghurst's planners predicted forty per cent losses for the Arnhem portion of Market. In the event, both estimates proved wildly inflated. Just twenty of the 805 aircraft employed in Normandy were lost, and no aircraft at all were lost from the first British lift into Arnhem.[13]

The RAF's insistence on controlling the planning process may have been marginally acceptable in the early days of airborne operations, when the British airborne force restricted its activities to small-scale raiding. The problem was that the procedure was not updated in parallel with the expansion in scale of airborne operations and, most crucially, there was absolutely no machinery to force the RAF to change its operating procedures. The army has to accept some of the blame for not adequately challenging the RAF's planning monopoly, even when it became a matter of life and death as at Arnhem. The bulk of the responsibility, however, lies squarely with the RAF, and not merely for putting its own narrow service interests first and imposing unsuitable landing zones with no regard for the men who would have to use them, and indeed suffer the consequences.

As with the ludicrous planning arrangements, the location of 1st Airborne's landing zones has attracted surprisingly little attention from writers on Arnhem. Most minimise the importance of the distance between landing zones and objectives,[14] and it has been claimed that the remoteness of the landing areas was a positive advantage, on the grounds that landing closer would have shortened the reaction time for nearby German units.[15] However, these views are based on the received wisdom that Market Garden failed because 30 Corps did not reach the Arnhem road bridge within the allotted time frame. They are thus rooted firmly in hindsight, heavily coloured by the deservedly epic status accorded events at the Arnhem Bridge, and after the remainder of 1st Airborne became encircled at Oosterbeek. The simple fact is that Market Garden failed in the first twenty-four hours, long before 30 Corps was supposed to have ridden to the rescue, and it failed because the bulk of 1st Airborne Division did not reach the Arnhem road bridge at all. This was almost overwhelmingly due to the excessive distance between the landing zones and the target bridges, which flew in the face of all airborne experience to date, not to mention Brereton's instruction to seize the bridges with thunderclap surprise. More crucially, it gave the German defenders ample time to deduce 1st Airborne's objective and react accordingly, and thus robbed the comparatively lightly armed airborne troops of their sole advantage of surprise.

It is therefore no exaggeration to say that the RAF planners' insistence that 1st Airborne use the landing zones near Wolfheze, and by extension the ludicrous arrangement that accorded them the power to do so, was the single most significant factor in the failure of Market Garden. If those planners had been less blinkered, and had they exhibited just a modicum of flexibility or even common sense, events might well have turned out very differently. Had the Arnhem road bridge been seized by glider *coup-de-main* at the outset, followed by the delivery of the bulk of 1st Airlanding Brigade with its heavy weapons onto the polder south of the bridge, there is every chance that an adequate perimeter could have been established in Arnhem proper before nearby German units could react in sufficient strength to interfere. It should be remembered that a scratch force of less than 700 men, built around two companies of Lieutenant Colonel John Frost's 2nd Parachute Battalion, succeeded in holding out around the north end of the Arnhem road bridge for three and a half days. Consider what a single, or indeed two full brigades might have achieved had they been delivered almost directly to the same location at the outset of Market.

The third factor to consider in this section is Urquhart's plan for 1st Airborne. As we have seen, the air planners' decision to stagger the delivery of 1st Airborne over three days and the selection of the landing zones around Wolfheze sharply narrowed his options. They were subsequently narrowed yet further. On 15 September, Urquhart was playing a round of golf on the course adjacent to 1 British Airborne Corps HQ at Moor Park when Lieutenant Colonel Charles Mackenzie, 1st Airborne's Operations Officer, informed him that 'a few' gliders were being trimmed from the Division's first lift. Urquhart acquiesced with the proviso that the allocation of anti-tank guns remained unchanged.[16] In fact, thirty-two Horsas were to carry an advanced HQ from 1st British Airborne Corps into the landing area south-east of Nijmegen.[17]

This was the vehicle by which Browning intended to rectify his lack of airborne combat experience. That Browning was willing to remove so many gliders from a Division already strapped for airlift resources merely underlines his lack of compunction in putting his personal goals ahead of the greater good. Browning's presence in Holland in the initial stages of Market was superfluous, and in any case the Advanced Corps HQ did not have sufficient communications equipment or personnel to allow him properly to exercise command. Browning would therefore have been better placed to do his job had he remained at Moor Park.[18] Even if his presence had been necessary after the initial assault, there is no reason why Browning could not have gone in on a subsequent lift, or even by road with 30 Corps. The blunt fact is that Browning did not fly into Holland with the first lift to exercise control over his airborne corps, but as part of a self-publicity exercise aimed at creating the appearance that he was both indispensable and at the forefront of events.

The equanimity with which Urquhart appears to have accepted this is curious, given that a shortage of infantry was arguably the most pressing problem facing the first lift. The decision to deliver 1st Airborne in increments meant that the first lift's infantry component was split between going for the bridges and defending the landing areas for the second lift. The latter was assigned to 1st Airlanding Brigade, which had to leave part of the 2nd South Staffs for the second lift because there were insufficient gliders and tugs to transport them. An airlanding infantry battalion required fifty-six Horsa gliders, and only twenty-two were available.[19] The thirty-two Horsas Browning needlessly diverted for his self-serving side-show would thus have been far better employed in permitting 1st Airlanding Brigade to be delivered in its entirety in the first lift.

However, it would be mistaken to push this point too far. As Brereton's single-lift decision ruled out additional parachute transports, the only way Urquhart could have significantly increased the proportion of infantry in the first lift was to send in all or part of 4th Parachute Brigade or the 1st Polish Independent by glider. Given that gliders were almost universally regarded as death traps by parachute troops, the reception such a move would have received can be imagined. More importantly, the parachute units were billeted too far from the glider airfields for easy transfer, and the short lead-time between Market being proposed and launched effectively ruled out the necessary reorganisation. None of this excuses Browning's behaviour, but it does put it in perspective.

In the event, the unavoidable shortage of infantry in the first lift seriously handicapped 1st Airborne's ability to carry out the Arnhem portion of Market. Urquhart and his Division were thus paying the price for decisions not of their taking, and not just those of Williams and Brereton. First, the decision to keep 6th Airborne Division in Normandy as normal infantry until the beginning of September effectively removed the only additional source of trained, and experienced, glider infantry. Had 6th Airborne been withdrawn from Normandy at the same time as the two US airborne divisions, Urquhart would have been able to borrow part or all of 6th Airlanding Brigade to augment his strength. Second, Urquhart and 1st Airborne were also suffering for the British army's concentration on parachute troops at the expense of glider troops. While the standard British airborne division contained twice as many paratroopers as glider infantry, the RAF could not move more than a fraction of the parachute troops, and the Air Ministry never had any intention of increasing its transport organisation to alleviate the situation. Given that the largely obsolete bombers that made up the bulk of the RAF's transport fleet were best configured for glider towing, and that the Horsa glider could carry more troops than any RAF aircraft including the C-47 Dakota, it would have been far more logical for the army to reverse, or at least balance the ratio of paratroops to glider infantry.

Urquhart briefed his brigade and other commanders on Market Garden at British 1 Airborne Corps Headquarters at Moor Park in the late afternoon of Tuesday 12 September. D-Day for Market was finally set for 17 September. The assembled commanders appear to have received the rather unpromising briefing without adverse comment, although this may have been due to the presence of Browning, who attended but did not contribute. It may also have been because they thought Market would be cancelled like all the previous operations for which they had been briefed. Nonetheless, they appear to have been well aware of the drawbacks of the proposed scheme. Hackett, for example, later warned 4th Parachute Brigade's battalion commanders to expect losses of around fifty per cent, and Lathbury appears to have disseminated similar warnings to 1st Parachute Brigade's battalion and company commanders.[20] Whichever, most of 1st Airborne's personnel were dispatched on forty-eight hours leave while the various planners went to work. Detailed briefings and glider loading were to commence on Friday 15 September.

Urquhart chose to divide his Division over the three lifts as follows. Urquhart's tactical HQ, 1st Airborne Reconnaissance Squadron, 1st Parachute and the bulk of 1st Airlanding Brigades, 1st Airlanding Anti-Tank Battery RA, the bulk of 1st Light Artillery Regiment RA, 1st Parachute Squadron and 9th Field company RE, and 16th Parachute and 181st Airlanding Field Ambulances were to go into Drop Zone (DZ) 'X' and Landing Zones (LZ) 'S' and 'Z' on the first lift. The second lift consisted of the balance of 1st Airlanding Brigade, 4th Parachute Brigade, the 2nd Airlanding Anti-Tank Battery RA, one battery from 1st Airborne Light Regiment RA, 4th Parachute Squadron RE, 133rd Parachute Field Ambulance, and the remainder of Divisional HQ. The parachute units were to land on DZ 'Y', and the gliders on LZs S and X; the latter was switched from parachutes to gliders for the second lift.

The third lift consisted of 1st Polish Independent Parachute Brigade, which was to use two previously unused landing zones. The parachute element of Sosabowski's brigade was to land on DZ 'K', just south-east of the Arnhem Bridge, while the Pole's heavy equipment landed by glider on LZ 'L'. Urquhart decided to set up his Division HQ on LZ Z, and assigned 1st Airlanding Brigade to protect the various landing areas for use by the second lift. Once the Polish gliders were down, 1st Airlanding was to concentrate and establish a defence line on the western edge of Arnhem proper. Seizing the Arnhem bridges was entrusted to Lathbury's 1st Parachute Brigade supported by the 1st Airborne Reconnaissance Squadron. The three-lift arrangement thus halved the infantry force available to Urquhart at a stroke, and obliged 1st Airborne to attempt to achieve a divisional task with a single brigade. In effect therefore, it reduced the Arnhem portion of Market from a divisional task to the original Comet concept, minus the *coup-de-main*.

Because intelligence reports indicated that he would be facing only light opposition, Lathbury decided to advance from the landing area on a broad front, sending each of his three battalions along separate but parallel routes. These routes were codenamed, running north from the Lower Rhine, 'Lion', 'Tiger' and 'Leopard'. Thirty-one of the Reconnaissance Squadron's armed Willy's jeeps were to move along Leopard to seize and hold the Arnhem road bridge.[21] Frost's 2nd Parachute Battalion was to move into Arnhem along the north bank of the Lower Rhine on the Lion route, securing the rail and pontoon bridge west of the town on the way, before relieving the Recce Squadron and cross-ing the road bridge to establish a perimeter facing south. The 3rd Parachute Battalion, commanded by Lieutenant Colonel John Fitch, was to take the central Tiger route and assist Frost's men in securing the Arnhem road bridge. Lieutenant Colonel David Dobie's 1st Parachute Battalion was to be Lathbury's reserve until the other two battalions were on their way, after which it was to follow the Reconnaissance Squadron along the Leopard route. Instead of going to the road bridge, however, Dobie was to secure an area of high ground to the north of Arnhem. Lathbury's Brigade HQ was to follow the 2nd Parachute Battalion along the Lion Route. All three battalions were to be accompanied by parties of Royal Engineers and single troops of anti-tank guns, while the remainder of 1st Parachute Squadron RE, 16th Parachute Field Ambulance and a variety of other administrative elements were to travel with Lathbury's Brigade HQ.

As we have seen, Browning deliberately suppressed intelligence showing the presence of SS troops and armour near Arnhem. Urquhart and Lathbury thus based their planning on the assump-tion that they were facing the equivalent of a low-category brigade, possibly bolstered by a few mobile battalions and flak troops.[22] Even so, Lathbury's plan was still over-confident in spreading 1st Parachute Brigade so wide and thin without a desig-nated and substantial reserve, a fact he acknowledged as a mistake after the event.[23] This was especially surprising given Lathbury's experience at the Primasole Bridge, where he had had to contend with the unexpected presence of German airborne troops from the 1st *Fallschirmjäger* Regiment. The plan was also a typical British airborne effort, insofar as it was overly complicated and dispersed a large proportion of the available combat power on peripheral tasks.

1st Parachute Brigade as a whole was only marginally strong enough to achieve its primary objective of securing the Arnhem bridges, yet the 1st Parachute Battalion was not even tasked to assist in their seizure, being directed to occupy high ground north of Arnhem instead. More importantly, while the 2nd Parachute

Battalion was tasked to make all speed to Arnhem, it was also detailed to seize the two secondary objectives, the rail and pontoon bridges, on the way. It is doubtful that single companies would have been strong enough to hold these secondary objectives against determined opposition, and their detachment would have cut the 2nd Parachute Battalion's strength by half before it even got into Arnhem. It would have made much more sense to despatch two battalions on the southern Lion route, tasking one to seize and hold the pontoon and rail bridges while the other pushed on to Arnhem for the main objective. In fact, Lathbury's plan for 1st Parachute Brigade would have been more appropriate for three brigades rather than three battalions, which raises the suspicion that its authors had cut corners by merely adapting a larger original plan for a smaller force.

To an extent, however, this is being wise after the event. In the circumstances, Lathbury's plan probably had as much chance of success as any other, given that the remoteness of the landing areas stacked the odds against 1st Parachute Brigade whatever plan it followed. Over-confident or not, Lathbury made his plan based on the available intelligence, and his immediate superior, Urquhart, approved it. There were two more factors on which success or failure hung. These were the battle-worthiness of 1st Parachute Brigade and the reaction of the German defenders. The former has already been discussed in detail above. It may therefore be advisable to put the latter in context with a brief examination of the strength and location of the German forces facing Market Garden, and, more specifically, facing 1st Airborne in the Arnhem area, before moving on to examine how events unfolded.

NEITHER OLD MEN ON BICYCLES
NOR ELITE SS PANZERS

THE GERMAN DEFENDERS FACING OPERATION MARKET GARDEN

From the German perspective, the defining event between the destruction of Heeresgruppe B at Falaise and the beginning of Market Garden was the Allied liberation of Antwerp on 4 September 1944. At that point, there was only a single German Division, augmented by a few Dutch SS internal security units and some *Luftwaffe* and *Kriegsmarine* training units, available to cover the sixty-odd mile gap between Antwerp and Maastricht on the German border. This was the 719th Infantry Division, commanded by *Generalleutnant* Karl Sievers, which had been deployed on the Dutch coast since 1940. The loss of Antwerp also cut off the German 15th Army commanded by *General* Gustav von Zangen, which had been retiring from Normandy along the Pas de Calais coast. With Antwerp gone, 15th Army's only remaining line of retreat was across the Scheldt estuary into Holland.

The effort to rectify the situation created by the destruction of Heeresgruppe B began on the very day Antwerp fell to the British, and occurred simultaneously at a variety of levels. *Oberkommando der Wehrmacht* (OKW) at Hitler's Rastenburg HQ ordered the creation of a new front on the Albert Canal with the newly created 1st *Fallschirmjäger* Army, commanded by *Generaloberst* Kurt Student, and the 176th Infantry Division from the West Wall garrison near Aachen. The local German command in Holland ordered the 719th Infantry Division to the Canal from its coastal defences. These units were preceded by the remnants of the 85th Infantry Division, under *Generalleutnant* Kurt Chill. On learning of the fall of Antwerp, Chill had proceeded to the Albert Canal on his own initiative, set his men to preparing defensive positions along the north bank, and established reception stations at crossings to co-opt more men from the retreating throng. Within twenty-four hours *Kamfgruppe* Chill was ready to oppose British 30 Corps when it tried to establish bridgeheads over the Albert Canal. It was joined by the first elements of 1st *Fallschirmjäger* Army on 6 September, and by the 176th Infantry Division the following day.

Rapid though their response might have been, the character of the German units gave no grounds for complacency. In spite of its grand-sounding title, Student's Army consisted largely of units cobbled together from all branches of the *Luftwaffe*, reinforced with some light anti-aircraft artillery and a *Heer Kampfgruppe* equipped with twenty-five self-propelled guns. The 719th Infantry Division contained a high proportion of elderly personnel, and the 176th Infantry Division was a *Kranken* formation, made up of soldiers with a variety of disabilities that had hitherto barred them from regular field service. For all that, it took the British six days of fierce fighting starting on 7 September to cross the Albert Canal at Beeringen and push a narrow bridgehead twenty miles north to Neerpelt on the Meuse-Escaut Canal. Apart from this narrow penetration, by 12 September the Germans had succeeded in establishing a coherent defensive line along the Albert Canal, and additional reinforcements stiffened the defence yet further. Many of these came from the 15th Army, which began to filter out of the trap and over the Scheldt estuary on 4 September, virtually unmolested by the Allies. In the sixteen days that followed 65,000 men, 225 guns, 750 trucks and 1,000 horses were ferried to safety. Many of these evacuees were directed to the Albert Canal line, while the 245th and 591st Infantry Divisions regrouped to the west of Nijmegen.

Thus by 13 September, and by dint of excellent staff work at a variety of levels, 1st *Fallschirmjäger* Army succeeded in erecting a credible defence line where none had existed only a matter of days before. Behind that line Heeresgruppe B had been reconstituted under *Generalfeldmarschall* Walther Model and the Army Group's area of responsibility had been divided in two. The Forward Combat Zone ran north from the Albert Canal back to the River Waal, and thus included the objectives of the US 101st Airborne Division and most of those of the 82nd Airborne apart from Nijmegen, which lay on the border between the two zones. On the eve of Market Garden the Forward Combat Zone was manned by the 176th and 719th Infantry Divisions and *Kampfgruppe* Chill, in addition to Student's various *Fallschirmjäger* units and formations. It also included *Kampfgruppe* Walther, a mix of *Fallschirmjäger* and *Waffen* SS units drawn from II SS *Panzerkorps*. *Kampfgruppe* Walther's primary task was to contain the British bridgehead over the Meuse-Escaut Canal at Neerpelt.

The primary role of the Rear Combat Zone was to support the Forward one. To this end reception centres were established to sort out retreating troops at crossing points over the Waal and Maas, and preparing screening positions along the north bank of those rivers. All military units within its boundaries were considered the first line of reinforcement for the Forward Zone. Thus although the majority of these were depot, training and internal security units from all branches of the German armed forces, they were nonetheless organised for combat and most were relatively well armed and equipped. There were two such units in the immediate environs of Arnhem. These were the impressively named training unit, SS *Panzergrenadier Ersatz und Ausbildungs* Battalion 16, which was based just outside the western Arnhem suburb of Oosterbeek, and an internal security unit, SS *Wacht* Battalion 3. The latter was based at Ede, also to the west of Arnhem, and was composed largely of Dutch SS volunteers. Finally, the Arnhem rail bridge was defended by an eleven-strong demolition team billeted on the south bank, and three 20mm flak guns, while the road bridge was defended by around twenty-five elderly or very young soldiers manning two bunkers and more light flak.

These, however, were not the only German units within striking distance of Arnhem. The area north and east of the town was the designated concentration area for II SS *Panzerkorps*, commanded by *Obergruppenführer* Wilhelm Bittrich, and consisting of the 9th SS

Panzer Division 'Hohenstaufen' and the 10th SS *Panzer* Division 'Frundsberg'. II SS *Panzerkorps* had been committed to battle in Normandy at the end of June 1944, and had been in action almost constantly thereafter. Both divisions narrowly avoided destruction at Falaise, and played a leading role in covering the retreat across north-east France. A hastily formed *Kampfgruppe* from the 10th SS was all but wiped out in a rearguard action at Albert on 1 September, and the 9th SS fought a similar battle at Cambrai the following day. The latter action ended with the 9th SS's commander, *Obersturmbannführer* Walther Harzer, cut off but undiscovered behind Allied lines. He only regained safety after laying up for two days and bluffing his way at night on roads packed with Allied vehicles; on occasion SS military police held up Allied convoys at junctions, and Harzer's men looted unattended Allied vehicles in villages along their route.

Both divisions concentrated briefly in the area of Maastricht. On 5 September 10th SS *Panzer* Division was ordered to the Arnhem area to refit, after detaching a *Panzergrenadier* Battalion to help contain the British bridgehead over the Meuse-Escaut Canal at Neerpelt. The 9th SS followed two days later, also after detaching units to *Kampfgruppe* Walther. By 17 September both divisions were billeted north and east of Arnhem, with 9th SS *Panzer's* units nearest Arnhem. To the north, *Kampfgruppe* Harder was billeted just outside the city, SS *Panzer Aufklärungs Abteilung* 9 was located ten miles further north at Hoenderloo, and 9th SS *Panzer* Division's HQ, logistic elements and the divisional anti-tank battalion, SS *Panzerjäger Abteilung* 9, were located around Apeldoorn. The rest of 9th SS *Panzer* Division was located along the eighteen miles leading to Zutphen. SS *Panzergrenadier* Regiment 20 was camped on a training area near Rheden, six miles east of Arnhem. Five miles further on, SS *Panzer Artillerie* Regiment 9, an SS *Panzergrenadier* battalion commanded by *Hauptsturmführer* Karl-Heinz Euling, and a detachment of SS anti-aircraft gunners under *Obersturmführer* Heinz Gropp were concentrated around Dieren. Next came SS *Panzer Pionier Abteilung* 9, commanded by *Hauptsturmführer* Hans Möller, based at Brummen, and finally SS

Panzergrenadier Regiment 19 located in Zutphen proper. The 10th SS *Panzer* Division's sub-units were located generally east and north of the Hohenstaufen, at Deventer, Vorden and Ruurlo, and II SS *Panzerkorps* HQ was located at Doetinchem, around seventeen miles east of Arnhem.

This force looks formidable on paper, but it should be noted that both divisions had only around a quarter of their authorised establishment. Shortly after they arrived at Arnhem it was decided to retain and refit 10th SS *Panzer* Division in Holland, and to withdraw the 9th SS to Germany to be re-equipped. The latter was ordered to hand over its vehicles and heavy equipment to the former, although some units declared working vehicles unserviceable in order to hang on to them. SS *Panzer Aufklärungs Abteilung* 9, commanded by *Hauptsturmführer* Viktor Gräbner,[1] was a particular offender in this regard, removing weapons, optical equipment, wheels and tracks from its vehicles. Thanks to this administrative sleight of hand, Gräbner's unit was relatively well-equipped, with thirty armoured half-tracks of various types and ten eight-wheeled armoured cars, although some of its personnel had to travel in open trucks equipped with oil drums full of sand or grain as rudimentary armour. Other units were less fortunate. SS *Panzerjäger Abteilung* 9, commanded by *Hauptsturmführer* Klaus von Allwörden, had a maximum of two *Panzerjäger* IV self-propelled guns and a handful of towed 75mm PAK 40 pieces. *Kampfgruppe* Harder was a composite battalion made up of dismounted tank crew, fitters and logistic personnel from the Hohenstaufen's SS *Panzer* Regiment 9, reinforced with a draft of *Kriegsmarine* personnel. Transportation of all types was in short supply.

The matter of transport was important because only two German units were closer to the Arnhem bridges than 1st Airborne's drop zones. These were SS *Panzergrenadier Ersatz und Ausbildungs* Battalion 16, commanded by *Hauptsturmführer* Sepp Krafft, and *Kampfgruppe* Harder. The two next nearest units were not well configured for action by the time 1st Airborne arrived. SS *Panzergrenadier* Regiment 20 had handed in its personal weapons and field equipment in preparation for the move back to Germany, while Gräbner's recce battalion had loaded most of its vehicles onto railway wagons for transport to Germany too. All Hohenstaufen's and Frundsberg's units were similarly handicapped to a greater or lesser extent.

All this should have offset the disadvantage conferred on the British by the distant location of their drop zones. Unfortunately for 1st Airborne, however, the German defenders in the Arnhem region possessed two force multipliers with the potential to tip the odds decisively against 1st Airborne. First, they were *Waffen* SS. The ethos of this organisation, with its emphasis on aggression and personal initiative, meant that Hohenstaufen and Frundsberg were guaranteed to respond rapidly to any threat, personnel and equipment shortages not withstanding. Second, II SS *Panzerkorps* had been raised for service in the West and, because Allied airborne operations were considered a very real possibility, both divisions had been trained in counter-airborne measures. Indeed this had been an early training staple while they awaited the arrival of their heavy equipment in the summer of 1943 and, ironically, Hohenstaufen carried out a large-scale anti-airborne exercise in September of that year. Most importantly, leaders at all levels were thoroughly schooled in the need for speed in countering airborne landings, and thus in acting swiftly on their own initiative even when spread over widely dispersed locations. These, of course, were precisely the conditions under which II SS *Panzerkorps* was operating in mid-September 1944.

The presence of troops of such calibre in the Arnhem area, even depleted and poorly equipped as the Hohenstaufen and Frundsberg were, obviously had implications for 1st Airborne Division. These implications should not be overestimated, however, and it would be overstating the case to suggest that the mere presence of Hohenstaufen and Frundsberg doomed 1st Airborne's mission to failure. What the presence of the two depleted SS divisions did do was tilt the odds yet further against 1st Airborne. Generally speaking, the initial stages of any airborne operation can be characterised as a race pitting the airborne interlopers against the speed of defender's reaction, and the presence of

Hohenstaufen and Frundsberg significantly narrowed 1st Airborne's chances in this respect. It should be noted, however, that this merely exacerbated the underlying problem, which was the needless handicap created by the RAF's airborne planners in insisting that 1st Airborne use landing areas so remote from its objectives. Speed was therefore going to be of the essence once 1st Airborne was on the ground. Given what we have seen of its battle-worthiness by early September 1944, the leading question has to be whether or not 1st Airborne Division was capable of moving with the requisite speed on arrival in Holland.

THE FIRST LIFT IN
THE CORRIDOR

Sunday 17 September dawned with light mist of the kind that heralds fine weather, and no cancellation. Operation Market was on, although as far as RAF Bomber Command was concerned, the operation had been underway for several hours. During the previous night 282 RAF bombers had raided German airfields and flak positions to prevent them interfering with the airborne transports. Because take off was scheduled for mid-morning, the airborne soldiers assigned to Market's first lift were able to enjoy an early hot breakfast before being driven to their designated airfields. For most this was the last cooked meal for a considerable period. For some it was to be their last meal on earth.

The following participant account from a US veteran provides a vivid picture of this period. Then Private William J. Stone was half of a two-man Forward Observer team from Battery B, 321st Field Artillery Battalion, attached to the 3rd Battalion, 506th Parachute Infantry Regiment. He parachuted into Holland on 17 September in the same stick as the 3rd Battalion's commander, Lieutenant Colonel Robert G. Cole:

> Take off for D-Day was 1015 on September 17th. I knew that this would be a go when at dinner on the 16th we were served steak and fruit cocktail. The latter was a delicacy in the ETO and when it and steak – which never made our menu – were served, while I wouldn't say that we were being fattened up for the slaughter, the air did take on an ominous quality. My feeling was reinforced when

the C-47s began landing as dinner was ending. Those pilots wanted their share of the steak and fruit cocktail.

The next day... we were up early, drew our parachutes and other equipment. I drew an equipment bag and packing for our radio and batteries. The packing would line the equipment bag and cushion the radio when the bag hit the ground. The bag was going to be hung on an equipment rack under the wing of the aircraft in which we would fly to Holland. It would be released when we jumped... I carried my individual and personal equipment in a musette bag hanging in front of my chest and from a web belt. I don't remember what I had in the musette bag other than rations. I carried my folding carbine in a scabbard from my web belt on which I also carried a canteen, ammunition, a compass and a wound dressing. Shortly before boarding the aircraft we put on our parachutes, the main on our backs and the reserve on our chests.

After we boarded the pilots fired up the engines of the many C-47s on the field that day. The roar was unimaginable... We taxied to the end of the runway, got the signal to take off and the pilot gunned that ship down the runway... I was off on my first combat jump and the adrenaline was racing through my body. I was sitting on a bucket seat and just beside my ears those piston-powered engines were vibrating fiercely and hammering... And so I was off to the wars again.

September 17th was a Sunday, another beautiful day by which to remember an England of which I was growing fonder all the time. Many airborne soldiers had made dates for the 16th, a Saturday. At that time we were locked into airfields and we could not let anyone know where we were on that evening. A lot of young women must have had evil thoughts about their dates on that Saturday, thoughts which were probably dispelled when on Sunday morning they saw the airborne armada thundering eastward.[1]

A total of 1,534 aircraft and 491 gliders, the largest single concentration of transport aircraft ever gathered to date, were waiting at twenty-three separate airfields to carry the first lift to their drop and landing zones in Holland. Fourteen of these airfields lay around fifty miles west of London, in the area of Basingstoke and Reading. It was from these that the US 53rd Troop Carrier Wing would lift the 101st Airborne, and the RAF's 38 and 46 Groups the 1st Airlanding Brigade and almost all of 1st Airborne's other glider-borne elements. Some of the latter were also to leave from RAF Manston in Kent, which acted as a forward operating base for Albemarles from 296 and 297 Squadrons, towing gliders containing infantry from the 2nd South Staffs and elements of 1st Airborne's various artillery units. The remaining eight airfields were located around 100 miles north of London, in Leicestershire and Lincolnshire. These were the preserve of the US 52nd Troop Carrier Wing, which was to deliver the 82nd Airborne's first lift and the 1st Parachute Brigade.[2]

Take offs commenced in mid-morning, the exact timings being staggered to take into account the precise distance of the various airfields from their forming-up points and routes. Because it took the unwieldy tug-glider combinations longer to manoeuvre into formation, the RAF glider serials began to take off at 09:45, whereas the 82nd Airborne's parachute transports waited until 10:09.[3] The air plan was thus extremely complex, and a masterpiece of staff work in its own right. The two clusters of airfields were each assigned a forming-up point, those to the west over Hatfield north of London and those in the north over March near Peterborough. The formations were then directed down two five-mile wide air corridors to carry them to the English coast and beyond. Coincidentally, 17 September had been designated a Day of Thanksgiving for the RAF victory in the Battle of Britain four years before. There can have been no more eloquent expression of how far British fortunes had shifted since the dark days of summer 1940 than the sight of the vast Market force throbbing across the sky, for almost an hour and a half in places, carrying an airborne army to strike directly at the heart of German-occupied Europe. The noise of these massed formations of aircraft was of sufficient volume to drown out church organs, and drew onlookers from churches and their homes all across south and east England.

The two air corridors were designed to carry the troop carriers between the densest concentrations of German flak. The Northern Route was assigned to the aircraft carrying the 82nd Airborne and British 1st Airborne. It crossed the English coast at Aldeburgh, proceeded south-east across the North Sea to the Dutch island of Schouwen before dog-legging east to a point just north of Eindhoven. There the route split, with the aircraft carrying the 82nd Airborne moving north-east to Nijmegen, and those carrying 1st Airborne flying almost due north to Arnhem. The Southern Route, which was reserved exclusively for the 101st Airborne, crossed the coast in the region of Colchester in Essex, ran south-east across the Thames Estuary and over the tip of Kent, where it dog-legged over the English Channel to Belgium. It then ran east to Antwerp, and then north over the British lines, and on to the landing zones just to the north of Eindhoven. Navigation was assisted by marker beacons placed at rendezvous, coastal crossings and waypoints, and by marker and rescue boats on the oversea stretches.

The transport aircraft were preceded by an intensive flak suppression effort by bombers and fighter-bombers from the RAF and USAAF. Bomber Command added to its night time effort by attacking flak installations on Walcheren and along the Scheldt estuary, and a force of 117 bombers from the US 8th Air Force delivered 3,139 tons of bombs on seventeen separate flak sites along the Market route. Many of these targets were hit again, along with selected targets in the immediate vicinity of the Market landing areas, by fighter-bombers and light bombers from the British 2nd Tactical Air Force and the US 9th Air Force. In the course of the day, twenty-three of these machines were lost to a variety of causes, and seven German fighters from a force of just over twice that number which appeared near the 82nd Airborne's landing area were also shot down. The German aircraft were presumably scrambled because their early warning system misidentified the airborne armada as a bombing raid. Including those assigned to protect the transport fleet, almost 1,000 Allied fighters were in the air with Market's first lift.[4]

The pathfinders from the three airborne divisions were the first to reach the landing areas in Holland. Twelve Short Stirlings from 190 Squadron RAF delivered the 21st Independent Parachute Company west of Arnhem at 12:40. Six US C-47s carrying the 82nd and 101st Divisions' contingents, two for the former and four for the latter, arrived over their respective target areas seven minutes later. One of the 101st Airborne's C-47s was shot down with only four survivors from its stick, but the rest made successful drops. By 12:54, four minutes short of the deadline for the arrival of the main force, all the Garden landing zones save one had been located and marked with day-glo panels, coloured smoke canisters and Eureka electronic homing beacons.[5]

The 101st Airborne Division had been tasked to seize seven separate bridges, and a further four bridges within Eindhoven if possible. From south to north these were the road and rail bridges over the Wilhelmina Canal near Son and Best respectively, approximately seven miles north of Eindhoven; the road bridge over the River Dommel at St Oedenrode; and the road and rail bridges over the Willems Canal and River Aa near and in Veghel. To achieve this, three separate landing areas had been selected. The largest, combining two parachute DZs codenamed 'B' and 'C' was located in the triangle between Best, Son and St Oedenrode. A glider landing zone, codenamed LZ 'W' lay tight between the two parachute DZs, an arrangement made possible by scheduling the 101st Airborne's glider landings an hour after the parachute drop. The 506th Parachute Infantry Regiment, tasked to seize the Son Bridge before moving south to Eindhoven, was assigned DZ C, while DZ B went to the 502nd Parachute Infantry Regiment. The latter's main objectives were to seize the road bridge at St Oedenrode and guard the LZ for the glider landing and the second lift, with a secondary mission of detaching a small force to seize the railway bridge near Best. Because its target bridges at Veghel lay around seven miles from the 101st Airborne's other objectives, the 501st Parachute Infantry Regiment used two smaller nearby DZs, codenamed 'A' and 'A2', on either side of the Willems Canal.

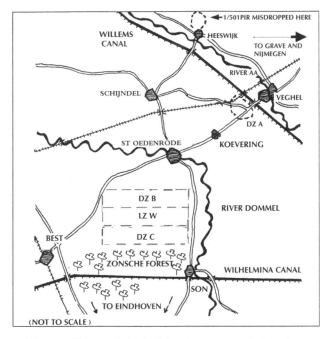

US 101st Airborne Division's landing zones and objectives.

The 101st Airborne's air route ran directly over the German front line, and thus attracted a good deal of anti-aircraft fire in spite of the flak suppression effort. This thickened considerably on the five-minute run in to the DZs for the 13:00 deadline, but the C-47 pilots held their formations in what appears to have been a conscious and courageous effort to make up for past failures over Sicily and Normandy. Consequently, the 101st Airborne's drop, again led by General Taylor in person, was its most compact and accurate of any to date, including training jumps. The sole exception was one of the 501st Parachute Infantry Regiment's battalions at Veghel, which was dropped three miles from its assigned DZ; presumably this was due to the loss of the planeload of 101st pathfinders. In all, sixteen C-47s were shot down, but none of them before disgorging their sticks of paratroopers, and the pilots of at least two were lost after remaining at the controls of their burning aircraft to ensure their passengers got out. Within thirty minutes 6,769 men were on the ground, and within a further hour all the 101st Airborne's battalions were fully assembled and moving on their objectives.

The 101st Airborne's glider landing, which commenced at 14:00 hours, fared less well. Seventy gliders left England, but six aborted for technical reasons en route, six more were cast off early when their tugs were shot down, and three crash-landed on the LZ. Two more were unaccounted for, and had presumably either crashed short due to mechanical failure or been shot down by flak. Once again, the transport aircrew exhibited considerable dedication and courage. Forty-six glider tugs were damaged by anti-aircraft fire, six of them so badly they had to be scrapped. The fifty-three gliders that landed intact delivered 252 men, thirty-two jeeps, thirteen trailers and a war correspondent named Walter Cronkite. Many of the soldiers were observer teams for the airborne artillery units slated for the second lift, which fought as infantry until their arrival.

The 506th Parachute Infantry's 1st Battalion was tasked to seize the Son road bridge. The Battalion's commander, Major James L. LaPrade, had arranged for his men to advance directly on the objective bridge without pausing to regroup fully. Lead elements of the 1st Battalion were thus well on the way within forty-five minutes of landing, possibly spurred on by the presence of General Taylor who elected to accompany them. As the 1st Battalion filtered through the Zonsche Forest, which screened the drop zone from the Wilhelmina Canal, the lead company came under direct fire from three 88-mm flak guns emplaced along the north bank of the canal. Within minutes the company commander was seriously wounded, and many other officers and men were killed. Those remaining unscathed responded with a spontaneous bayonet charge across open ground, which overran two of the 88s and carried the advance to within 100 metres or so of the bridge, but at cost of almost a third of the company's strength. Unfortunately they were unable to prevent the defenders blowing the bridge, but Major LaPrade swam the canal accompanied by two of his men and established a lodgement on the south bank. Airborne engineers were then able to erect a rope bridge across the demolished bridge, using the undamaged central pillar. This was subsequently augmented with a commandeered rowing boat and an improvised raft, but it nonetheless took until midnight to get the 506th Regiment across the Wilhelmina Canal. The Regiment's commander, Colonel Robert F. Sink, decided to dig in for the night and push on to Eindhoven at first light.

Things ran more smoothly for the 502nd Parachute Infantry Regiment, despite one of its battalions being mis-dropped on the 506th Regiment's DZ. Two *Panzer* IV tanks which might have interfered with the Regiment's advance north-east to St Oedenrode were destroyed by fighter-bombers, and the Regiment's lead elements reached the town without mishap. There they seized their assigned bridges over the River Dommel and prevented German engineers from destroying an additional one they had not been briefed about, killing a score of defenders and capturing a further fifty-eight. The exception to this relatively easy run was Company 'H' from the 502nd Regiment's 3rd Battalion, which had been detailed to secure the two bridges over the Wilhelmina Canal near Best, south-west of the main landing areas. Curiously, the Market planners had ignored these bridges even though they lay only around five miles west of those at Son. They were included in the 502nd Regiment's list of objectives on the initiative of its commander, Colonel John H. Michaelis. Company H planned to bypass Son to the south and move directly on the bridges, but a navigation error led to a costly fight with the town garrison, which considerably outnumbered the paratroopers. By 18:00 Company H had been obliged to dig in just inside the western fringe of the Zonsche Forest. Part of a detached platoon managed to reach the Wilhelmina Canal after midnight following a series of skirmishes, and dug in on the embankment just east of the bridges. In the meantime, the rest of the 3rd Battalion had been sent to reinforce Company H, but darkness and enemy mortar fire forced it stop about a mile east of Best. Like the 506th to the east, the 502nd Regiment dug in and waited for daylight.

While all this was going on, the 501st Parachute Infantry Regiment, commanded by Colonel Howard R. Johnson, was securing the four bridges over the parallel Willems Canal and River Aa in and near Veghel, seven miles or so to the north-east of St Oedenrode. The 501st Regiment's 1st Battalion managed to seize the railway bridge over the Aa despite being mis-dropped three miles north-west of its DZ, using commandeered bicycles and civilian motor vehicles, and pressed on to Veghel proper. Unfortunately, a party of forty-six left to guard heavy equipment at the landing site was overwhelmed by German forces later in the afternoon of 17 September. The remainder of the Regiment took only forty-five minutes to reorganise on the main DZ to the west, before rapidly seizing the road and rail bridges over the Willems Canal and linking up with the 1st Battalion's lead scouts in the centre of Veghel. German resistance in the town was quickly overcome, and the road bridge over the Aa was secured. After accepting the enthusiastic thanks of the locals for their liberation, the 501st Regiment established a defensive perimeter and dug in to await relief.[6]

Twenty-five miles further to the north-east, the focus of the 82nd Airborne Division was slightly different. The 82nd Airborne's most important objectives were the huge road and railway bridges across the River Waal on the northern outskirts of Nijmegen. However, Browning considered the Groesbeek Heights, a wooded plateau to the south and east of the city, to be more important because they overlooked Nijmegen and the Garden route. Consequently, on 14 September Browning specifically forbade Gavin from moving on the Nijmegen bridges until the Groesbeek Heights were secured, and the 82nd Airborne's plan thus assigned two of its parachute infantry regiments to that task. The 505th Regiment, commanded by Lieutenant Colonel William E. Ekman, was to drop onto the southern end of the high ground, sharing their DZ with the 376th Parachute Artillery Regiment, Gavin's divisional HQ and then the gliders carrying Browning's Corps HQ. Ekman's task was to secure the town of Groesbeek, establish a perimeter along the southern edge of the Heights, and link up with the 504th Parachute Infantry regiment to the west. The second regiment assigned to the Heights was Lieutenant Colonel Roy E. Lindquist's 508th Parachute Infantry Regiment. The Regiment's primary tasks were to establish a perimeter along the east and north of the plateau, and to hold its landing area for the arrival of the 325th Glider Infantry Regiment on 8 September. However, while Gavin agreed with Browning about the importance of the Groesbeek Heights, he was also uneasy about not going after the Nijmegen bridges. Consequently, not long before take off on 17 September Gavin orally instructed Lindquist to despatch a battalion to the bridges as soon as the situation allowed.[7] He also took more practical measures to reinforce the 82nd Airborne's combat power, based on the experience gained in Normandy 700 men spread over all three regiments were to carry an anti-tank mine as well as all their other gear, and every man was deliberately overloaded with ammunition of various types.[8] As we shall see, Gavin was to regret not making his instructions to Lindquist more explicit, and the 82nd Airborne was subsequently to pay a very high price for Browning's fixation on the Groesbeek Heights to the exclusion of all else. The 82nd Airborne's third regiment was the 504th Parachute Infantry Regiment, commanded by Lieutenant Colonel Reuben H. Tucker. Tucker's primary task was to seize the nine-span bridge over the River Maas at Grave, and four bridges over the Maas-Waal Canal, all of which lay south and west of Nijmegen. Tucker thus chose a main DZ between the River Maas and the Maas-Waal Canal, and a smaller one for a single company at the south end of the Grave Bridge.

Like that of the 101st, the 82nd Airborne's jump went extremely well. There was only scattered flak and Gavin, who jumped from the lead C-47, considered it to be one of the best jumps he had experienced. The accuracy of the 504th Regiment's drop permitted the 2nd Battalion to seize the Grave Bridge very quickly after landing, and by nightfall had secured Grave itself after driving out 400 defenders. Matters did not proceed quite so successfully at the four bridges over the Maas-Waal Canal. The 504th Regiment successfully seized the southernmost bridge at Molenhoek, but the two centre ones were demolished as Tucker's men approached. The most northerly was a substantial combined road and rail affair at Honinghutie, protected by pillboxes, trenches and mines. The German garrison held out against elements from the 508th Regiment until mid-morning on 18 September, when they ignited demolition charges that destroyed the railway bridge and badly damaged the road bridge. Events were similarly mixed on the Groesbeek Heights. Ekman's 505th Regiment rapidly secured Groesbeek, established their perimeter facing the Reichswald, and were somewhat relieved when reconnaissance patrols established that reports of German armour in the forest were false. Tucker's 504th Regiment linked up with Ekman's on crossing the Molenhoek Bridge after nightfall.

Matters proceeded less smoothly for the 508th Parachute Infantry Regiment. The Regiment's 2nd Battalion was dispatched west to link up with the 504th Regiment and assist in securing the Maas–Waal Canal bridges. The remaining two battalions were tasked to establish a perimeter along the eastern edge of the Groesbeek Heights, but ran into determined German resistance while setting up roadblocks and securing the village of Wyler, two miles north-east of Groesbeek town. This was because, unknown to the paratroopers, the selected positions lay just inside the German border. Thus it was not until around 18:00 that Lindquist felt the situation was sufficiently safe to despatch the 508th Regiment's 1st Battalion, commanded by Major Jonathan E. Adams, on a reconnaissance in force toward the main Nijmegen bridges. More time was lost in reorganising the battalion for the move, and it was decided to send one company ahead, followed shortly afterward by another. Despite the assistance of at least one Dutch guide, the leading company did not reach the vicinity of the Nijmegen rail bridge until around 22:00 hours, where it arrived at the same time as *Kampfgruppe* Euling from 10th SS *Panzer* Division.

Euling's force had been dispatched to secure the Nijmegen bridges by II SS *Panzerkorps'* initial warning order in the early afternoon. However, fulfilling this order was delayed by the unex-

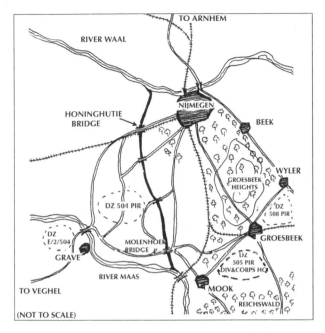

US 82nd Airborne Division's landing zones and objectives.

pected seizure of the Arnhem Bridge by British airborne troops, which obliged *Kampfgruppe* Euling to detour to a secure crossing further east. They arrived in Nijmegen in the nick of time, and immediately engaged in a brutal close-quarter fight in near pitch-darkness with paratroopers from the 2nd Battalion of the 508th Regiment. The post office building housing the controls for the bridge demolition charges was overrun and the controls destroyed, but Adams and a small party were cut off by an SS counter-attack and remained besieged for a further two days. By dawn on 18 September Lindquist had called his 3rd Battalion into the fight from Wyler, but the 508th Regiment remained unable to make any progress toward the Nijmegen bridges in the face of an aggressive and stiffening German defence. The presence of Euling's SS troops from the Frundsberg gave Gavin his first inkling that the intelligence reports on which he had based his plan had missed something.[9]

There is one further matter to detail briefly before moving on
to examine the progress of the British 1st Airborne Division at
Arnhem. The Allied airborne attack came as a complete surprise,
but the supporting ground attack out of the Neerpelt bridgehead
did not. The German defenders around the bridgehead reported
traffic noise and dimmed headlights during the nights leading up
to 17 September. They also noted the British troops opposite were
highly alert. On the night of 15–16 September a *Kriegsmarine*
combat swimmer team attempted to destroy the Neerpelt Bridge
with a modified 500 kilogram sea mine, but both mission and
mine were abandoned when the noise of manhandling it down the
bank of the Maas-Escaut Canal attracted a heavy British mortar
barrage.[10] In all, British 30 Corps mustered around 20,000 vehicles,
which were concentrated in the five nights leading up to 17
September, and an additional 2,000 truckloads of bridging equipment dumped just behind the front at Neerpelt. Given preparations on this scale, it was hardly surprising that the Germans had
noticed something was brewing.

The British plan was relatively simple. The attack would be led
by the Guards Armoured Division, commanded by Major-General
Allan Adair, followed by Major-General Ivo Thomas's 43rd
(Wessex) Infantry Division. The Guards would lead until Arnhem,
after which the 43rd Division would move up and occupy the area
around Apeldoorn. The 43rd Division, which had trained exten-
sively in assault water-crossing techniques prior to the Normandy
landings, had the extra bridging troops and equipment under
command. 30 Corps' third formation, the 50th (Northumbrian)
Infantry Division, was holding the Neerpelt bridgehead, and was
thus designated Corps reserve. Once Arnhem was secured, the
50th was to move across the Lower Rhine and form a link
between 1st Airborne and the 43rd Division at Apeldoorn. In addition, 30 Corps also had the Dutch Princess Irene Brigade and the
4th Armoured Brigade, detached from the 11th Armoured
Division, under its command. The formation chosen to spearhead
the Guards Armoured Division's breakout from the Neerpelt
Bridgehead was the Irish Guards Brigade Group, commanded by

Lieutenant Colonel J.O.E. Vandeleur. This consisted of the 2nd (Armoured) and 3rd Battalion, The Irish Guards, the former carrying the latter on the decks of its tanks. Vandeleur's men had secured the bridge over the Maas-Escaut Canal, subsequently dubbed 'Joe's Bridge', on 7 September. The breakout was to be supported by 350 guns from nine Royal Artillery regiments and fighter-bombers from the RAF's 2nd Tactical Air Force.

The Germans may have been aware of 30 Corps' preparations for Garden, but the latter appear to have been completed only just in time. Montgomery had briefed the Corps commander, Lieutenant-General Brian Horrocks, on 12 September, but Horrocks did not brief his senior officers until 16 September, in a cinema at Bourg Leopold just behind the Neerpelt bridgehead. More importantly, the Garden advance did not commence until two whole hours after the first airborne troops had arrived at their various landing areas. According to one account, Horrocks was not informed that Market was on until shortly before 13:00 on 17 September, as the Market transport serials were actually passing over his forward observation post near the Maas-Escaut Canal.[11] On the other hand, Horrocks' own account claims that he was ensconced in the observation post from the late morning of 16 September, and that he deliberately withheld the order for Guards Armoured to advance until the aircraft were actually overhead. This does not sound like the actions of a man unaware that Market had been launched, and it is also rather unlikely because marshalling and preparing the Garden assault force, to say nothing of organising liaison between the ground and air forces, had to be done well in advance.

In fact, another source provides a more plausible explanation directly connected to the latter point. The ground assault plan incorporated eleven squadrons of ground-attack aircraft from RAF No. 83 Group, which were tasked to operate in direct support of 30 Corps and the Guards Armoured Division. Unlike the airborne transport fleet, these aircraft were based on the continent as part of the British 2nd Tactical Air Force. Apparently in order to minimise the risk of collision, the ground-attack machines were forbidden to venture within twenty miles of the operational area until well after the transport aircraft had delivered their loads and cleared the area.[12] If this were the case, it would be yet another instance of overconfidence and poor staff work on the part of the 1st Allied Airborne Army, which, as we have seen, also had a reputation for poor liaison with ground formations. It would also provide a further example of Brereton's rather shaky grasp of the realities of airborne operations to set alongside his agreement to restrict Market to a single lift on the first day. This does not necessarily mean that 30 Corps had fully completed its preparations for the advance toward Eindhoven earlier, but it would absolve Horrocks' and the Guards Armoured of blame for the tardy start of the ground advance.

Be that as it may, the preparatory bombardment for Garden commenced at around 14:00 hours and the Irish Guards tanks began to advance at 14:35. The barrage wiped out *Kampfgruppe* Walther's contingent of towed anti-tank guns, largely because a lack of all-terrain prime movers had obliged their crews to site them in vulnerable positions along the roadside. Initially the tanks made good progress behind the rolling barrage, but then ran into a carefully sited close ambush by *Fallschirmjäger* armed with *Panzerfausts* that left eight or nine tanks and two armoured cars ablaze on a half-mile stretch of road. The British response was to call down Typhoons, send in the infantry from 3rd Irish Guards to dig out the troublesome *Fallschirmjäger*, and call up bulldozers to clear the road, a time-consuming process that set the pattern for the next few hours. When they halted at nightfall, the Guards Armoured had reached the village of Valkenswaard, seven miles from their start point but still six miles short of Eindhoven and ten miles short of the 506th Parachute Infantry Regiment dug in just south of the Wilhelmina Canal at Son.

Guards Armoured should have reached Eindhoven just after 17:00 hours given the schedule to reach Arnhem within forty-eight hours, and the advance was thus around four hours behind schedule when a halt was called for the night. This was a rather inauspicious start considering the defence consisted of hastily formed and poorly equipped German units. However, the ferocity of the German response can hardly have been a surprise, as those same troops had fought Guards Armoured to a standstill after the latter had forced the bridgehead across the Maas–Escaut Canal on 7 September. Guards Armoured's tardy performance thus appears to have been largely due to three interlinked factors. First, it should be noted that the Garden plan envisaged an advance by the whole of the British 2nd Army all along the line of the Maas–Escaut Canal. 30 Corps should therefore have been flanked by Lieutenant-General Sir Neil Ritchie's 12th Corps to the west, and Lieutenant-General Sir Richard O'Connor's 8th Corps to the east. For a variety of reasons, some of which remain unclear, this did not happen and 30 Corps was left to go it largely alone. Consequently the German defenders were able to concentrate all their resources against 30 Corps' advance in the opening stage of the battle.

The second factor was Guards Armoured Division's late jump-off time. There was little utility in timing the attack to coincide with the commencement of Market, and none at all for beginning two hours after the first airborne troops were on the ground, which in effect allowed the Germans an uninterrupted two-hour breathing space to organise counter-measures against the airborne landings. Consequently, it would have made much more sense to launch Garden in the early hours of 17 September. An earlier start might possibly have drawn German attention, and indeed reserves away from the airborne landing areas. It would certainly have allowed Guards Armoured more operating time before nightfall, which leads to the third factor.

By the time the British Liberation Army set foot on the European mainland, the dictum that armour fought only by day and carried out maintenance and rearming after dark appears to have become set in stone. It is unclear where this originated. The practice may have grown out of the unreliability and heavy maintenance demands of British tanks earlier in the war,[13] although the advent of the US-produced M4 Sherman, with its exemplary reliability, should have done much to offset this. It may also have been a carry over from the long years of training in the UK between Dunkirk and the Normandy invasion. Certainly, British tank crew training in the run up to the Normandy invasion had to make a conscious effort to break potentially lethal habits engendered by peacetime-training regulations.[14] During the static phases in the Normandy fighting it became standard practice for British tanks to move up to the line in the pre-dawn darkness and to withdraw after dark.[15]

This practice appears to have been largely based on an assumption that tanks were too vulnerable to operate in darkness. However, the Germans, and more especially the Soviets, did not subscribe to this view. Nor, incidentally, did everyone in the British and Canadian armies in North-West Europe. Operation 'Totalize', launched by the 2nd Canadian Corps on the night of 7–8 August 1944, saw a large force of Canadian and British tanks and armoured infantry pass virtually unscathed through strong German defences along the Caen-Falaise road. They achieved what they had repeatedly failed to do in daylight, because the darkness nullified the expertly sited German anti-tank guns. But the Guards Armoured Division being Guardsmen, and thus not the most flexible of formations, preferred to limit their offensive activities to the hours of daylight. To be fair, there is evidence that the Irish Guards Group were willing to push on after clearing Valkenswaard toward 22:00, but they were ordered to remain in place until first light when a prearranged relief by another infantry battalion was countermanded.[16] Be that as it may, the combination of 30 Corps' late start time and fierce German resistance put the Garden advance four hours behind schedule by nightfall, and the decision to stop increased the shortfall to twelve hours. It was not an auspicious start, although it was the beginning of an unfortunate pattern.

THE LANDINGS AND
IMMEDIATE GERMAN
REACTIONS AT ARNHEM

The first inkling of what was to come at Arnhem was a series of bombing raids around the 1st Airborne Division's landing area, beginning in the late morning. Deelen airfield was hit again, along with several barracks and other military installations in Arnhem proper and on the roads leading away from the town. Targets further west were hit too, in particular the SS barracks at Ede and the village of Wolfheze. The former was bombed at the specific request of Hackett, whose 4th Parachute Brigade would be dropping only two miles east of Ede on the second lift. Wolfheze, which lay only yards from both 1st Airlanding Brigade's glider landing zones, was hit because German troops were known to be billeted there. Unfortunately, so were a large number of Dutch refugees, and almost fifty were killed. The bombing nearer Arnhem also had an unintended side effect. In order to minimise casualties *Hauptsturmführer* Sepp Krafft, the commander of SS *Panzergrenadier Ersatz und Ausbildungs* Battalion 16 (hereafter referred to as Battalion Krafft) stood his men to and moved them and most of their equipment into the nearby woods west of Oosterbeek for additional and unscheduled training. This unwittingly moved them closer to 1st Airborne's landing areas.

As we have seen, 1st Airborne was starting with the odds stacked against it, and Krafft's decision was the first of several bits of ill luck that were to tip the scales decisively. While all the US C-47s carrying 1st Airborne's parachute elements and all but one of the glider tugs got off safely, twenty-two Horsas were lost over the UK mainland mainly due to tow-line failure. This was by no means an uncommon phenomenon, and all but one of those over the mainland landed safely, allowing their occupants to go in on later lifts. The unfortunate exception was a Horsa carrying men from 9th Airborne Field Squadron RE which according to eye-witnesses came apart in the air near Weston-Super-Mare. There were no survivors. Of the remaining twenty-one, fourteen were carrying infantry from 7th KOSB and 1st Border, including the commander and part of the HQ of the latter battalion. In effect, this reduced 1st Airlanding Brigade's infantry component to two battalions. Four more gliders fell out of the formation over the North Sea and a further eight after making landfall in Holland. However, there were lighter moments during the fly in, even for those that force-landed. The passengers of one Horsa that landed at a US airfield were delighted to be provided with ham and eggs for breakfast.[1] The second pilot of another Horsa was alarmed to see his passengers blithely boiling water on a chemical stove set up on the glider's plywood floor, next to a trailer loaded with mortar bombs. The tea-makers were unimpressed by his alarm, as was the senior pilot, who merely asked if the pilots were to be included in the prospective brew-up.[2]

The first British airborne soldiers to arrive as planned in Holland were the 186 pathfinders from 21st Independent Parachute Company, who were dropped at 12:40. Their landing was unopposed, although two men were injured on landing. Within twenty minutes they had marked out two glider LZs and one parachute DZ with Eureka electronic homing beacons, and white panels and smoke canisters to denote wind direction. At 13:00 hours 1st Airlanding Brigade began to land on LZ S, just north of Wolfheze, and nineteen minutes later another 150 gliders began to land on LZ Z, to the west of Wolfheze and just over the railway line from LZ S. With the heavily laden machines coming in at a rate of around six per minute, accidents were inevitable. A few gliders overshot and ended up in the trees surrounding the LZs, and others dug their noses into the soft soil of potato fields and overturned. This was a particularly serious hazard for the giant

Hamilcars, of which there were at least thirteen in the first lift,[3] because the cockpit was mounted in a blister on the top of the fuselage. Three Hamilcars nosed over, and the crew of at least one was crushed. Such accidents were the exception rather than the rule, however, and in around forty minutes 283 gliders were down. The landing zones were a hive of activity as men and vehicles were unloaded from their gliders and began to move to their unit rendezvous points. 7th KOSB, predictably, rallied to a piper playing 'Blue Bonnets over the Border'.

The parachute drop onto DZ X, which lay along the western edge of LZ Z, began ten minutes behind schedule, at 13:50. 143 US C-47s, divided into two almost equal formations, delivered 2,278 paratroopers in around twenty minutes. The RAF airborne planners may have sold 1st Airborne short by obliging them to use the Wolfheze landing area, but their assurances that they would have a safe landing were certainly borne out on the first day. There was no flak, not a single aircraft was lost, and only one sadly unidentified paratrooper was killed by a parachute malfunction. Once on the ground the paratroopers made for their own unit rallying points, which were marked by coloured smoke along the eastern side of the DZ. All accounts agree that it was a near perfect drop, and many participants remarked on the similarity to training exercises, an impression heightened by the near total lack of enemy activity. Thus by 14:10, 1st Airborne Division's first lift was safely on the ground in Holland. The Arnhem part of Market would now be a straight race between 1st Airborne and the reactions of the German defenders.[4]

The German reaction was swift indeed. The key to this was the HQ of II SS *Panzerkorps* at Doetinchen, west of Arnhem, which received its first report of Allied airborne activity at 13:30 hours. Its commander, *Obergruppenführer* Wilhelm Bittrich, issued a warning order to all units under his command a mere ten minutes later. Bittrich then rapidly and correctly assessed the intent of the Allied operation, identified Arnhem and Nijmegen as the key objectives, and formulated and issued orders to his divisions. That his hasty appreciation was correct is clear from the fact that his orders and appreciation were fully endorsed by *Generalfeldmarschall*

Walther Model, commander of *Heeresgruppe* B, when he arrived at Doetinchen from Oosterbeek at around 15:00 hours. The 9th SS *Panzer* Division, whose units lay closest to Arnhem, was to stop its planned withdrawal to Germany to refit. Instead, it was immediately to secure the Arnhem road bridge, defeat the airborne landings near Oosterbeek, and scout south toward Nijmegen to ascertain the extent of enemy activity in that direction. The 10th SS *Panzer* Division was to secure the Nijmegen bridges as quickly as possible and form a defensive bridgehead at their south end. By 14:40 these orders had been transmitted and acknowledged by all the widely dispersed elements of both divisions.[5]

The commander of 9th SS, *Obersturmbannführer* Walther Harzer, was with his Division's reconnaissance battalion, SS *Panzer Aufklärungs Abteilung* 9 at Hoenderloo when he received Bittrich's warning order. Harzer was decorating the battalion's commander, *Hauptsturmführer* Viktor Gräbner, with the Knight's Cross of the Iron Cross for gallantry in Normandy. Gräbner's forty vehicles, thirty armoured half-tracks of various marks and ten heavy-armoured cars, were already loaded aboard a train for shipment to Germany. He was ordered to unload them with all speed, and refit the missing parts and equipment removed to render them 'unserviceable' as a ploy to avoid transferring them to the 10th SS *Panzer* Division. The first ten vehicles were to be dispatched to reconnoitre the airborne landings west of Oosterbeek, while the remainder were to move south over the Arnhem Bridge and set up a blocking position at Elst, mid-way between Arnhem and Nijmegen. Immediate lack of equipment was also an issue for SS *Panzergrenadier* Regiment 20, which had handed in all its personal weapons and field equipment in readiness for the move back to Germany. The unit's personnel were hastily issued rifles and ninety rounds per man and, lacking web equipment or even steel helmets, moved off toward Arnhem.

Many of Hohenstaufen's sub-units moved out toward Arnhem on their own initiative on receiving Bittrich's warning order. SS *Panzerjäger Abteilung* 9, renamed *Kampfgruppe* Allwörden after its commander, was on the move with its two *Panzerjäger* IVs and whatever transport it could muster between 14:30 and 15:00. *Obersturmführer* Heinz Gropp's mobile anti-aircraft detachment and SS *Panzer Pionier Abteilung* 9, commanded by *Hauptsturmführer* Hans Möller, were similarly swift off the mark. The latter were in contact with British paratroopers on the outskirts of Oosterbeek by 16:30. Ironically, Möller had fought in exactly the same area with another *Waffen* SS formation during the invasion of Holland four years previously.[6]

In the event, the first two German units to make deliberate contact with 1st Airborne did so without any specific orders at all. 213 *Nachrichten* Regiment was a *Luftwaffe* signals unit based at Deelen. Having witnessed the arrival of the gliders to the south the unit commander, *Hauptmann* Willi Weber, put together a scratch force of ninety men and went to investigate. Weber's little band, or part thereof, filtered through the woods to the north edge of LZ S and opened fire on the troops and gliders before withdrawing to report what they had seen. It appears that this information, disseminated through the *Luftwaffe's* highly efficient communication system, was the basis of the reports that arrived with such despatch at II SS *Panzerkorps* HQ. Weber's men may have been responsible for the death of four men from 1st Airlanding Brigade killed in this area, possibly from 7th KOSB.

The second unit was Battalion Krafft. A platoon from 9th (Airborne) Field Company RE, moving to establish a roadblock to catch German stragglers fleeing from Wolfheze, ran into some of Krafft's men in the woods south-east of the town. The British lost their platoon commander killed and two seriously wounded in the resulting firefight. Krafft, it will be remembered, was with his men training in the woods near Wolfheze because of the preparatory bombing. He quickly deduced the objective of the British landings to be the Arnhem bridges, and made his dispositions accordingly. Reconnaissance patrols were dispatched to gather information, one of his two available companies was ordered to advance and attack the landing areas, while the other established a line to the east and south of Wolfheze, blocking the two most direct routes to Arnhem. Krafft also called forward his third company from the outskirts of Arnhem as a reserve, and set up his battalion HQ in the Hotel Wolfheze, in the woods south east of the town proper. There is some doubt over Krafft's subsequent claim that the company advancing on the landing area machine-gunned LZ Z, but it did fight some skirmishes before retiring to the blocking position. It was this company that clashed with the platoon from the 9th Field Company RE.

It is thus clear that the immediate German reaction to the arrival of 1st Airborne Division was exceedingly swift. For its part, 1st Airlanding Brigade made equally fast progress toward its collective objective of securing and preparing to defend the landing areas for the second lift. The 2nd South Staffords cleared Wolfheze, with the assistance of 9th Field Squadron RE. 1st Airlanding Brigade HQ was established in the town, and 181 Airlanding Field Ambulance set up a Dressing Station nearby. Meanwhile 1st Border moved south and secured the village of Heelsum at the southern edge of DZ X, ambushing a truckload of German troops in the process. The battalion then dispersed into company groups to the west, south and south-east of the southern landing area, one of them as a forward observation post position in a brickworks at Renkum, to cover the riverside road. 7th KOSB moved in company groups almost three miles west of the rest of 1st Airlanding Brigade, and took up similar positions around the as yet unused DZ Y. This was completed by around 17:00 hours, at which time a rather inept probe from SS *Wacht* Battalion 3, moving east from its barracks in Ede, was ambushed by A Company. The largely Dutch SS unit lost twenty-five dead and over twice as many wounded, and the survivors fled in disorder. A series of similar probes by other sub-units from the hapless *Wacht* Battalion were similarly handled through the night.

Unfortunately, the remainder of 1st Airborne Division was less prompt and markedly less rapid than 1st Airlanding's infantry component or their German opponents. The worst offender in this regard was the 1st Airborne Reconnaissance Squadron. Given that this unit's mission was to speed ahead of 1st Parachute Brigade and seize the Arnhem road bridge, it would have been logical to assume that it would have been among the first off the landing zone. In fact it was the last, and did not begin to move from its forming-up area at the north east corner of LZ Z until 15:40, two hours after its gliders had landed. Even allowing that it took an average of thirty minutes to unload a Horsa, that one of the Squadron's troops had an unusually large number of bad landings that complicated vehicle recovery, and that some of the Squadron's personnel arrived by parachute, this was an inordinately long period for which no satisfactory explanation has yet appeared. According to John Fairley, who served with the Recce Squadron at Arnhem, there was some confusion over elements of 9th Field Squadron RE detailed to join the Recce troops for the run in to Arnhem, but which failed to show up.[7] Some time may therefore, have been lost to this misunderstanding, but it is difficult to see how this factor could justify a delay of more than an hour in total.

For whatever reason, the performance of the bulk of the Recce Squadron did not improve substantially after its twenty-eight jeeps of a planned thirty-one left the landing area. They had travelled less than a mile east of Wolfheze Station when the lead section of two jeeps ran into the northern end of Battalion Krafft's defensive screen, at around 15:45. All nine occupants of the lead section's vehicles were killed or captured, and the advance came to an abrupt halt as the following section moved forward on foot to ascertain what had happened, and then became embroiled in a long and fruitless firefight with Battalion Krafft. In the middle of all this the Recce Squadron's commander, Major Freddie Gough, was recalled to divisional HQ by Urquhart, receiving the radio message at around 16:30. The reasons for, and wisdom of Gough's recall, will be examined in more detail below. The point here is that the ambush and removal of the Recce Squadron's commander effectively ended the *coup-de-main* effort against the Arnhem Bridge, leaving 1st Parachute Brigade to manage on its own. The Recce Squadron remained in place at Wolfheze until around 18:30, when it was relieved by a detachment of glider pilots and moved back to the main landing area for fresh orders.

It is difficult to avoid the conclusion that the Recce Squadron did not try very hard. No attempt appears to have been made to ascertain the size or location of the enemy blocking force, or to find alternative routes around it, all of which were routine reconnaissance tasks. In effect therefore, a vital mission was abandoned after a skirmish led to the loss of two jeeps and nine men. The reason for this lack of push may well have lain with Gough. He was unhappy about the *coup-de-main*, and had attempted to persuade Urquhart and Lathbury to deploy his men in their more accustomed role as scouts ahead of the three parachute battalions instead, although the performance near Wolfheze raises doubts as to how effective this might have been.[8] If the Recce Squadron's personnel had picked up on Gough's doubts, it would explain why they appear to have quietly abandoned the *coup-de-main* idea once Gough was called away. The irony is that the Recce Squadron might have avoided Battalion Krafft altogether if it had displayed a little more haste in leaving the landing area.

Lack of haste was by no means the sole preserve of the Recce Squadron, for 1st Parachute Brigade's three battalions were not especially swift in leaving their forming-up areas either. The 2nd and 3rd Parachute Battalions spent almost an hour on the ground before moving off at around 15:00, followed half an hour later by the 1st Battalion and then Brigade HQ. In part, the delay was due to the time it took for the various glider-delivered vehicles and anti-tank guns to link up with the parachute battalions. The insistence that the battalion groups assemble fully before moving off came directly from Lathbury, and was presumably based on 1st Parachute Brigade's bad experience at the Primasole Bridge. Even so, at least one battalion commander at Arnhem was unhappy about the resultant delay, and chafed at having to await permission from 1st Parachute Brigade HQ to proceed.[9] Nor were matters helped by the easy landing and lack of tangible opposition, which may well have lulled some into a dangerously false sense of security. The British performance compared poorly with that of their US counterparts, most of which were well on their way within forty-five minutes of landing. The more recent combat experience of the US units was doubtless a major factor in this divergence. It would also appear that the British commanders recognised this, for

1 Garden preparations: 30 Corps vehicles near Helchteren, moving between the Beeringen crossing on the Albert Canal and the Neerpelt bridgehead on the Meuse-Escaut Canal. The burned out Sherman was a casualty of the fighting to secure the Neerpelt bridgehead, between 7 and 12 September 1944.

2 Operation Garden: a British-manned M10 crosses a Bailey Bridge over the Meuse-Escaut Canal during the build-up to Market Garden. This was the type of bridge erected by the Guards Armoured Division over the Wilhelmina Canal at Son.

3 Ready for take off: paratroopers from the Mortar Platoon, 1st Parachute Battalion aboard a C-47 belonging to the US 61st Troop Carrier Group at Barkston Heath, 17 September 1944.

5 LZ Z at Wolfheze, with paratroopers from 1st Parachute Brigade advancing east from DZ X. The glider in the left foreground is a US Waco CG4, one of four machines carrying radio teams from the US 306th Fighter Control Squadron attached to 1st Airborne Division. The raised nose of the CG4 shows it was used to carry a jeep.

4 Covering the Garden jump-off: British infantry with Vickers medium machine-guns emplaced to provide fire-support for Guards Armoured Division's breakout from the Neerpelt bridgehead toward Valkenswaard.

6, 7 Seven miles in: Dutch civilians turn out to greet tanks from the Guards Armoured Division in Valkenswaard, where the Garden force halted for the night of 17-18 September, ten miles short of their first objective at Son.

8 1st Parachute Brigade dropping on DZ X, 17 September 1944. The landed Horsa gliders in the top left are on LZ Z, with overshoots on the parachute drop zone at the bottom left.

9 British Airborne medic paying respects at the temporary grave of Trooper William Edmond, 1st Airborne Reconnaissance Squadron. Trooper Edmonds was mortally wounded in the clash between his unit and Battalion Krafft east of Wolfheze Station in the late afternoon of 17 September. He is now interred in the Commonwealth War Graves Commission cemetery at Oosterbeek.

10 The first lift into Wolfheze: Paratroopers from 1st Parachute Brigade drop onto DZ X, with LZ Z and unloaded Horsa gliders in the foreground. That the Horsas carried jeeps or artillery pieces of some kind is evident from their detached tail sections.

11 LZ Z littered with abandoned gliders, 17 September 1944. The parachute DZ X is just off the picture to the left, and the woods visible to the right are where 9 Field Company RE clashed with Battalion Krafft shortly after the landings. The circled machines are the large Hamilcar gliders.

12 Late afternoon, 17 September: HQ troops from 1st Airlanding Light Regiment RA unloading their equipment from Horsa gliders on LZ Z. The officer in the beret is Lieutenant Colonel W.F.K. Thompson, CO of the Light Regiment. Lt. Col. Thompson was instrumental in establishing the eastern side of the Oosterbeek Perimeter on 19 Sepember.

13 Locals greet British Cromwell tanks and Universal Carriers from 30 Corps in Eindhoven after the city was liberated on 18 September 1944.

14 *Below Left*: Hell's Highway: US paratroopers seek cover as vehicles from a stalled 30 Corps convoy burn following a German attack.

15 *Below right*: Hell's Highway: British and US airborne medics tend the wounded in a ditch alongside a British convoy stalled between Eindhoven and Nijmegen.

16 British M4 Sherman, probably from the Guards Armoured Division, overlooking the River Waal at Nijmegen.

17 75mm Pack Howitzer from the 1st Airlanding Light Regiment RA firing in support of 4th Parachute Brigade's attack north of Oosterbeek, 19 September 1944.

18 Some got through: men from 1st Airborne Division recovering small-arms ammunition from a re-supply drop in, or near, the Divisional perimeter. One of the wicker hampers used alongside light metal containers for such drops is visible to the left of the centre soldier.

19, 20 Vehicles from 30 Corps crossing the Nijmegen road bridge.

21 Street-fighting in the Oosterbeek Cauldron. An Airborne patrol, armed with pistols and Sten guns, moves cautiously through the rubble.

22 Three members of the British army's Film and Photographic Section who parachuted into Arnhem with 1st Airborne Division, pictured after their return to the UK on 28 September 1944. Many of the photographs reproduced in this book were taken by these men. Left to right: Sgt D.M. Smith (wounded at Arnhem); Sgt G. Walker; and Sgt G.M. Lewis.

both Urquhart and Lathbury expended a good deal of energy in the first few hours after the landing urging their subordinates to greater haste. Despite their efforts, the British performance still compared unfavourably with that of their German opponents, which was the difference that mattered. Even at this early stage it is therefore possible to identify the factor that was to become the leitmotif of 1st Airborne in the crucial initial stages at Arnhem: a marked lack of urgency.

The final area in which 1st Airborne was found wanting in comparison with its German opponents was that of command, as the following brief examination of Urquhart's activities once on the ground in Holland shows. Urquhart originally planned to remain with 1st Airborne HQ at the landing area until the arrival of the second lift. However, this eminently sensible course was rapidly undermined by a combination of radio problems, garbled reports and rumour. Much has been made of the first, and while there were undoubtedly some problems, the role played by radio difficulties has been much overplayed, a point made by Louis Golden, who served at Arnhem as a signals officer with the 1st Parachute Brigade. The root of this problem was a total lack of purpose-designed airborne radios, a situation that went unchanged throughout the war. Because most standard army radio equipment was too big and too heavy for airborne use, airborne signallers were thus forced to rely on radio sets with reduced power and range. This compromise was originally justified on the grounds that airborne units would only be required to fight in restricted perimeters of up to three miles radius, which was the limit of the No.22 sets used for internal brigade and battalion communications. The problem was compounded by technological constraints that required radio sets to be dropped disassembled which meant they could not be 'netted in' until after landing, always assuming that the necessary components could be located in an undamaged condition. Reliable radio communications were therefore the exception rather than the rule long before 1st Airborne Division arrived in the vicinity of Arnhem.[10] Indeed, Urquhart himself made this very point in a post-war interview.[11] Consequently, any problems cannot have been a total surprise, and alternative arrangements and procedures should and could have been made.

Urquhart was especially concerned over unsubstantiated reports that the 1st Airborne Reconnaissance Squadron had lost so many vehicles on the fly-in that it was incapable of carrying out its *coup-de-main* mission. Urquhart's response to this was to summon Gough, the reconnaissance commander, to Divisional HQ to clarify matters. This, as we have seen, led directly to the collapse of the *coup-de-main* effort by removing Gough from his unit at a critical moment. Urquhart's summons to Gough was curious, and not merely because he instructed the latter to report to him while shuttling between divisional HQ and 1st Airlanding Brigade HQ, but without arranging a firm rendezvous location. Allegedly, Urquhart's concerns were based on a total lack of contact with Gough. Consequently, he had no way of knowing that the Recce Squadron had not left the landing area on time. As far as Urquhart was concerned, therefore, Gough should have been well on his way to Arnhem, and Urquhart had no way of knowing this was not the case.

The implicit assumption of Urquhart's order was thus twofold. First, Gough lacked the commonsense to contact him in some manner had there really been a problem. Second, it was perfectly safe for the recce commander to motor back and forth sixty miles behind enemy lines at the whim of his superior. This strongly suggests that Urquhart had not fully grasped the realities of airborne operations. He then compounded his error yet further. First, he ordered his personal radio operator to attempt to contact Gough directly, which involved retuning the set in Urquhart's jeep and thus severing his sole link with divisional HQ. The procedure of retuning contemporary British army radio equipment was by no means the effortless exercise permitted by even the most primitive modern radio. Second, at some point between 16:30 and 17:00, he suddenly decided to leave the landing area and go after 1st Parachute Brigade, accompanied only by his driver, radio operator and the divisional artillery commander, Lieutenant Colonel Robert Loder-Symonds. Ostensibly, Urquhart's purpose was to urge Lathbury to greater speed, but the main imperative was undoubtedly Urquhart's desire to see what was happening for himself. After locating Lathbury, Urquhart elected to remain with him within the 3rd Parachute Battalion's perimeter for the night, on the western edge of Oosterbeek.

Urquhart stayed with the 3rd Parachute Battalion until 16:00 hours on Monday 18 September, by which time the battalion was bogged down in street-fighting only a mile from the Arnhem road bridge. Urquhart then decided to make his way back to Divisional HQ, accompanied by Lathbury and the latter's intelligence officer, Captain Willie Taylor. In the process, they became separated from the 3rd Battalion's command group, lost themselves in a maze of streets and walled backyards, and were obliged to abandon Lathbury in the care of a courageous Dutch civilian after a spinal wound left him unable to walk. Urquhart shot a German soldier who happened upon them while ministering to Lathbury. Shortly thereafter Urquhart and Taylor, accompanied by Lieutenant Cleminson from the 3rd Parachute Battalion, whom they picked up during their brief and confused odyssey, were cut off by German troops and obliged to seek refuge in the attic of another Dutch civilian. There they stayed, with a German assault gun parked directly outside, for the next twelve hours, until the German troops re-deployed to the east in the early hours of Tuesday 19 September.

All this clearly raises questions about Urquhart's judgement. To put it bluntly, he did not make a single correct decision from the time he arrived in Holland until he finally decided to abandon the fruitless and costly attempts to reach the Arnhem Bridge and concentrate the remnants of 1st Airborne in Oosterbeek on 19 September. The problems began with his endorsement of Lathbury's plan, which, as we shall see, merely diffused and squandered 1st Parachute Brigade's combat power to no good effect. Urquhart's ill-judged interference with Gough effectively ended the Recce Squadron's *coup-de-main* effort before it began. His badly thought-out decision to leave his divisional HQ with no inkling of his intentions or destination and without a clearly defined chain of command, ultimately left 1st Airborne Division without leadership for the first forty hours of the battle. This was precisely when leadership was most needed, as it became apparent that events were rendering the original plan increasingly unworkable.

Going forward from semi-permanent brigade or divisional command posts may have been standard practice in normal ground operations, but it was an extremely hazardous undertaking in an airborne context. Urquhart's behaviour in this regard is almost invariably excused by referring to his personal courage, but Urquhart was not there to prove his personal courage. He was there as a divisional commander; his first duty was to the several thousand men reliant upon his judgement and decisions, and this meant his place was in his divisional command post, however personally frustrating that might have been. In the event, Urquhart was very lucky not to have shared the fate of General Friedrich Kussin, the town commandant of Arnhem, who was killed after inadvertently driving into elements of the 3rd Parachute Battalion at the very time Urquhart was driving around unescorted in search of Lathbury. Finally, Urquhart's mere presence, along with Lathbury, had an extremely disruptive effect on the actions of the 3rd Parachute Battalion, which otherwise might well have reached the Arnhem Bridge on the night of 17–18 September.

The irony is that Urquhart was not an incompetent commander. This is clear not only from his record before December 1943, but more relevantly from his handling of the second phase of the Arnhem battle, when it had devolved into a conventional defensive infantry battle. In the initial phase, however, Urquhart clearly had a very poor grasp of the realities of airborne operations, and of his situation generally. He was demonstrably very much out of his depth, placed in an extremely demanding situation for which he had virtually no training and absolutely no experience. The real fault for this lay not with the hapless Urquhart, but with those who had put him in such an invidious position. Montgomery and Browning had been quite happy to place patronage above mere experience and technical competence in choosing a commander for the 1st Airborne Division. Urquhart and the men of 1st Airborne paid the price for their arrogance at Arnhem and Oosterbeek.

COURAGEOUS BUT TOO SLOW
AND TOO LITTLE

1ST PARACHUTE BRIGADE'S ATTEMPTS TO SECURE
THE ARNHEM ROAD BRIDGE

As we have seen, 1st Parachute Brigade's plan involved dispatching its three reinforced battalions along individual parallel routes to Arnhem. The most northerly of these was the 1st Parachute Battalion, which was tasked to move along the main Arnhem–Ede highway (Leopard Route) and secure the high ground to the north of Arnhem. After finally being released from acting as Brigade reserve by Lathbury at around 15:30, Lieutenant Colonel Dobie's battalion moved off along the route previously followed by the Recce Squadron, to Wolfheze Station and then east to the Arnhem–Ede road. However, Gough passed the 1st Parachute Battalion as it left the landing area on his way to answer Urquhart's summons, and he informed Dobie that his intended route was blocked. In order to circumvent this, Dobie therefore elected to change his path by following another road north from Wolfheze that intersected with the Arnhem–Ede highway north of LZ S.

However, his new line of approach brought Dobie's men into contact with *Hauptmann* Weber's scratch force of *Luftwaffe* signal personnel. This prompted the first in a long and confusing series of firefights that continued until after dark, and effectively stymied the 1st Parachute Battalion's advance. Repeated attempts to bypass German opposition by filtering east through the woods and then north to reach the main Arnhem–Ede road failed. After clashing with Weber, Dobie's men came into contact with the ten half-tracks detached by Gräbner's reconnaissance battalion and then *Kampfgruppe* Allwörden with its two self-propelled anti-tank guns and dismounted armour crews acting as infantry. Finally, after dark the 1st Parachute Battalion ran into a solid German line erected across the approaches to Arnhem north-east and east of Oosterbeek. This was the work of *Sturmbannführer* Ludwig Spindler, who took command of the effort to seal off the British landing areas from Arnhem late in the afternoon of 17 September. By midnight *Kampfgruppe* Spindler had succeeded in doing just that, incorporating Battalion Krafft when the latter finally fell back from its own blocking position at around 21:30. How well Spindler had succeeded did not become fully apparent until the following day.

Meanwhile, the 1st Parachute Battalion, badly scattered and having lost eleven dead and over 100 wounded, had abandoned the idea of getting through to the high ground north of Arnhem and was heading south-east toward the Arnhem Bridge. This level of loss, which accounted for almost a quarter of the battalion's effective strength, shows that Dobie's men had displayed more application than the Recce Squadron. Precisely how much more is a matter of debate, however, because until it finally came up against *Kampfgruppe* Spindler's properly configured blocking line, the 1st Parachute Battalion had only been in contact with German units of far inferior size and capabilities. Dobie's men should have made short work of Weber's band of *Luftwaffe* signalmen, and the battalion's PIATs and gammon bombs, to say nothing of the attached troop of six-pounder anti-tank guns, should have given them the edge over the ten hastily re-assembled half-tracks belonging to Gräbner's recon-naissance battalion in the close wooded terrain. The reluctance of the 1st Battalion to close with the opposition was largely down to Dobie, who ordered his company commanders to avoid heavy contact with the enemy in order to avoid squandering the battalion's fighting power before it reached its objective. This was a logical course, if not necessarily the most appropriate in the circumstances, but it is also interesting to speculate to what extent, if any, Dobie was influenced by the discipline problems that had led to him replacing the 1st Battalion's previous commander earlier in 1944.

Dobie's decision to abandon his mission was prompted by a radio signal from the 2nd Parachute Battalion, which had reached the

Arnhem road bridge at around 20:00 and requested reinforcements. 1st Parachute Battalion thus finally embarked, on its own initiative and after significant losses, upon the task it should have been assigned from the outset, that of directly supporting the 1st Parachute Brigade's drive for its main objective. However, despite moving for the rest of the night and fighting numerous confused skirmishes on the way, Dobie's men were still short of the western outskirts of Arnhem by first light.

The 3rd Parachute Battalion, commanded by Lieutenant Colonel John Fitch, moved off at 15:00 for the central Tiger Route. This followed the road between Arnhem and Utrecht, which ran along the south edge of the landing area. The 3rd Battalion thus struck off on a south-easterly course for the road, which incidentally also provided the southern boundary of the blocking line established by Battalion Krafft not very far to the east. Once on the Arnhem–Utrecht road, the British airborne troops made good progress, slowed only by Dutch civilians enthusiastically celebrating their liberation, until they reached the junction with the road running north-west to Wolfheze. The battalion's lead scouts were just past this junction when a camouflaged Citroën saloon appeared from the direction of Wolfheze, and was promptly shot up by B Company's 5 Platoon. The car was carrying the town commandant of Arnhem, General Friedrich Kussin, who had left Krafft's HQ at the Hotel Wolfheze only moments before. Kussin was killed outright, along with his batman and driver.

This small success was followed by a hit-and-run attack against the 3rd Battalion column by Krafft's mobile reserve, which knocked out a PIAT section and shot up a jeep towing a six-pounder anti-tank gun, killing one of the crew. The attack lasted about ten minutes, and was over by about 17:15. There was then a further delay as Fitch rejigged his advance in an effort to avoid further ambushes. He was 'assisted' in this by Lathbury, who arrived on the scene by jeep accompanied by the Brigade intelligence Officer, Captain Willie Taylor. The brigade HQ group proper was following Frost's 2nd Parachute Battalion on the southernmost route, and Lathbury had gone off alone to harass his battalions to

greater haste. Fitch dispatched his B Company, commanded by
Major Peter Waddy,[1] to filter south of the current route, while
Major Lewis's C Company was to try a side route to the north. C
Company was hurried on its way in no uncertain terms by
Lathbury. At around 18:30, in the vicinity of Kussin's car, Lathbury
was joined by Urquhart, who was also engaging in the highly
dangerous practice of driving unescorted between his subordinate
units. This coincided with another attack by Battalion Krafft, this
time on the 3rd Battalion's rear company, which went on for
around two hours. Prompted by this, the accompanying German
mortar barrage, the gathering darkness and possibly the graphic
example of Kussin, both senior officers decided to remain with the
3rd Parachute Battalion until the next day. At this point the battalion had covered approximately half the distance to the Arnhem
road bridge, and the decision was taken to remain in place for the
night.

This decision is usually attributed to Fitch acting with Lathbury's
approval, although this is rather unlikely. Lathbury appears to have
been virtually running the 3rd Battalion since arriving at Fitch's
command group and he is therefore unlikely to have allowed Fitch
any such latitude. That said, deciding to stop for the night flew in
the face of all Lathbury's actions to that time, which had been
focused exclusively on urging his battalions on to ever-greater
haste. The key to Lathbury's about-face must therefore have been
the arrival of Urquhart, and he (Lathbury) must have decided that
Urquhart's safety took precedence over further offensive action.
Urquhart presumably went along with the halt decision to
minimise the disruptive effects of his presence. Fitch, even if he
were consulted, was doubtless relieved not to have to fight his
battalion with his brigade and divisional commanders looking over
his shoulder. We can have no way of knowing what Fitch really
thought about the decision to halt because he was killed later in the
battle, although the evidence suggests that, left to his own devices,
he would have continued to move toward Arnhem. Ironically, the
3rd Battalion's C Company got through to the Arnhem road bridge
later than night after following the railway line into the town.

Whoever decided and whatever the rationale, the result of all this was the absolute worst of all worlds, and all those concerned must have known it. As Major Tony Hibbert, then Brigade-Major of 1st Parachute Brigade, put it in a recent television documentary, there should have been no question of halting because the 3rd Parachute Battalion had only been fighting for six hours or so.[2] Hibbert, incidentally, reached the Arnhem Bridge with 1st Parachute Brigade's HQ group just after Frost's 2nd Parachute Battalion, at around 20:45. Thereafter he succeeded in contacting Lathbury by radio, but the Brigade commander rejected his suggestion that the 3rd Battalion be immediately directed along the same (southern) route. The outcome was even more serious than Hibbert's criticism suggests, for with hindsight it is clear that the decision to halt marked the point at which 1st Airborne Division lost the race to reach the Arnhem Bridge, and at which the Arnhem portion of Operation Market failed. Because the 1st Parachute Battalion was fully engaged in its own running fight to the north, Fitch's 3rd Parachute Battalion was the only unit in a position to help, and every second the 3rd Battalion remained immobile the balance tilted further and further in favour of the German defenders. By the time Fitch's men moved off shortly before dawn on 18 September, the narrow window of opportunity had gone.

As with the Recce Squadron and the 1st Parachute Battalion, the defining characteristic in the 3rd Parachute Battalion's performance was thus also a lack of urgency and push. While it can be argued that this was due largely to the presence and actions of superiors on the spot, the fact remains that the 3rd Battalion allowed the comparatively minor activities of Battalion Krafft seriously to slow its advance. For evidence that it should not and indeed did not have to be that way, it is necessary to look no further than the performance of the 1st Parachute Brigade's third infantry battalion.

Lieutenant Colonel John Frost's 2nd Parachute Battalion left the landing area at the same time as the 3rd Parachute Battalion. Reaching its assigned Lion Route involved moving south to Heelsum, then east through the woods and along the north bank of the Nether Rhine, through the southern outskirts of Oosterbeek and into Arnhem proper. Major Digby Tatham-Warter's A Company led off, and almost immediately ambushed a group of German vehicles, possibly from Battalion Krafft, killing some and taking thirty prisoners. Another clash as the battalion's lead elements exited the woods onto the riverside road was decided equally quickly. Interestingly, Tatham-Warter had trained his men to communicate via bugle calls in advance to contact operations, a system that appears to have functioned very well in the close terrain.[3] At this point the 2nd Battalion passed close to the Heveadorp ferry, about which it had not been briefed despite the fact that the ferry was capable of carrying several light vehicles at a time. This omission was further evidence of the over-optimistic attitude of the Market planners, and underscored the flaws in Lathbury's plan, which tasked Frost's men to seize and hold three widely spaced objectives. This was a rather tall order for a single battalion.

Within three hours of leaving the landing area, Frost's men had covered around half the distance to the Arnhem road bridge, fighting two major skirmishes and running the gauntlet of enthusiastic Dutch civilians eager to celebrate their liberation. The latter became a particular problem in the built-up areas of Heveadorp and Oosterbeek, and orders were issued to prevent the heavily laden paratroopers imbibing the alcoholic beverages on offer. This problem, however, resolved itself once more shooting began near Oosterbeek Church, where Tatham-Warter's men cleared scattered German rearguards and killed or captured three truckloads of newly arrived reinforcements. At this point Frost dispatched C Company, commanded by Major Victor Dover and accompanied by a detachment of airborne REs, to seize the railway bridge. Apart from some light flak guns at the north end, the crews of which fled as C Company approached, the bridge was undefended except for a demolition party of ten men. However, as the lead British platoon set foot on the bridge itself, the NCO in charge of the demolition party detonated the charge and dropped the centre span of the bridge.

The destruction of the railway bridge was witnessed by the remainder of the 2nd Parachute Battalion, and stymied Frost's plan

to put C Company across the river to seize the south end of the
Arnhem road bridge. The 2nd Battalion thus continued east, fighting a skirmish with a German armoured car as it passed under the
railway line leading to the blown bridge from the Oosterbeek Laag
railway station. Once through the underpass, however, an area of
high ground called Den Brink dominated the river road, forming a
natural firebreak between Oosterbeek and Arnhem. Den Brink
appears to have been occupied by engineers from *Hauptsturmführer*
Hans Möller's SS *Panzer Pionier Abteilung 9*. The weight of fire
directed at the river road prompted Frost to send his B Company,
commanded by Major Douglas Crawley, to deal with it at around
19:00 hours. B Company used the twilight and a railway cutting
running north to approach the high ground unseen, and spent the
next four hours embroiled with Möller's engineers in the parkland
crowning Den Brink. A combination of B Company's efforts and
the gathering darkness allowed the remainder of the 2nd Parachute
Battalion to pass east along the river road unmolested. It was around
this time that Frost's men witnessed the thirty hastily reassembled
armoured cars and half-tracks from Gräbner's SS *Panzer Aufklärungs
Abteilung 9* crossing the Arnhem road bridge to the south, en route
to Elst to set up the blocking position ordered by Harzer.

The lead elements of the 2nd Parachute Battalion moved into
Arnhem proper in near darkness at around 17:30. A small party
secured the north end of the pontoon bridge, a large section of
which was moored to the north bank, and remained to act as a guide
for C and B Companies. The Arnhem road bridge was reached
without further incident around half an hour later, and the 2nd
Battalion's HQ, A and Support Companies rapidly set up a defensive
perimeter under the bridge's huge north ramp, preparatory to
attempting to seize the bridge itself. They were joined at around
20:45 by the 1st Parachute Brigade's HQ group. Despite all this activity, the German defenders remained blissfully unaware of the British
presence. In part this was because Frost's men allowed several vehicles
to cross the bridge unmolested, and because of the inexperience of
the twenty very young and over-age German soldiers guarding the
bridge. In their ignorance these soldiers remained ensconced inside

two bunkers, one at each end of the bridge, rather than patrolling. This error was shortly to cost those at the north end their lives.

The first effort to secure the bridge, by a rifle section from A Company, ran into a group of German troops on the ramp and was rebuffed. A second attempt, by a full platoon led by Major Tatham-Warter, also failed with the loss of eight wounded when a machine-gun in the north bunker caught the airborne troops exposed on the bridge ramp. A third attempt, at around 22:00 was more successful. A jeep reversed a six-pounder anti-tank gun part way up the ramp embankment, allowing it to be manhandled the rest of the way onto the top. Nearby a PIAT was used to blow a hole in the wall of one of the buildings level with the pillbox, for use by a RE flame-thrower team. The six-pounder put several armour piercing rounds into the pillbox, and the blast of fire from the flame-thrower deto-nated an ammunition dump just behind it and set fire to the newly painted bridge superstructure. With that, the north end of the bridge was secured, and Frost's men set about fortifying the upper floors of buildings overlooking the bridge and ramp.

While this was going on there was also fighting under and on the approaches to the bridge ramp, as the British airborne troops setting up their perimeter clashed with German troops in the darkened streets and buildings. Some of the latter were from the 10th SS *Panzer* Division's *Panzergrenadier* Battalion 21, who had pedalled all the way from Deventer on bicycles commandeered at gunpoint from Dutch civilians. At the same time a V2 launch unit, relocating north by truck after firing off all their missiles, was captured. These prisoners, perhaps wisely, kept quiet about their recent activities. Among the first to discover that the British held the north end of the bridge were armoured cars from SS *Panzer Aufklärungs Abteilung* 10 which approached from the north at around 20:00, and a small German ammunition convoy that attempted to cross from the south shortly thereafter. The former withdrew and requested instructions after coming under fire, thus giving the German command its first inkling that the British had reached the bridge, and the latter exploded with spectacular effect after being shot up by Frost's men. The British presence thus caused something of a traffic-jam for the Frundsberg's units ordered south to Nijmegen. Like SS *Panzergrenadier* Battalion 21, elements of *Hauptsturmführer* Karl-Heinz Euling's *Kampfgruppe* also became embroiled in an unexpected battle with the British airborne troops as they unsuspectingly approached the bridge.

Not all this fighting and consequent German confusion was down to Frost's little band. The 3rd Parachute Battalion's C Company reached Arnhem after a series of skirmishes and then navigated its way through the darkened streets virtually intact with a mixture of bluff and aggression, but then lost almost half its number in a confused fight near the 2nd Battalion's perimeter. A platoon from the 9th Field Company RE also got through without mishap, as did two jeeps from the Recce Squadron commanded by Major Gough, who was still looking for Urquhart after his summons from Wolfheze. Even more remarkable were the exploits of two more jeeps belonging to Major Dennis Munford from the 1st Airlanding Light Regiment RA, who was accompanying Major Hibbert's Brigade HQ group. In order to re-establish failed radio communication with his guns, Munford led two jeeps back to the landing area through the German positions, had the radios in the vehicles renetted, collected fresh batteries and left a report for the absent Urquhart at Division HQ before returning to the bridge. Unfortunately, only Munford's vehicle made the second leg of the fourteen-mile round trip safely; the other was shot up and its occupants taken prisoner.

The 2nd Parachute Battalion's other two rifle companies did not enjoy Munford's luck. C Company was tasked to seize the German headquarters in Arnhem after being foiled in its attempt to take the railway bridge. However, after dealing with a force of German troops debussing near the St Elizabeth Hospital in the west of the town, Major Dover and his men went to ground for the night just short of their objective and around a mile from the bridge. They were overwhelmed the following morning, apart from a single platoon that broke through to meet the 3rd Parachute Battalion, by then fighting in the western outskirts of Arnhem. Major Crawley's B Company successfully disengaged from the fight at Den Brink at around midnight, and reached the guide party at the north end of the pontoon bridge without incident. A scheme to cross the Lower Rhine to take the south end of the road bridge was stymied when no boats could be found, and almost all Crawley's men subsequently filtered into the bridge perimeter, apart from a rearguard platoon cut off by the Germans. A small group from this platoon succeeded in reaching the bridge later, but the rest were obliged to surrender after running out of ammunition after a twenty-four hour siege. A similar fate befell a group of military policemen from the 1st Airborne's Provost Company, which took over the main police station as a POW holding centre. There they remained with twenty German prisoners for two days, surrounded by unsuspecting German troops until, for reasons best known to himself, one of the MPs opened fire on them on the morning of 19 September. German troops then stormed the station, killing one of the MPs and taking the rest prisoner, apart from one who hid in the attic. He remained there until 31 October before escaping with the help of a Dutch police officer.[4]

Despite these setbacks, by dawn on Monday 18 September a force of around 740 British airborne soldiers had gathered around the north end of the Arnhem road bridge.[5] They were spread around a perimeter the base of which ran along the riverbank, approximately 300 yards either side of the bridge. It extended north to just short of the end of the ramp leading onto the bridge, around 700 yards from the river. The force available to defend this perimeter equated to roughly a battalion and a half. The largest contingents came from Frost's A Company and Hibbert's brigade HQ group, but virtually every unit from the Division was represented, including parachute and glider engineers, artillerymen, glider pilots, airborne military police and men from 1st Airborne's REME, RASC, RAOC and Intelligence Corps detachments. Thus only around half of airborne troops in the perimeter were infantrymen, although the rest were shortly to receive a crash-course in close-quarter battle. Once it became clear that the British had actually seized the north end of the Arnhem Bridge, II SS *Panzerkorps* HQ immediately began organising the removal of the interlopers as swiftly as possible.

That Frost's men succeeded in reaching and securing the north end of the bridge would appear to support the RAF airborne planners' sponsorship of the landing areas west of Arnhem. This view, however, overlooks two key factors. First was the exceptional performance of the 2nd Parachute Battalion, which exceeded reasonable expectations even allowing for the fact that it encountered marginally less effective resistance than the remainder of 1st Parachute Brigade. This seems to have been largely due to Frost's training and leadership, which probably also explains why the 2nd Battalion does not appear to have suffered as severely from the disciplinary problems that afflicted the 1st and 3rd Battalions earlier in 1944. Frost's battalion moved more swiftly than the latter on the forced march from the drop zone, and certainly handled its clashes with the enemy in a far more effective manner, at least until it was in Arnhem proper. The second and more important factor was pure luck. The 2nd Parachute Battalion unwittingly profited from the German policy of not stationing troops in built-up areas to minimise the risk of what they regarded as a terrorist attack. This meant there were no German troops in a position to block the riverside route from the east, and the 2nd Battalion was shielded to the north by the remainder of 1st Parachute Brigade, which attracted virtually all of the German immediate reaction forces from north of the town.

An even more significant piece of luck was the German failure to organise a proper defence at the Arnhem road bridge. This rather surprising oversight was the result of poor communications between the various German commands involved in the immediate reaction to the British landings. All of these erroneously assumed that another was responsible for the defence of the bridge, which allowed Frost's little band to slip through the crack. This was indeed fortunate, for it is unlikely that Frost could have overcome a properly organised defence. He arrived at the bridge with only around a third of his battalion's combat power to hand, as a direct result of the 2nd Parachute Battalion's plan, which was the only black mark against its performance in the initial stages of the battle. It is unclear who was responsible, but the plan was a microcosm of 1st Parachute Brigade's, insofar as it dispersed the battalion's combat power on peripheral tasks at the expense of the main effort. The clearest example of this was the loss of the 2nd Battalion's C Company in its abortive effort to seize the main German HQ in Arnhem, which was a waste of troops that would have been far better employed at the Arnhem road bridge.

Be all that as it may, the important point was that part of the 2nd Parachute Battalion had succeeded in reaching and partially securing its primary objective, against the odds and within eight hours of landing. If this success was to be maintained, Frost's group at the bridge needed rapid reinforcement, which left the ball firmly in 1st Parachute Brigade's court.

After conferring with Lathbury and Urquhart, Lieutenant Colonel Fitch received permission to do what he would have probably done nine hours before if left to his own devices, which was to abandon his assigned route and move south onto the riverside road followed by Frost's 2nd Parachute Battalion the previous evening. Led by B Company's 5 Platoon, the 3rd Parachute Battalion moved off from its night perimeter before dawn at 04:30 and, shielded by the darkness, rapidly covered the two and a bit miles into the western outskirts of Arnhem without incident. By first light 5 Platoon had reached a riverside building called the Rhine Pavilion, just over mile from the Arnhem road bridge. However, the cohesion of the battalion column was adversely affected when daylight exposed it to the attention of Möller's SS engineers at Den Brink, and riflemen and machine gunners infiltrated south through the wooded firebreak that divided Oosterbeek and Arnhem.

This unwelcome attention split the 3rd Battalion's column, resulting in HQ and A Companies moving on a more northerly route to that taken by B Company, and some of the battalion's support elements remaining pinned down in the region of the Oosterbeek Laag underpass. The latter were picked up by Dobie's 1st Parachute Battalion when it arrived there an hour or so later. The 3rd Battalion's B Company halted when it realised it had lost those following at around 07:00, and went to ground in houses near the Rhine Pavilion. Unfortunately they were observed by *Kampfgruppe* Harder, which had set up a backstop line in the western outskirts of

Arnhem to supplement that established by *Kampfgruppe* Spindler a few hundred metres to the west and north. When Harder's men sent forward a tank, possibly a Panther, to investigate, a six-hour stand-off ensued, with the British paratroopers being unable to move without drawing heavy fire, and the German armoured vehicles and infantry wisely preferring to stand-off rather than close with them.

B Company's predicament mirrored that of the remainder of the battalion, and the situation was exacerbated by the continued presence of Lathbury and Urquhart, the protection of whom detracted from the 3rd Battalion's ability to operate as an effective fighting force. Additional ammunition and reinforcements, presumably from the elements cut off earlier near the Oosterbeek Laag, reached the battalion at 14:30. Unfortunately B Company's commander, Major Peter Waddy, was killed while unloading ammunition from the Bren Gun Carrier that carried it in. At 16:00 hours Urquhart and Lathbury finally left the 3rd Battalion in their ill-fated attempt to regain their respective HQs, and Fitch then launched another attempt to break the stalemate. However, the weight of German fire directed against anyone moving on the streets rapidly obliged Fitch to abandon the attack, and defensive positions were set up in houses to the west of St Elizabeth's Hospital. The 3rd Parachute Battalion lost fifteen dead and approximately fifty wounded in the course of the day's fighting, which reduced it to the strength of a reinforced company. Nonetheless, Fitch was determined to continue the fight the next day.

The bulk of the 1st Parachute Battalion, consisting of a little over two rifle companies, reached the northern outskirts of Oosterbeek before dawn on Monday 18 September. Assuming that the 3rd Parachute Battalion had already passed on the Arnhem-Utrecht road, Lieutenant Colonel Dobie decided to follow that route into Arnhem too. Good progress was made until the battalion's lead scouts left Oosterbeek and approached the railway embankment dividing the town from Arnhem at around 05:00 hours. Here they almost literally bumped into German troops deployed along the embankment, and in the ensuing firefight seven men were killed and several wounded. Dobie decided to pull back and side step again to the south, aiming for the riverside route. This was achieved without incident, but when the 1st Battalion attempted to move east of the Oosterbeek Laag underpass at around 08:00 they came under heavy fire from German defenders already stirred up by the passage of the 3rd Battalion. As well as reinforcing the Den Brink, the Germans had also set up blocking positions in houses to the east and in industrial buildings south of the river road behind the 3rd Battalion.

With no further room to manoeuvre, Dobie attacked straight down the river road, sparking a day of close-quarter fighting that carried the 1st Battalion into the western outskirts of Arnhem alongside the 3rd Battalion, and to within a mile of Frost's perimeter at the bridge. By late afternoon, however, Dobie's men had fought themselves to a standstill, and the survivors set up a night perimeter near that established by the 3rd Battalion, just west of the St Elizabeth Hospital. In the course of the day the 1st Battalion was, like the 3rd Battalion, effectively reduced to a single operational company. T Company, which had led the fight, lost all its platoon commanders and the battalion as a whole lost twenty-five dead, the highest single battalion loss of the Arnhem battle.

By last light on Monday 18 September the situation was therefore unpromising for 1st Airborne Division. The bulk of the 1st Parachute Brigade had, thanks to a combination of the distance from the landing areas, an unsuitable plan and a marked lack of push, been comprehensively beaten in its race with II SS *Panzerkorps* within the first ten hours after landing. The Brigade's courageous attempts to reverse the result over the next twelve hours or so succeeded only in destroying it as an effective fighting force, with the 1st and 3rd Parachute Battalions being reduced to around a third of their original strength. Consequently, there was no prospect of 1st Parachute Brigade reaching the Arnhem road bridge unaided. Frost's force at the bridge thus had two possible sources of relief. These were Hackett's 4th Parachute Brigade, which had arrived during the afternoon of 18 September, although realistically its prospects against the German defences that had stopped Lathbury's brigade were not bright. The other was the prompt arrival of 30 Corps.

THE BATTLE IN THE CORRIDOR

While the 1st Parachute Brigade was fighting itself to destruction in the western outskirts of Arnhem, the US airborne divisions were fighting doggedly in the airborne corridor, the southern portion of which was dubbed 'Hell's Highway' by the 101st Airborne Division. This chapter will examine the latter's fight to hold the road open before and after relief by 30 Corps.

Colonel Robert F. Sink's 506th Parachute Infantry Regiment moved off toward Eindhoven from its overnight positions south of Son at around 06:00 on 18 September. Resistance was light until the lead battalion ran into a pair of flak guns in the outskirts of the city, but these were quickly outflanked and overrun, and the objective bridges over the River Dommel were seized intact shortly thereafter. Radio contact was made with 30 Corps, and General Taylor warned of the destruction of the Son Bridge and requested the British to be prepared with bridging equipment, a precaution that already appears to have been made by Guards Armoured's CRE, Lieutenant Colonel C.P. Snow. Armoured cars from the Household Cavalry arrived in the city from the north at around midday, having bypassed the German blocking position and the city itself. However, it took the main body of Guards Armoured Division the entire day to cover the six miles from Valkenswaard, linking up with the 506th at 18:30, and reaching Son thirty minutes later.

This was a dilatory performance considering that Guards Armoured was faced by a single, hastily established blocking position on the outskirts of Aalst, just south of Eindhoven proper. This consisted of eleven towed PAK 40 anti-tank guns, again deployed in unsuitable roadside positions due to a shortage of prime movers, backed with a handful of *Panzerjäger* IVs surviving from the previous day's fighting. The root of the problem would again appear to have been a simple lack of urgency. According to British accounts, the Irish Guards Group was ordered to resume the advance at 06:30.[1] While this may have been the case, the fact remains that German accounts claim that no British activity was detected until the late morning and contact was not made until midday.[2] Whatever the reason, when Guards Armoured linked up with the 506th in Eindhoven at 18:30 the ground advance had slipped twenty to twenty-four hours behind schedule, depending on the account consulted. This delay was extended yet further by the need to erect a Class 40 Bailey Bridge at Son, to thirty to thirty-six hours.

While all this was going on, the 502nd Parachute Infantry Regiment's 1st Battalion, dug in around the bridges at St Oedenrode, enjoyed what appears to have been the quietest Monday of all the 101st Airborne's units. Some small German probes were repulsed during the night of 17–18 September, and the only daylight action concerned what the troops christened the 'Incident of the Seven Jeeps', which involved the rescue of a party of staff officers from 1st Allied Airborne Army. The latter took a wrong turning travelling through St Oedenrode en route from Son to Veghel and became pinned down just outside Schijndel. A party from the 1st Battalion's Company C, led by Lieutenants Joshua A. Mewborn and Troy Wall managed to extricate the party and its vehicles at a cost of two wounded. The remainder of the 502nd Regiment, however, had a rather more active time at Best, five miles to the west of Son, not least because their activities appear to have attracted German reinforcements away from Eindhoven and Son. The 502nd Regiment's 3rd Battalion, it will be recalled, had spent the night pinned down in woods east of Best, with a detached platoon isolated by the bridges over the Wilhelmina Canal to the south. The Regiment's 2nd Battalion was brought up to assist in the early hours of the morning, but the town's reinforced defenders rebuffed a hasty attack with heavy casualties, and pinned the 3rd Battalion in place with artillery fire. An attempt to suppress the German defence with air support led to the loss of the 3rd Battalion's commander, Lieutenant Colonel Robert Cole, to a German sniper.

The 101st Airborne's second lift arrived while the 502nd Regiment's 2nd Battalion was reorganising. Beginning at 14:30 428 gliders landed on LZ W, carrying 2,579 men, 146 jeeps and 109 trailers. The largest contingent was made up of the 2nd and 3rd Battalions, 327th Glider Infantry Regiment. The 3rd Battalion was tasked to protect the landing area for future resupply drops, while the 2nd Battalion was dispatched to assist the 502nd Parachute Infantry in its fight for Best. While these reinforcements were en route, the 502nd Regiment's 2nd Battalion launched another attack in the late afternoon. Beginning at around 17:00, the new attack was routed south-west through the 3rd Battalion's positions toward the bridges over the Wilhelmina Canal. This too was rebuffed, largely by direct fire from flak artillery positioned along the Canal, and the 2nd Battalion withdrew to the nearest woods and dug in for the night.

Although they had no way of knowing, the 2nd Battalion's gallant effort was a futile one, because the Canal bridges south of Best had been demolished by the German defenders at 11:00 on 18 September. The isolated platoon from the 3rd Battalion near the north end of the bridges, commanded by Lieutenant Edward L. Wierzbowski, lacked the strength to interfere, and had no radio to report the destruction. The 2nd Battalion only learned of the demolition after another abortive attack on the morning of 19 September, and they were too late to save Wierzbowski's isolated platoon. The latter were finally overwhelmed later that morning, and the survivors captured. In the process, Private Joe E. Mann earned a posthumous Medal of Honor. Despite being wounded, Mann deliberately smothered a German grenade with his body, thereby saving six other men in the same trench. The battle for Best was finally decided on the afternoon of 19 September, by a joint attack from 502nd Regiment's 2nd and 3rd Battalions and the 2nd Battalion 327th Glider Infantry Regiment. The airborne troops were supported by a squadron of tanks from the 15th/19th Hussars, which had been attached to the 101st Airborne by 30 Corps, and the Corps' artillery. The town fell with 1,000 prisoners and fifteen artillery pieces, and the survivors from Lieutenant Wierzbowski's platoon were liberated in the process.

At Veghel, Colonel Howard R. Johnson's 501st Parachute Infantry Regiment was holding the 101st Airborne's most isolated objectives, the road and rail bridges over the Willems Canal west of the town and the River Aa within its boundaries. A thick fog arose after dark on 17 September, and the Germans used it to cover a series of attacks against the western side of the 501st Regiment's perimeter, beginning with a company-sized assault down the east bank of the Willems Canal at around 02:00. The US troops only repulsed the heaviest attack, which began at 04:00, with the assistance of daylight and the deployment of its reserve infantry platoon. The Germans kept up the pressure, to the point where Johnson was obliged to shorten his perimeter by pulling his 3rd Battalion back from positions at Eerde, west of the Willems Canal. The arrival of the Guards Armoured Division did little to alleviate the situation. The Son Bailey Bridge was complete by 06:00 on the morning of Tuesday 19 September. The Grenadier Guards Brigade Group began to cross between 06:10 and 06:45, and enjoyed a clear run through the first section of the airborne corridor, passing through Veghel by mid-morning.

This, however, did not deter an *ad hoc Fallschirmjäger* unit from launching two determined attacks on the 501st in the late morning and early afternoon, and the pressure continued to mount against the 101st Airborne's perimeter. The German hand was strengthened by the fact that, contrary to security regulations, a copy of the 101st Airborne's Market Garden operation order recovered from a crashed Waco glider was in the hands of Model's Heeresgruppe B HQ by midnight on 17 September.[3] In the early evening of 19 September tanks from *Panzer* Brigade 107 overran the 101st Airborne's divisional HQ and almost reached the Son Bridge. They were only driven off after a US 57mm anti-tank gun, rushed down from the landing area, knocked out the lead Panther tank just yards from the Bailey Bridge at around 22:00 hours. Another attack on the same axis, made under cover of dawn mist on 20 September, was only repulsed with the assistance of British tanks.[4]

The near miss at the Son Bridge was the first of a series of determined German attempts to cut the airborne corridor in the 101st Airborne's area. On 22 September the reconstituted *Kampfgruppe* Walther and *Kampfgruppe* Huber attacked toward Veghel from both sides of the corridor, and succeeded in cutting it for a time. Communications difficulties prevented the German forces from properly co-ordinating their efforts, but they nonetheless presented the American defenders with a very serious threat, not least because the US force in Veghel had been reduced to a single battalion from the 501st Regiment. The 506th Parachute Infantry's 2nd Battalion, en route to Uden further up the corridor and reinforced by a squadron of British tanks, arrived at Veghel in the nick of time to block *Kampfgruppe* Huber from reaching the Willems Canal Bridge, just west of Veghel from the south-west. In the ensuing battle two battalions from the 501st Regiment, which had occupied Schijndel earlier in an effort to widen the corridor, swung back and took *Kampfgruppe* Huber in the rear. Virtually surrounded, *Kampfgruppe* Huber was driven back with heavy losses after savage close-quarter fighting in the woods south-west of Veghel.

Kampfgruppe Walther reached the road north of Veghel, but was prevented from entering the town by a battalion from the 327th Glider Infantry Regiment, reinforced with a platoon of 57mm anti-tank guns. The US force arrived literally minutes before German armour approached the outskirts of the town, and knocked out the lead Panther tank. This prompt action persuaded the German armour it was facing a properly established defence, and it pulled back to await infantry support before trying again in the late afternoon. This attack came close to reaching the railway bridge over the River Aa, but was driven back by elements of the 501st and 506th Regiments. By nightfall the road north of Veghel remained cut, but *Kampfgruppe* Walther had suffered so heavily that some units began to melt away, while those that remained were critically short of ammunition and desperately in need of reinforcement.

Fallschirmjäger Regiment 6, commanded by Crete veteran *Oberstleutnant* Friedrich Freiherr von der Heydte, was supposed to have attacked with *Kampfgruppe* Huber on 22 September, but was unable to reach the start line in time. The Regiment was thus directed to renew the attack on Veghel from the west, with the same objective of capturing the Willems Canal Bridge. The attack began at 07:00, but was fought to a standstill by late morning, and a second attempt in the afternoon was no more successful. Detecting no sign of a supporting attack to the north of Veghel, von der Heydte broke off the attack on his own initiative, and ordered his men to dig in just west of the village of Eerde, effectively bringing the western thrust against Veghel to an end.

There had been no attack from *Kampfgruppe* Walther in the north because the lead elements of the reinforcements assigned to make it – a battalion each of SS *Panzergrenadiers* and *Fallschirmjäger,* supported by a handful of SS *Jagdpanzer* IVs – did not begin to arrive until midday. The attack was thus postponed until late afternoon, by which time it was too late. The German attack was pre-empted by the 2nd and 3rd Battalions of the 506th Regiment, which advanced north from Veghel at 15:00 and linked up with elements of the Grenadier Guards Brigade Group moving south from Uden. The 506th Regiment's two battalions then swung south-east and attacked the rear of *Kampfgruppe* Walther, disrupting the attack preparations and forcing a rapid German withdrawal to the south-east. US commanders on the spot, including divisional commander General Taylor, felt that the German force should, and could, have been destroyed had the Grenadiers' armour been willing to leave the main road and accompany them.[5] This, however, they declined to do in a further example of the rigidity and lack of initiative that characterised the Guards Armoured's involvement in the battle. Even so, the threat to Veghel from the north had been removed and was not to reappear, for *Kampfgruppe* Walther, having lost twenty per-cent of its tanks and a quarter of its infantry, was withdrawn to a blocking position near Venlo.[6]

The threat still lingered south of Veghel, however. The remnants of *Kampfgruppe* Huber were reinforced during 23 September, and launched another attack on 24 September. *Fallschirmjäger* Regiment 6, supported by *Jagdpanther* tank destroyers from *Panzerjäger* Battalion 559 attacked the 501st Parachute Infantry's 1st

Battalion at Eerde at 10:00. The US airborne soldiers held the German attack with the help of tanks from the British 44th RTR, several of which were knocked out, but could not prevent two *Jagdpanthers* from cutting the highway with fire just south of Eerde. Even more seriously, during the night of 24–25 September a battalion of *Fallschirmjäger* commanded by Major Hans Jungwirth seized the village of Koevering, astride the road between Veghel and St Oedenrode, destroying a convoy of fifty vehicles and taking forty prisoners. Jungwirth's force managed to hold onto their lodgement on the highway in the face of repeated attacks and heavy shelling for twenty-four hours, and mined the road before withdrawing toward Schijndel with the rest of *Kampfgruppe* Huber in the early morning of 26 September. The road was reopened at 14:00 that day, after the mines and other debris had been cleared. The attack of 24–26 September was the last serious German attack on the airborne corridor in the 101st Airborne's sector, and the last time they succeeded in cutting the road. Thereafter German interdiction efforts were restricted to artillery fire.

It is clear from this brief account that the 101st Airborne Division's fight to keep open its section of the airborne corridor was an epic in its own right. As an airborne Division, the 101st Airborne should have been too small to cover the necessary frontage, and too lightly armed to face the kind of opposition the Germans were increasingly able to muster against it. However, the Screaming Eagles offset these paper disadvantages with their experience, skill and aggression. In combination, these factors allowed them consistently to outfight the German troops ranged against them, no mean feat even allowing for the variable quality and command and control problems that dogged the latter. Fitness also played an important part, as the US airborne troops were frequently obliged literally to run from fight to fight as the Division shuttled its units back and forth along the airborne corridor to meet the enemy threats as they appeared. All in all, the battle fought by the 101st Airborne Division in its sector of the airborne corridor was at least as fierce as that fought by British 1st Airborne at Arnhem, although it has received far less recognition.

SO NEAR BUT SO FAR

THE 82ND AIRBORNE AND THE SEIZURE
OF THE NIJMEGEN BRIDGES

The experience of the 82nd Airborne Division was similar to that of the 101st, although it was focused more on securing water crossings than maintaining the integrity of the airborne corridor. The night of 17–18 September passed relatively peacefully for the 504th and 505th Parachute Infantry Regiments, after the former had successfully secured the Grave Bridge on the west of the Division's perimeter, and linked up with the latter at the Molenhoek Bridge on the southern side. The same was the case with the 508th Regiment's 2nd Battalion, which was tasked to link up with the 504th Regiment on the Maas-Waal Canal. The 508th Regiment's 1st Battalion, however, became embroiled in a close-quarter fight with newly arrived German reinforcements on the approaches to the Nijmegen railway bridge just before midnight, into which the 508th Regiment's 3rd Battalion also became drawn in the early hours of the morning. Interestingly, at around dawn a German railway train passed oblivious through the 82nd Airborne's perimeter near Groesbeek and continued over the Nijmegen Bridge to safety, because no-one had thought to block the line. A second train was stopped with the aid of a bazooka an hour or so later, after which the German rail traffic control presumably realised that the line was cut. The underlying problem was that the 508th Regiment's expanding fight in Nijmegen left the eastern edge of the divisional perimeter dangerously vulnerable, and especially the landing zone for the 82nd Airborne's second lift, scheduled for 13:00 on the afternoon of 18 September.

By dawn on 18 September the local German command nearest the Groesbeek Heights had assembled an *ad hoc* force under the operational control of the German 406th Division, totalling around 2,300 men supported by five armoured cars and three half-tracks mounting 20mm flak guns.[1] This force was grouped into four *Kampfgruppen* which were ordered to move against the south and east side of the Groesbeek Heights at 06:30 on the morning of 18 September, oriented roughly on the villages of Beek, Wyler, Mook and Groesbeek. Fortunately for the Americans, the German advance was extremely slow, because the bulk of the German troops were very badly equipped and untrained in infantry work. One contingent consisted of over-age men recently called up for POW guard duties. Nonetheless, while the thinly stretched 505th Regiment succeeded in keeping the main German thrust out of Groesbeek town, other German troops penetrated the absent 508th Regiment's section of the divisional perimeter and reached the landing areas.

Gavin had recognised the implications of the situation after clarifying the 508th Regiment's status just after dawn, and he directed Colonel Lindquist to send the 3rd Battalion back to the perimeter as quickly as possible. Gavin's divisional reserve consisted of the 2nd Battalion, 505th Parachute Infantry Regiment, commanded by Colonel Benjamin Vandervoort. As the situation deteriorated in the late morning Gavin reinforced Vandervoort with two companies of engineers and dispatched him to clear the landing zones, with a warning to avoid clashing with the 508th Regiment's 3rd Battalion when it arrived. Moving from the reserve position to the landing area involved an eight-mile forced march, and Vandervoort's battalion was thus still fighting to clear the periphery of the landing zones when the second lift arrived.

The 82nd Airborne's second lift consisted almost exclusively of the Division's artillery assets; thirty-six 75mm Pack Howitzers and 1,866 men from the 456th Parachute Field Artillery Battalion and the 319th and 320th Glider Field Artillery Battalions, a battery of eight 57mm anti-tank guns, and some engineer and medical units. Poor weather in the UK put the lift an hour behind schedule, and the first gliders thus arrived at the Groesbeek LZ at 14:00. The 2nd

Battalion of the 505th Regiment launched a bayonet charge as a
last ditch effort to clear at least part of the LZ as the first gliders
began to land. This combination prompted many of the inexperienced German troops to break and run, hurried on their way by
Vandervoort's men who killed fifty and captured a further 150. The
rout was only stemmed by the personal intervention of the 406th
Division's commander, *Generalleutnant* Scherbenning and his
immediate superior, General Feldt.[2]

Of the 444 Waco gliders that lifted off from the airfields in the
UK, 385 avoided technical or mechanical failure and flak to reach the
release point. 250 landed on, or close to, the designated LZ, and the
remainder were scattered around the surrounding area, some over-
shooting the LZ to land inside Germany; the passengers in most of
these strays nonetheless succeeded in making their way back to the
divisional perimeter. The landing was complete by 14:30.
Considering it took place on an active battlefield, and that many of
the attacking German troops engaged the landing gliders with small-
arms and light flak, the landing was remarkably successful. Thirty of
the thirty-six 75mm Pack Howitzers were recovered, along with
seventy-eight of the 106 jeeps and all the 57mm anti-tank guns.

It was just after this that Browning, who had come into the
82nd Airborne's landing zone with his entourage of thirty-six
gliders with the first lift on 17 September, had his first direct
involvement in the battle he had taken such pains to initiate.
Hitherto his activities appear to have been confined to crossing the
LZ immediately on landing to urinate on German soil, theatrically
unfurling a specially embroidered Pegasus pennant on his jeep, and
impressing the Americans with his immaculate Guards turnout.[3]
His Advanced Corps HQ succeeded only in establishing radio
contact with the nearby 82nd Airborne HQ and 1st British
Airborne Corps HQ at Moor Park. The former was largely superfluous given the proximity of the two HQs, and the latter was
rendered the same by a lack of cipher operators, which prevented
the transmission of operationally sensitive material. Browning was
thus effectively reduced to an ineffectual bystander capable only of
looking over the already hard-pressed Gavin's shoulder.

Browning, however, was not content to remain a passive bystander. After the second lift was down, he asked Gavin to refocus his Division's efforts from the Groesbeek Heights to seizing the Nijmegen bridges as quickly as possible. Considering that Browning issued his request at sometime after 14:30 and that the Guards Armoured Division was scheduled to reach the Nijmegen bridges at 18:00, this was arguably not before time. It is interesting to speculate what Gavin made of the request, given that he had been trying to accomplish this on his own initiative with elements of Lindquist's 508th Regiment since the early hours of 18 September. Whatever he thought, Gavin responded in his unfailingly correct manner by rapidly drawing up a plan for a three-pronged assault using the 508th Regiment reinforced with a battalion from the 504th. However, when presented with this, Browning vacillated, and switched back to his original preoccupation with holding the Groesbeek Heights. Despite the urgency of the matter therefore, the deliberate effort to reach the Nijmegen bridges was thus effectively postponed for a further eighteen hours or so, and did not get underway until well after the arrival of the Guards Armoured Division in the 82nd Airborne's perimeter.

Browning and Gavin greeted the Grenadier Guards Brigade Group in person at Grave in the late morning of 19 September. Gavin immediately organised a hasty attack toward the Nijmegen bridges, teaming the Grenadiers' tanks with the 2nd Battalion, 505th Parachute Infantry. However, this attack did not go in until the late afternoon, partly because the Honinghutie Bridge, the most direct route to Nijmegen, was too badly damaged to take traffic. This obliged the Grenadiers to take the roundabout route over the Maas-Waal Canal via the Molenhoek Bridge, and picking up Vandervoort's battalion at the 82nd Airborne's landing area caused further delay. When the attack did go in, the German defence, manned largely by *Panzergrenadiers* from the 10th SS *Panzer* Division, stopped it several hundred yards short of the bridges, destroying at least five of the Grenadier Guards' tanks. They and Vandervoort's battalion fell back to organise a more

deliberate attack for 20 September, while the SS set fire to buildings to illuminate the approaches to their positions.

Given the earlier experience of the 508th Regiment in the same
area, the failure of this hasty attack cannot have come as a great
surprise. From Gavin's perspective, it was one more adverse development to add to a growing list that had dampened the morale boost
provided by the arrival of Guards Armoured. The 82nd Airborne's
third lift, scheduled for the afternoon of 19 September and carrying
much-needed infantry reinforcements from the 325th Glider
Infantry Regiment, was postponed due to bad weather in the UK.
Of more immediate concern, small groups of German troops,
having recovered from their trouncing on the afternoon of 18
September, were beginning to infiltrate the Division's landing area
and the Groesbeek heights once again. It is also highly likely that by
this time Gavin was beginning to feel the strain. He had been
running back and forth between his divisional HQ at Groesbeek
and his various regimental, battalion and in some cases platoon
commanders virtually non-stop since arriving in Holland, advising,
cajoling and inspiring his men by personal example. This would have
been no mean feat in itself, but Gavin had damaged several vertebrae
on the 17 September jump, and had been in severe pain ever since.

Despite this, Gavin also managed to deal courteously and diplomatically with the collection of high-ranking officers that gathered
in the 82nd Airborne's area, which by 20 September consisted of
three corps commanders and his opposite number from Guards
Armoured, Major-General Allan Adair. The corps commanders
were Browning, Lieutenant-General Brian Horrocks, commanding British 30 Corps, and US Lieutenant-General Matthew
Ridgeway, commanding the US XVIII Airborne Corps. The latter,
like Browning, had no real business there, but arrived unannounced at Gavin's Groesbeek HQ in the early afternoon of 20
September. Ridgeway was brimming over with resentment at
perceived British failings witnessed on the journey up the airborne
corridor, and his temper was not improved when Gavin all but
dismissed him into the care of a staff officer.[4] Gavin, however,
had more pressing matters to deal with than placating sightseeing

superiors. On 19 September Browning's Advanced Corps HQ received a brief situation report from the GHQ Liaison Regiment, or 'Phantom' team attached to 1st Airborne Division, during a fleeting period of clear communication. This indicated that things were not going well at Arnhem, a verdict reinforced by occasional, brief reports from the Dutch resistance coming through the local civilian telephone network. This prompted Browning to button-hole Gavin and urge him in the strongest terms to get across the Waal by the following day at the absolute latest.[5]

Browning's action in issuing these instructions to Gavin is invari-ably attributed to his concern for 1st Airborne Division, which may have been the case. However, as Browning's motivation for insinuat-ing himself into Holland was pure self-interest with no operational, or indeed military justification whatsoever, it is not unreasonable to conclude that he was also driven by less altruistic motives. By 19 September he confronted the prospect of being saddled with the responsibility for a costly failure, and it is therefore quite possible that Browning issued his uncompromising instructions to Gavin as a contingency measure intended to deflect future blame. The fact that the operation looked set to fail at that time because of the failure to secure the Nijmegen bridges at the outset, and that this oversight arose largely because Browning had specifically ordered Gavin not to move on the bridges, might also be relevant. If this sounds far-fetched, it should be noted that Browning was later to make an even more blatant attempt to pass the buck for the failure of Market Garden. At the very least, the episode says little for Browning's man-management skills. Gavin was already operating under extreme pressure, he was hardly sitting on his hands with regard to getting across the Waal, and his operational airborne experience meant he had a far better idea of what 1st Airborne was up against at Arnhem than Browning could ever have. Significantly, Gavin's account of events makes no references to Browning's urgings.

Nonetheless, Browning's urgings appear to have inspired Gavin to come up with an imaginative plan to break the deadlock at the Nijmegen bridges and get 30 Corps over the Waal to Arnhem. At a meeting with Browning, Horrocks and Adair on the evening of

19 September, Gavin enquired whether 30 Corps' engineer train contained any boats. On being informed that it held twenty-eight folding canvas assault boats, Gavin suggested using them to ferry the 504th Parachute Infantry across the River Waal to seize the north end of the Nijmegen bridges. This was an impressive piece of lateral thinking, although it says little for Browning, Horrocks and Adair or their combined staffs that it was left to a hard-pressed airborne commander fully occupied with fighting his own Division to come up with it. The crossing was to be co-ordinated with the renewed assault on the south end of the bridges by the 2nd Battalion of the 505th Regiment and the Grenadier Guards' tanks. When his plan was accepted, Gavin returned to his Groesbeek HQ, surveyed the map for suitable crossing points and briefed the 504th Regiment's executive officer at around 23:00 on 19 September.

At 08:30 on 20 September Lieutenant Colonel Reuben Tucker's 504th Parachute Infantry Regiment, supported by tanks from the Irish Guards, began the task of clearing the way to the bank of the River Waal downstream from the target bridges. At the same time the 505th Regiment and the Grenadiers' tanks began clearing German positions covering the approaches to the Nijmegen road bridge. This involved the paratroopers mouseholing, or blowing holes through dividing walls in the upper storeys of the buildings, while the tanks covered the street. Once the block was secured, the tanks would move up and the process would be repeated. Tucker's regiment reached the riverbank just before noon, but there was no sign of the boats, which were still being threaded through the traffic on the Eindhoven-Nijmegen highway. The crossing was postponed to 13:30, and then to 15:00.

Twenty-six boats finally arrived at around 14:30, each capable of carrying thirteen paratroopers and a crew of three engineers. This was sufficient to lift Companies H and I from the 504th Regiment's 3rd Battalion, commanded by Major Julian Cook. The engineers swiftly assembled and loaded the boats with the assistance of Cook's men, and then carried them to the water's edge for launching. The shallow water complicated rather than eased matters and some became stuck in the mud and were only extricated with difficulty.

By that time the pre-planned artillery preparation and smokescreen was already falling on the north bank, thickened up by strafing attacks by RAF Typhoon fighter-bombers and direct fire from the Irish Guards' tanks. The crossing began at around 15:00, observed by Browning, Horrocks and Adair from on top of a nearby power station. Gavin had rushed back to the Groesbeek Heights, where a renewed German attack from the Reichswald Forest was threatening to overwhelm the south-eastern portion of the 82nd Airborne's perimeter and cut the route over the Molenhoek Bridge.

The paratroopers had no boat training, and their clumsy efforts to row caused many of the frail craft to spin on the spot rather than go forward. An eight-knot current and a shortage of paddles, which obliged many of the paratroopers to use their rifle butts, exacerbated the situation yet further. Major Cook vocally encouraged his men, and appropriately set up a cadence using a shortened Roman Catholic prayer – 'Hail Mary/Full of Grace.'[6] When the frantically paddling, bobbing and circling armada was part way across the 400-yard wide river, the wind began to disperse the smokescreen. The German defenders dug in on the north bank then opened fire with rifles, machine guns and mortars, and 20mm flak guns wheeled forward from their permanent emplacements. Some boats were swamped by the backwash from the explosions or the effect of dead and wounded falling across the gunwales. The passengers of those that remained afloat were obliged to bail with their helmets as bullets and shrapnel tore the flimsy canvas sides of their craft.

In spite of this, and to the amazement of observers, at least half of the first wave of boats made it to the north bank. This consisted of a mud beach extending back from the waterline for several hundred yards to an embanked road running parallel with the river. As soon as the boats grounded, their cargoes of paratroopers disembarked, some vomiting from dizziness, fear or their exertions. One soldier made a rather less conventional landfall after falling overboard, holding his breath and walking up the riverbed and onto the beach, still clutching a can of .30 calibre machine-gun ammunition in each hand.[7] The boats immediately began the return crossing to collect the next wave, and Cook's paratroopers launched themselves over the beach toward the embankment without pausing to reorganise, intent on extracting retribution for their ordeal. They were aided by the fact that the German light flak guns and some of the machine guns were unable to depress sufficiently to hit them. The trenches and gun pits on top of the embankment were overrun, most of their occupants being given no opportunity to surrender, and the momentum of the charge carried the first wave over the road. There they overwhelmed a row of houses and many German defenders attempting to pull back to secondary positions behind the embankment.

Cook paused briefly to reorganise as more of his men were ferried over the Waal, and then launched a two-pronged advance. The smaller was directed toward the Fort Hof Van Holland, a moated pre-war Dutch fortification lying about a kilometre north of the river. The remainder, led by Captains Moffatt Burriss and Karl W. Kappel, swung south-east and went for the north end of the bridges. The paratroopers reached the northern approach to the railway bridge at the same time as the 505th Regiment and the Grenadiers' tanks, reinforced by Irish Guards infantry, launched their final drive toward the south end of both bridges at around 17:00. The northern German defence held firm against Cook's men until the pressure grew too great at the Nijmegen, and troops began to stream back over the bridge seeking safety. They ran into the fire from Cook's exultant paratroopers instead, and over 260 were killed before the remainder began to surrender and the north end of the railway bridge was secured. However, while the Allies held both ends, the German flak positions along it were still manned, and the British were reluctant to send tanks across for fear of German demolition charges. Urged on by the arrival of Lieutenant Colonel Tucker, Cook's men therefore turned their attention to the road bridge, the north end of which lay 1,000 yards further east.

The overwhelming Allied concern at this point was that the Germans would simply blow the Nijmegen bridges and bring the Garden advance to an abrupt and premature halt. This had been the fear since Lindquist's men had first approached them on the night of

17–18 September, and the German failure to do so had been a matter of increasing puzzlement to the American and British leadership. The reason was simple. The commander of *Heeresgruppe* B, *Generalfeldmarschall* Walther Model, had categorically forbidden the destruction of the Arnhem and Nijmegen bridges, the preservation of which he considered vital for a subsequent German counter-offensive. Model's view on the matter was not universal, however. *Obergruppenführer* Bittrich, commanding II SS *Panzerkorps*, was sceptical of the likelihood of any such counter-attack, and felt that the bridges should have been demolished as a precautionary measure. His view was shared by *Brigadeführer* Heinz Harmel, commanding the 10th SS *Panzer* Division, who was watching developments from his command post in the village of Lent, at the north of the Nijmegen road bridge. Harmel was aware of Model's edict, but resolved to destroy the bridge rather than let it fall intact into Allied hands. To this end he had the permanently manned firing trigger for the demolition charge set up near his command post, and SS engineers on the bridge made courageous efforts to maintain the integrity of the charges and their all-important wiring.

While the success at the railway bridge spurred the 504th and 505th Regiments and the Grenadier tanks to redouble their efforts against the road bridge, it had the same effect on the German defenders. In practical terms the latter consisted of the 100 strong remnants of *Kampfgruppe* Euling, who were stubbornly holding on to the approaches to the road bridge in a mirror image to events at the Arnhem Bridge eleven miles further north. As dusk gathered, Euling's men were finally prised far enough away from the bridge ramp to allow a troop of four Grenadier Guards' Sherman tanks, commanded by Sergeant Peter Robinson, to move onto the bridge. An 88mm anti-tank gun emplaced just off the north end of the bridge was knocked out in a brisk exchange of fire, and the tanks then motored right across the bridge, manoeuvring around concrete roadblocks and spraying German troops in the steel upper works with machine-gun fire.

By this time Harmel had moved to the demolition firing post and was monitoring events through binoculars. On seeing

Robinson's tanks, Harmel waited until they reached the centre of the bridge and then ordered the SS engineer to detonate the charges. Nothing happened. The engineer tried the plunger again, but with the same result, and Harmel watched helplessly as the Shermans continued to move across the bridge and off the north ramp. Harmel then issued orders to his staff to block the roads leading to Arnhem from Lent and Elst with whatever forces they could muster, ordered his signaller to inform II SS *Panzerkorps* that the Nijmegen bridges had been captured intact, and hastily evacuated his command post. The time was around 18:30. Why the demolition charges failed remains a mystery, although it is popularly attributed to a Dutch resistance fighter named Jan van Hoof, who had been working with the 82nd Airborne as a guide. Whatever the reason, it was fortunate indeed for Robinson. Captain Tony Jones, a RE officer travelling with the second wave of tanks across the bridge, found that it was wired with six or eight specially configured individual charges totalling 500 pounds of explosive. Sergeant Robinson was subsequently awarded the Distinguished Conduct Medal, and two of his men received the Military Medal for their part in the action. The reprieve was brief for two of Robinson's tanks, which were knocked out in another exchange with German anti-tank guns at the north end of the bridge. The two survivors pushed on a few yards to positions where they could cover the bridge approaches, and in the process linked up with the paratroopers from the 504th Regiment at around 19:15. The remainder of the Grenadier tank squadron moved over the bridge to reinforce them shortly thereafter.

The link up between Tucker's paratroopers and the Grenadier Guards north of the Nijmegen road bridge did not bring the fighting at either end of the bridge to an immediate halt, however. In Lent, resistance from the remnants of a company of SS engineers from the 10th SS *Panzer* Division was not finally quelled until midnight, and the isolated pockets of German troops on the south bank of the Waal also continued to fight. Fighting around the command post of one SS unit next to the road bridge ramp went on until 20:30, when the small band of defenders were overwhelmed by paratroopers from the 505th Regiment. A handful of survivors who escaped to link up with *Kampfgruppe* Euling claimed that the vengeful Americans had shot a number of SS prisoners and wounded out of hand. Euling held on for a further two hours before leading his remaining sixty men in a breakout.[8] Using a combination of stealth and sheer bluff – at one point Euling formed his men up and marched them openly through British units in the dark – they passed under the road bridge ramp while Allied troops and vehicles moved north overhead and reached the south bank of the Waal. Moving east, Euling's little band finally crossed the river at Haalderen and regained the German lines and safety. *Hauptsturmführer* Euling later received the Knight's Cross in recognition of his leadership during the battle in Nijmegen and the breakout.

The problem from the Allied side was that none of the activity noted by Euling's little band was concerned with pushing on to Arnhem, eleven miles further up the road. Lieutenant Colonel Tucker and his paratroopers had assumed that the British would start moving north as soon as the Nijmegen Bridge was open. Nothing of the kind happened, however, and Tucker was drawn into an acrimonious exchange with British officers on the spot when he learned that they had been ordered to remain in place and wait for infantry support. The frustration of Tucker and his men was understandable, given their unstinting and costly efforts, and the failure of Guards Armoured to capitalise on their sacrifice was widely considered a betrayal by the paratroopers. Quite how strongly Tucker felt is clear from the fact that he briefly considered advancing north alone with his depleted battalion, and Gavin found him still livid with rage when he reached Tucker's command post twelve hours after the bridge had fallen.[9]

American incomprehension was matched by that of their German opponents, although the latter were grateful for the respite. In Harmel's view, the British failure to advance rapidly north from the Nijmegen Bridge squandered the last chance to reach Arnhem and relieve the British airborne troops who were at that time still holding on to the north end of the Arnhem road bridge. Harmel's opinion was based on the fact that when the

Nijmegen Bridge fell, there were virtually no German troops between Nijmegen and Arnhem. Nor were there for around sixteen hours, until the Germans were able to push armour over the Arnhem Bridge after finally overwhelming the British force clinging to the north end at midday on 21 September. The delay at Nijmegen handed the initiative to the Germans and allowed them once again to erect an effective defence where none had existed in time to counter Guards Armoured's leisurely advance. It also therefore, again with the benefit of hindsight, marks the point where Operation Market Garden failed.

Quite why the British squandered this opportunity remains controversial. Apologists invariably cite the problems of passing reinforcements up the airborne corridor, and more specifically the fact that Guards Armoured was badly stretched in defending the corridor between Veghel and Nijmegen, the 82nd Airborne's perimeter, and supporting the fight to secure the Nijmegen bridges. These are of course valid points, but they are mitigating factors rather than explanatory ones. The real reason appears to have been the result of two interlinked factors. The first of these was the Guards' inflexible operating procedures, of which there is ample evidence. As we have seen, the performance of the Guards Armoured from the outset of Market makes it difficult to disagree with Tucker's disgusted verdict that the Guards were fighting the war by the book. Certainly, they appear to have been unwilling, or unable, to adapt their operating procedures to reflect the urgency of the situation, a mindset that might have been rooted in ignorance of the realities of airborne operations. In halting for the night after crossing the Nijmegen Bridge, the Grenadier Guards were merely following the same routine as the previous two nights, when the situation had been no less urgent. The only difference was the presence of the less hidebound and more vociferous Americans to draw attention to the inappropriateness of their behaviour.

To be fair, Tucker may not have been focusing his spleen entirely on the right target. The Grenadier tanks that crossed the Nijmegen Bridge had been fighting for the best part of a day, and they are therefore likely to have been running low on fuel and ammunition. It was also understandable that the commander of Guards Armoured, Major-General Adair, was wary of launching tanks into unknown territory without infantry support, although his claim that he delayed the advance after seeing the terrain north of Nijmegen is rather unlikely.[10] It was almost dark when the Nijmegen road bridge was taken, and Adair cannot therefore have had a clear look at what lay ahead until after dawn on 21 September. By that time the advance had been stalled for at least eight hours, and the initiative had once again all but passed to the Germans. Nonetheless, even allowing for the fact that the Grenadiers' tanks may have been incapable of mounting a full-blooded advance to Arnhem, it is difficult to see why they could not have reconnoitred forward at least some of the way, even if this involved redistributing fuel and ammunition between vehicles. The problem of close security could have been overcome by co-opting some of the 504th Regiment's paratroopers; given his reaction to the Grenadier's inactivity, it is hard to imagine Tucker refusing to participate in any advance, limited or otherwise. However, the Grenadiers appear to have been content to confirm Tucker's scathing verdict and they thus stand condemned not for failing, but for failing to try.

The tardiness of the Grenadier Guards was merely a visible symptom of the second factor. This was the failure of the British top *echelon* commanders and their staffs at Nijmegen to make the most efficient use of the units available. The most glaring example of this was the failure to create and maintain a ready reserve as a contingency insurance. Maintaining a reserve for unforeseen circumstances or exploitation is a basic military principle at every level of warfare, although it does not appear to have been one adhered to at Nijmegen.[11] Quite why this was the case is unclear. There was certainly sufficient staff machinery on hand to organise the necessary measures, as the HQs of the Guards Armoured Division and 30 Corps were ensconced within the 82nd Airborne's perimeter from 19 September. Nor does the problem appear to have been a shortage of troops. By the same date the Grenadier, Coldstream and Irish Guards Groups were all operating at various points within the

Nijmegen perimeter. These Groups, which teamed an armoured battalion with an infantry battalion from the same regiment, were in very good shape. When the Nijmegen road bridge was secured, Guards Armoured Division had only lost a total of 130 men killed, wounded and missing since the beginning of Operation Garden.

It should, therefore, have been perfectly possible to assemble a reserve by the simple expedient of drawing infantry companies or platoons from each of the Guards Groups. Given the rigid, regimentally compartmentalised fashion in which the Guards Groups operated this may not have been overly popular, but regimental idiosyncrasies should not have been permitted to stand in the way of operational necessity. The selected infantry elements could have been mated with the Irish Guards tanks, which do not appear to have been employed after shooting off all their ammunition in support of the 504th Regiment's river crossing in the late afternoon. With a little application these vehicles could have been rearmed, refuelled and prepared for further action, as they should have been in any event given the continuing German pressure on the 82nd Airborne's perimeter from the east and south.

In any event, the Guards Groups were not the only source for additional troops available by the time the Nijmegen Bridge was secured. 130 Infantry Brigade, the lead formation of the 43rd (Wessex) Infantry Division, arrived just south of the Grave in the afternoon of 20 September. Given that a German attack from the Reichswald Forest threatened the Molenhoek Bridge, and thus the road link between Grave and Nijmegen that same afternoon, one might have assumed that 130 Brigade would be rushed forward, if only as a precaution. This was not the case, however, and 130 Brigade remained south of Grave until well into the next day. It surely would have taken no great effort to move the brigade straight through to the Nijmegen Bridge, where at the very least it could have relieved the exhausted paratroopers and the Grenadier Guards' infantry even if it were not pushed up the road toward Arnhem with the Irish Guards tanks.

As it turned out, none of these measures was even attempted, and the sheer number of omissions, missed opportunities and lack

of apparent leadership raises the suspicion that the problem lay at
the top, with the commander of 30 Corps, Lieutenant-General
Brian Horrocks. Horrocks was a Montgomery *protégé* who established a reputation as a competent and thrusting commander after
being brought out to North Africa by the latter. He fought at El
Alamein, in Tunisia and at Salerno, where he was wounded in an
air raid, and commanded 30 Corps in Normandy and in the Great
Swan that followed the Normandy breakout and immediately
preceded Market Garden. This was a considerable period of front-
line command, and it is therefore possible that Horrocks was
reaching the end of his tether by September 1944. He was ill for
several days at the end of August 1944 with some unspecified
malaise, appeared far from fit to individuals who worked with him
during Market, and was forcibly dispatched on sick leave by
Montgomery at the end of December 1944.[12] If Horrocks was
unfit, this would certainly explain a great deal about the performance of 30 Corps in the advance up the airborne corridor, and in
particular why Guards Armoured and the 43rd Infantry Division
were seemingly able consistently to contradict his orders for haste
with impunity. Whatever the reason, the performance of 30 Corps
in Holland left a great deal to be desired, and contributed in no
small measure to the failure of Market Garden.

THE SECOND LIFT
AT ARNHEM

As we have seen, the bulk of the 1st Parachute Brigade spent Monday 18 September fighting itself to the point of destruction in courageous but fruitless attempts to catch up with the part of the Brigade that had reached the Arnhem road bridge. 1st Airborne Division's chief-of-staff, Lieutenant Colonel Charles Mackenzie, was able to monitor 1st Parachute Brigade's progress fairly closely, but in Urquhart's absence he lacked the authority to organise reinforcements from 1st Airlanding Brigade. Urquhart, it will be recalled, had spent the night of 17–18 September with the 3rd Parachute Battalion in Oosterbeek and then got himself trapped behind German lines while attempting to get back to his HQ. Mackenzie therefore persuaded the senior officer available, Brigadier Philip Hicks commanding 1st Airlanding Brigade, to assume command of 1st Airborne Division, and to dispatch the 2nd South Staffs to reinforce 1st Parachute Brigade in Arnhem. Only two-thirds of the 2nd South Staffs, commanded by Lieutenant Colonel Derek McCardie, were present because of the shortage of gliders in the first lift. The battalion left its positions north of Wolfheze at 10:30, was strafed by German fighters and then progressed in exactly the same manner as the 1st Parachute Battalion had experienced a few hours earlier. The railway underpass east of Oosterbeek on the Arnhem-Utrecht road (the Tiger Route) was still held by German troops, obliging the South Staffs to side-step south to the Oosterbeek Laag underpass, where they came under fire from snipers and machine guns placed on top of

Den Brink. The journey took around seven hours, to cover a notional distance of around six miles, and the 2nd South Staffs finally linked up with the remnants of the 1st Parachute Battalion at 17:00.

1st Airlanding Brigade's other two infantry battalions remained in their positions to protect the landing areas for the second lift, which was scheduled for the late morning of 18 September. The four companies of 7th KOSB were deployed around DZ Y on Ginkel Heath, almost three miles north-west of the main landing area, while 1st Border was deployed around DZ X, which was to serve as the glider landing zone for the second lift. The exception was 1st Border's B Company, which occupied an isolated position overlooking the riverside road in the Renkum brickworks, a mile and a half south-west of the remainder of the battalion at DZ X. The two airlanding battalions had a relatively quiet night, the only action being a series of inept probes against 7th KOSB by elements from the largely Dutch SS *Wacht* Battalion 3. The quiet was not to last. In the early evening of 17 September *Generalleutnant* Hans von Tettau had been ordered to organise counter-measures similar to those enacted by II SS *Panzerkorps* to the east. *Kampfgruppe* von Tettau consisted of a variety of hastily mobilised units including SS *Wacht* Battalion 3, SS *Unteroffizier-schule Arnheim*, several *Kriegs-marine* and *Luftwaffe* training units, and a *Heer* artillery battalion operating as infantry.[1] By dawn most of these units were deployed just west of 1st Airborne's landing zones and were making ready to launch a two-pronged attack. The northern thrust was aligned just south of the Arnhem-Ede road, which would carry into the northern edge of DZ Y, the southern prong was to advance east along the north bank of the Lower Rhine, and some of the *Kampfgruppe's* weaker units formed a thin screen linking the two attacks.

The first contact occurred sometime after 05:00, when *Schiffstamm* 10, a German naval training unit and a battalion from SS *Unteroffizierschule Arnheim* moved into Renkum. The SS unit moved through the north of the town and on to Heelsum, but B Company 1st Border ambushed an advance party from *Schiffstamm*

10, killing several and throwing the sailors into considerable confusion. A series of attacks on B Company's positions in the brickworks beginning at 09:00 were rebuffed with heavy casualties, after which the naval unit contented itself with long-range machinegun fire and mortaring. B Company held its position until ordered to withdraw east in the early afternoon, which it did successfully after spiking two attached anti-tank guns and disabling all but one of the company's seven jeeps. The exception was used to carry the wounded back to 1st Border's battalion HQ, where they were accorded a hero's welcome for their unsupported stand.

To the north, SS *Wacht* Battalion 3 attacked an isolated platoon from 7th KOSB's D Company at dawn, and succeeded in overrunning it by mid-morning, killing or wounding seven men and taking the rest prisoner. However, another foolhardy attempt by other elements of the same SS unit to advance down the Arnhem-Ede road with vehicles was stopped by the KOSB's B Company with the loss of at least one half-track and several killed. B Company also rebuffed several attempts to infiltrate its area, at one point by jacking a three-inch mortar up on sandbags to fire under the recommended safe range. On another occasion artillery fire from the 1st Light Artillery Regiment RA, which had set up its guns in Oosterbeek, was called down on a party of German troops digging in just north of the Arnhem-Ede highway.

However, while 1st Border and 7th KOSB's dispersed companies were able to keep von Tettau's troops out of their positions and away from their immediate environs, there were simply too few of them to prevent the Germans from infiltrating right up to the edges of the landing zones in places. Indeed, in spite of their best efforts, by the early afternoon *Kampfgruppe* von Tettau was well on the way to achieving its aim of encircling the British landing area. In the north SS *Wacht* Battalion 3 was making good progress along the Arnhem-Ede road toward Wolfheze, and had infiltrated through the woods to approach DZ Y from the east. In the south *Standartenführer* Hans Lippert's SS *Unteroffizierschule Arnheim*, having cleared and secured Renkum and Heelsum, turned its attention to the landing zones just north of the towns. The first attack was supported by six ex-French Char B tanks, operated by *Panzer Kompanie* 224; anti-tank guns attached to 1st Border knocked out all six in short order, and the attack fizzled out. Lippert then organised a second effort, which succeeded in getting onto the eastern side of LZ X.

The second lift was scheduled to arrive in the late morning, but mist over the airfields in England caused a four-hour delay and take offs did not commence until after 11:00. 4th Parachute Brigade was carried in 126 USAAF transports, while RAF aircraft towed 296 gliders carrying the balance of 1st Airlanding Brigade and 1st Airborne's divisional units. A further thirty-three Short Stirlings' were to drop eighty-six tons of supplies in 803 panniers and containers onto a specially designated DZ just north of Oosterbeek. Unlike the first lift, the parachute transports went in first, and they were greeted by a considerable amount of light flak. One C-47 carrying troops from 156 Parachute Battalion exploded in the air with no survivors. Five more aircraft, carrying paratroopers from the 10th and 11th Parachute Battalions were shot down on the run into the DZ, although at least some of their passengers were able to jump. Many more aircraft suffered hits, from flak and small-arms fire from the German infiltrators in the woods north and east of DZ Y. 7th KOSB's HQ and Support Companies launched an attack to clear German troops from the south edge of the DZ as the transport aircraft were running in from the south.

The jump commenced at 15:09, and an estimated 1,914 paratroopers were delivered in nine minutes. For some, the battle began as soon as they hit the ground. The 10th Parachute Battalion had to fight for its RV, a café on the north-east corner of the DZ, and many sticks of paratroopers overshot the DZ and landed in the woods to the north. Some were killed while still in their parachute harnesses, while others succeeded in fighting their way back to the DZ and their rally points. At least four sticks, dropped around eight miles north, were obliged to become evaders, with some men linking up with the Dutch resistance later. One soldier from 156 Parachute Battalion captured a truckload of German weapons and ammunition single-handed, and brought his prize back to the LZ.

Thirty-two men were killed in the drop or in action on landing, and there were also a higher than normal number of landing injuries, including the 10th Battalion's padre.

The glider landing ran a little more smoothly, although at least one glider disintegrated in the air after being hit by a shell, and two tug aircraft were shot down, one crashing with its glider. 273 gliders reached the release point, sixty-nine of which landed without mishap among the abandoned machines from the first lift on LZ S. The remainder came down on DZ X, which had been used by parachutists the previous day. There were few serious crashes, but Lippert's men shot up at least three gliders on the south end of the LZ despite attempts by 1st Border to suppress them with mortar fire. One of the gliders burned, and the Germans also captured a Hamilcar loaded with ammunition, part of an experiment with three such machines. Despite this, by 17:30 thirty-three jeeps, fifteen towing two trailers loaded with ammunition had been unloaded, along with five anti-tank guns belonging to the 1st Polish Independent Parachute Brigade. Eight men had been killed in the course of the landing.

Before leaving England the commander of 4th Parachute Brigade, Brigadier John Hackett, had warned his officers that events were unlikely to run according to plan, although whether he envisaged what he encountered on Ginkel Heath is a matter of conjecture. The situation was at once exacerbated by the immediate removal by acting divisional commander Hicks of the 11th Parachute Battalion to reinforce 1st Parachute Brigade's attack into Arnhem. Hackett was less than overjoyed at having the fighting power of his brigade reduced by a third, but the overall situation was too urgent for argument, so the 11th Battalion duly marched off toward Arnhem. The order was relayed by Lieutenant Colonel Mackenzie, who also requested that Hackett report to Hicks at Division HQ as soon as practicable. Hackett, however, turned his attention to extricating the 10th Parachute Battalion from the fight on the north edge of the LZ, and moving 156 Battalion toward Arnhem. The latter moved off at around 17:00, at the same time as 1st Airlanding Brigade began to gather in its far-flung units preparatory to establishing a tighter divisional perimeter closer to Arnhem.

Hackett did not reach divisional HQ until shortly after 23:00. On arrival he demanded confirmation and clarification of some ambiguously worded orders to move his brigade to an area of high ground just north-east of Oosterbeek, on the left flank of 1st Parachute Brigade. Hackett also made no secret of his dissatisfaction with what he famously labelled as a 'grossly untidy situation', and openly questioned Hicks's competence and authority to command 1st Airborne Division in Urquhart's absence, not least because he was senior to Hicks. In fact, Hicks was Urquhart's second choice to command the Division after Lathbury, who was wounded and missing in Arnhem. Hackett was third in line, a decision based on Hicks's longer infantry service; Hackett was a cavalryman prior to joining the Airborne Forces. The problem arose because of an oversight that provides further evidence of Urquhart's failure to grasp the realities of airborne operations. Urquhart appears to have informed his brigadiers that Lathbury was his official second-in-command, but he made no further arrangements until he was embarking for the glider flight to Arnhem, when he orally informed his chief-of-staff, Lieutenant Colonel Mackenzie, of his decision about Hicks and Hackett. Arranging details such as this should have been accorded a much earlier and higher priority, and widely disseminated among 1st Airborne Division's senior commanders, for the vagaries of airborne operations meant no officer was guaranteed safe arrival at the landing area. The failure to make such arrangements could easily have had much more serious consequences than it did.

In the event, Hackett was mollified to an extent when Hicks agreed to his outline plan for the employment of 4th Parachute Brigade, and Hackett returned to his brigade HQ at 01:30 on the morning of 19 September. By that time 156 Parachute Battalion had run into outposts of a new advanced blocking line set up north of Oosterbeek by *Kampfgruppe* Spindler. After unsuccessfully probing the German positions, 156 Battalion withdrew a short distance, set up a defensive perimeter and waited for daylight. The

7th KOSB ran into the same German line a little further north at around 04:00 on 19 September, and did the same. The 10th Parachute Battalion spent the night near Hackett's brigade HQ east of Wolfheze and moved off at 04:30, heading for a road junction on the Arnhem-Ede road to take up position on 156 Battalion's left flank. To the south, the 2nd South Staffs had linked up with the 1st Parachute Battalion near the St Elizabeth Hospital at 20:00 on Monday night, and the 11th Parachute Battalion arrived sometime around midnight. Dobie assumed control of this force, and briefed Lieutenant Colonels McCardie and Lea, commanding the South Staffs and 11th Battalion respectively, for another attempt to force the riverside route, which he scheduled to commence at 04:00. Unknown to Dobie, the 3rd Parachute Battalion was preparing to attack on the same axis at the same time. The stage was thus set for 1st Airborne's final attempt to break through to the 2nd Parachute Battalion at the Arnhem road bridge.

RAMMING A BRICK WALL

1ST PARACHUTE BRIGADE'S FINAL ATTEMPT TO BREAK
THROUGH TO THE ARNHEM BRIDGE

First off the mark in the second attempt to break through to the Arnhem Bridge was Lieutenant Colonel Fitch's 3rd Parachute Battalion, which moved off sometime before 04:00 on Tuesday 19 September. Unknown to the British paratroopers, the German defence line had been pulled back several hundred yards from the area of the Pavilion and St Elizabeth Hospital during the night, to take advantage of an area of open ground on a steep incline rising from the riverbank. One unintended result of this withdrawal was that it allowed Major-General Urquhart to escape the attic where he had been trapped since the late afternoon of 18 September. Urquhart made his way toward the river, where he came upon the 1st and 3rd Parachute Battalions near the Rhine Pavilion. He then commandeered a jeep and set out for his divisional HQ, which by that time had relocated from the landing area to the Hartenstein Hotel in Oosterbeek. Urquhart arrived at the Hartenstein at 07:25, having been absent and out of contact from his HQ for forty hours. After familiarising himself with the deteriorating situation, he dispatched Colonel Hilaro Barlow, deputy commander of the 1st Airlanding Brigade, to sort out the situation near the St Elizabeth Hospital and to co-ordinate the attacks along the riverside route. Unfortunately, Colonel Barlow was killed shortly after arrival as an officer from the South Staffs guided him forward near the Rhine Pavilion. A subsequent message from Urquhart at 09:00, ordering the 11th Parachute Battalion not to become involved in the attack along the river, did get through by the late morning.

1st Parachute Brigade's attack was directed down two parallel roads emerging from a fork junction just east of the Rhine Pavilion. The Onderlangs ran close to the riverbank, at the foot of a scrub-covered incline that grew steeper toward the east. It was overlooked by a brickworks on the south bank of the Lower Rhine, which was occupied by part of Gräbner's SS *Panzer Aufklärungs Abteilung 9*. Another road, the Utrechtsweg, ran along the top of the incline, which was topped at its steepest by the Arnhem Municipal Museum. An area of railway lines and sidings sited in deep cuttings bounded the left side of the Utrechtsweg, allowing a clear field of fire from the houses and buildings to the north. The 3rd Battalion advanced over the open ground in darkness until it ran into the new positions, and began to pull back after suffering a dozen casualties. In so doing it ran into the 1st Parachute Battalion moving east, and Fitch led his fifty or so survivors forward again to support Dobie's battalion.

The 1st Battalion advanced straight down the lower Onderlangs road. Some outlying German positions were overrun, but Dobie's men were unable to make any impression on the main German position. Flanking fire from automatic light cannon mounted in the SS recce vehicles in the brickworks across the river proved especially deadly. At around 06:30, under fire from three sides and after two hours of continuous action, Dobie called off the attack and led the survivors to shelter in houses on the left side of the Onderlangs road. The 1st Battalion had started the attack 140 strong, and the attack reduced this to thirty-nine, all of whom were wounded. By 07:30 the survivors were surrounded by SS troops supported by assault guns, and were obliged to surrender. The 3rd Battalion fared no better. Fitch's men tried to support the 1st Battalion by setting up a fire position on the scrubby slope above the Onderlangs road, but German automatic weapons and mortars systematically raked the area. Mortar bomb fragments killed Lieutenant Colonel Fitch, and the survivors of his battalion were forced back toward the Rhine Pavilion, where they were overrun and most captured.

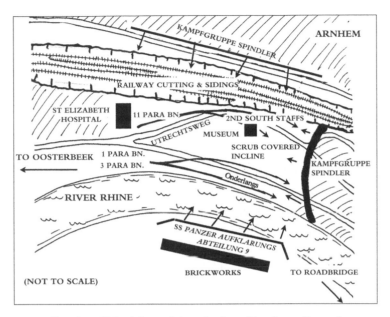

KAMPFGRUPPE SPINDLER

ARNHEM

RAILWAY CUTTING & SIDINGS

ST ELIZABETH
HOSPITAL

11 PARA BN

2ND SOUTH STAFFS

UTRECHTSWEG

MUSEUM

SCRUB COVERED
INCLINE

TO OOSTERBEEK   1 PARA BN.
3 PARA BN.

KAMPFGRUPPE
SPINDLER

Onderlangs

RIVER RHINE

SS PANZER AUFKLARUNGS
ABTEILUNG 9

(NOT TO SCALE)

BRICKWORKS   TO ROADBRIDGE

1st Parachute Brigade's attack into Arnhem, Tuesday 19 September.

The 2nd South Staffs began its advance along the Utrechtsweg about half an hour after the 1st Parachute Battalion began its attack up the Onderlangs road. The 11th Parachute Battalion, commanded by Lieutenant Colonel George Lea, trailed the South Staffs, ready to act in support. The South Staffs moved stealthily past the north side of the St Elizabeth Hospital which, bizarrely for the middle of a battlefield, was fully illuminated and past the debris from the battle fought by the 2nd Parachute Battalion's C Company the previous night. The glider soldiers then ran into and cleared a series of German outposts, and carried the advance to just past the Municipal Museum, over 600 yards from the start point. There the attack ran out of momentum under intense fire from mortars and assault guns from the newly arrived *Sturmgeschütz* Brigade 280 positioned in the buildings further up the road. The surviving South Staffs took up positions in the museum, in a hollow on the slope behind it and in houses on the north side of the road. A stalemate then ensued, which lasted until the scattered groups began to run out of PIAT ammunition. The German assault guns were then able to shell the British-held buildings at close range with impunity while their accompanying infantry closed in to clear them at leisure. By late morning it was all over and the South Staffs had been destroyed piecemeal, apart from one company which had held back near the 11th Parachute Battalion's lines after its commanding officer was killed. Most of the remainder were taken prisoner, including Lieutenant Colonel McCardie, although some scattered groups and individuals managed to escape to the west. Among these was Major Robert Cain, who had been prominent in the PIAT fight against the German armour near the museum. He took command of a separated company, which was about forty strong, and gathered in other survivors from his battalion.

The 11th Battalion was preparing to launch a supporting attack on the South Staffs' left flank, between the Utrechtsweg and the railway, when Urquhart's order not to become involved in the battle arrived. This resulted in the company deployed for the supporting attack being caught up and overrun by the German attack that overwhelmed the South Staffs, while the rest of the 11th Battalion held its positions near the St Elizabeth Hospital. Sometime before midday, another message from Division HQ arrived, ordering the 11th Battalion to secure an area of high ground to the north-west called the Heijenoord Diependal, in support of the 4th Parachute Brigade's advance north of Oosterbeek. Lea directed the stray company of South Staffs, now commanded by Major Robert Cain, to seize the Den Brink feature to anchor his left flank, and set about reorienting his battalion. Unfortunately, the Germans saw the 11th Battalion forming-up, and after a savage mortaring launched an armoured counter-attack that caught Lea's unit in the open and virtually destroyed it, before driving Cain's men off the Den Brink. The survivors fell back toward Oosterbeek, covered in some instances by anti-tank guns and other elements comprising the 1st Parachute Brigade's rear area. By the late afternoon the writing was clearly on the wall, and those who were able to decamped for Oosterbeek on their own initiative, singly and in groups. Those who could not were killed or captured as the German tanks and infantry system-atically cleared the area around the St Elizabeth Hospital. The 1st Parachute Brigade's effort to reach the Arnhem road bridge thus ended in a courageous but extremely costly failure, with the brigade literally fighting itself to destruction in the attempt.

While all this was going on, the 4th Parachute Brigade was making its own attempt to reach Arnhem from further north. It was led by 156 Parachute Battalion, commanded by Lieutenant Colonel Sir Richard des Voeux, which had spent the night in the woods north of Oosterbeek after running into the forward outposts of *Kampfgruppe* Spindler's blocking line. This line followed a road called the Dreijensweg, which ran north through woods from Oosterbeek for a kilometre and a half, and was perfect for defence. The wooded ground sloped up to the road from the west, which was bounded to the east by an earth bank that was ten feet high in places. Some of *Kampfgruppe* Spindler's armoured vehicles were positioned on the road, which allowed them to move back and forth in support of outpost positions set up west of the Dreijensweg. Other vehicles were placed east of the road among the *Kampfgruppe's* main infantry concentration, which effectively turned the road and the top of the embanked sections into a killing zone concealed from the west by the thickness of the woods. This was rendered even more deadly by the reinforcement of Spindler's collection of armoured half-tracks, armoured cars and self-propelled guns with a battalion of self-propelled flak, also mounted on half-tracks. Deployed in the ground role, this collection of single and quad-barrelled 20mm flak guns represented a deadly increase in firepower.

4th Parachute Brigade HQ gave 156 Battalion two objectives. The first was an area of high ground immediately east of its overnight position, about a quarter of a mile past the Dreijensweg. Once this was secured the advance was to swing south-east and seize another piece of high ground half a mile further on called the Koepel. The first objective was to be reached in two bounds. C Company, commanded by Major Geoffrey Powell, was to secure the area where it had run into a German position the previous night.[1]

Major John Pott's A Company, reinforced with a platoon of glider pilots, would then move through C Company, cross the Dreijensweg and move up the slope to secure the first objective. The attack began at dawn, and Powell's company swiftly occupied the German position, which had been abandoned. Major Pott and Lieutenant Colonel des Voeux then went forward to C Company's location in an effort to spy out what lay ahead, but were prevented from doing so by the thickness of the wood. They were joined there by Brigadier Hackett, who stressed the urgency of the situation in Arnhem and the consequent need for speed.

A Company's advance went according to plan until the lead platoon approached the Dreijensweg, where it came under fire from automatic weapons. The sheer volume of fire stopped the advance cold, and virtually the whole company was pinned down for a time in the roadside ditch until Major Pott led a rush across the road and into the woods on the other side. Pott was the only officer to survive the crossing, and he and the small group who made it with him then fought their way through the German positions. Incredibly Pott, despite being twice wounded, succeeded in getting onto his objective at around 10:00 accompanied by six of his men, but they were overrun by a counter-attack. The able-bodied among Pott's little group managed to escape, the walking wounded were taken prisoner and Pott was left alone on the battlefield for eighteen hours, before being picked up by two courageous Dutch civilians. Unknown to Pott, Hackett had dispatched 156 Battalion's B Company, commanded by Major John Waddy, to try a left flanking movement at 09:00. B Company did not even get across the Dreijensweg, which was by then occupied by several German vehicles moving back and forth and firing into the woods to the west. The fire from these extracted a fearful toll of B Company and the attack stalled when Waddy was wounded while stalking one of the flak half-tracks. The attack was called off at 14:00, by which time 156 Parachute Battalion had been effectively reduced to a single battle-worthy company.

The 10th Parachute Battalion was not supposed to have been involved in the initial attack on Spindler's blocking line, being assigned to protect 4th Parachute Brigade's left flank from a position on the Arnhem-Ede highway several hundred yards east of the Dreijensweg. At 10:00, however, Lieutenant Colonel Ken Smyth moved on from his designated position toward Arnhem. The reason for this is unclear. No order appears to have been issued by Hackett's HQ, and Smyth may have been influenced by the flow of wounded from 156 Battalion that passed through his position. The 10th Battalion's advance carried it straight into the north end of *Kampfgruppe* Spindler's line, near a water pumping station 300 yards west of the Dreijensweg. The lead company came under fire from automatic weapons and mortars, and was rapidly pinned down. Smyth responded by sending out recce patrols to locate the German positions and asking brigade HQ for permission to try a wide outflanking movement to the north of the Arnhem-Ede road. The battalion's A Company, commanded by Captain Lionel Queripel, was dispatched across the road when permission was received, but much time was lost in probing for German positions and, when the company did finally advance east, fierce resistance stopped it short. The attack was called off at around 14:00, and by 15:00 A Company had re-crossed the fire-swept Arnhem-Ede road to rejoin the rest of the 10th Battalion. In the process Queripel performed the first of a series of courageous actions by carrying one of his wounded men across the highway to safety.

The 10th Battalion's attack was called off at the same time as 156 Battalion's effort further south, and for the same reason. At 13:30 Urquhart, Hicks and Hackett conferred at the latter's HQ to review the situation. Hackett wanted to side-step his brigade south of the Arnhem-Ede railway for another attempt to break through to the Heijenoord Diependal feature in the outskirts of Arnhem and link up with the 11th Parachute Battalion. Urquhart was willing to sanction this, but was concerned that it would leave 7th KOSB isolated. The latter battalion was deployed around LZ Z just west of 4th Parachute Brigade to protect the third lift's glider component, which was scheduled to arrive that day. The problem was the railway embankment, which blocked direct vehicular access from LZ Z to Oosterbeek, and also presented a dangerous obstacle to men moving on foot. The obvious answer was to use properly configured crossing points, but there were only two of these within reach. These were the Oosterbeek Hoog Station, which lay at the southern end of the Dreijensweg, and Wolfheze Station, which lay over two miles to the west, in an area abandoned by 1st Airborne's withdrawal from the landing areas to Oosterbeek. The real danger, which remained as yet unrecognised, was that the railway embankment represented a backstop against which a determined German attack could pin 4th Parachute Brigade, 7th KOSB and any freshly landed glider elements and destroy them.

The danger was not yet clear, however, and Urquhart therefore ordered 7th KOSB to hold in place until the glider landing (which was already late) was down, gave Hackett permission to withdraw south of the railway line, and told Hicks to secure the Oosterbeek Hoog Station. He then crossed the railway embankment to reach his jeep and return to Division HQ, while Hackett set to work organising his brigade's disengagement and withdrawal. Although it was not apparent to those involved at the time, 4th Parachute Brigade's disengagement marked the end of 1st Airborne Division's attempts to get through to Frost at the Arnhem road bridge.

THE FIGHT FOR THE NORTH END OF
THE ARNHEM ROAD BRIDGE

As we have seen, a composite force built around part of Lieutenant Colonel John Frost's 2nd Parachute Battalion succeeded in securing the north end of the Arnhem road bridge by the late evening of 17 September. The presence of Frost's force disrupted II SS *Panzerkorps'* ability to dispatch forces to block the Allied advance from the south, and their removal was thus a matter of the highest priority, with preparations continuing through the early hours of Monday 18 September. To this end *Kampfgruppe* Brinkmann, built around SS *Panzer Aufklärungs Abteilung* 10, was tasked to attack at dawn from the industrial area east of the bridge, where there was sufficient room for vehicles to manoeuvre. Not long before dawn Brinkmann was reinforced by Major Hans-Peter Knaust's *Panzer-Grenadier Ersatz und Ausbildungs Bataillon,* a replacement training unit comprised of infantrymen in the final stages of convalescence following wounds. Knaust was assigned to relieve the portion of *Kampfgruppe* Euling still fighting alongside SS *Panzergrenadier* Battalion 21, so it could get to Nijmegen as assigned. The latter units had maintained the pressure on the airborne perimeter through the night. In the early hours of the morning they succeeded in forcing a party from the 1st Parachute Squadron RE commanded by Captain Eric Mackay to fall back from an exposed building to a school on the east side of the embanked section of the bridge ramp. The airborne soldiers also spent the night in preparation, those positioned in buildings smashing the glass from windows, building furniture barricades and collecting water in baths and sinks as a precaution against future need. Those stationed in the open dug slit trenches wherever possible.

The first interloper into the British perimeter appears to have been a municipal refuse truck that appeared near buildings occupied by Major Hibbert's brigade HQ just after first light, and was promptly shot up for its pains. At around the same time Brinkmann's infantry began infiltrating into the industrial area east of the bridge ramp held by elements of the 3rd Parachute Battalion's C Company and Brigade HQ Defence Platoon. The paratroopers were too few to provide mutual support, but defended their own buildings stubbornly as the Germans tried to force their way in. Where they succeeded in gaining entry vicious close-quarter fights occurred, with men fighting in stairwells and from room to room. Brinkmann's men were unaware of where the British actually were, and may also have been misled by a report from II SS *Panzerkorps* suggesting that their strength was limited to 120 troops.[1] This might explain why their next move was to try and rush three trucks full of soldiers under the elevated section of the bridge ramp. They were riddled by British fire as they emerged into the wide, open road junction on the west side. There were few survivors.

After a short but intense mortar barrage, the next attack followed the same route, but used some of Brinkmann's armoured cars and half-tracks. According to an eye-witness, they were led by a tank of some kind, although it is unclear what type or where it might have come from. Brinkmann's unit had no tanks, German sources show that the first tanks did not arrive at the Arnhem Bridge until the evening of 18 September, and it may, therefore, have been a misidentified armoured car.[2] Whichever, two airborne six-pounder anti-tank guns sited in the open street engaged the lead German vehicle under the bridge ramp, but with no noticeable effect. The paved road surface prevented the gun trail digging in to absorb the recoil, and the gun thus skidded back fifty yards, injuring some of the crew. Undaunted, the survivors re-laid the gun and knocked out the vehicle as it emerged fully from under the ramp. Several half-tracks were dealt with as they tried to negotiate their way past the burning wreck, some by airborne soldiers in the surrounding buildings tossing hand grenades into their open troop compartments, and their crews were shot down as they attempted to escape their wrecked and burning vehicles. The time was around 09:00, and *Kampfgruppe* Brinkmann then paused to regroup and consider its next move.

The next attack on the airborne perimeter came over the bridge from south of the river. *Hauptsturmführer* Viktor Gräbner's SS *Panzer Aufklärungs Abteilung* 9 had crossed the Arnhem Bridge the previous evening, en route to set up a blocking position midway between Arnhem and Nijmegen. By dawn he had returned to the south end of the bridge, from where he watched *Kampfgruppe* Brinkmann's unsuccessful attacks and then launched his own unit across the bridge. Gräbner's reason for acting as he did is unclear, given that it ran contrary to his orders; he did not survive the attack to enlighten anyone. Presumably he assumed, in typical *Waffen* SS fashion, that rapid and violent action would carry the day. Gräbner's force consisted of twenty-two vehicles; five eight-wheeled heavy armoured cars, nine armoured half-tracks and eight trucks with their cargo beds armoured with fuel drums filled with sand or grain to protect their passengers.

Some accounts claim that the British airborne troops initially mistook Gräbner's vehicles for the lead elements of 30 Corps. In fact, they were correctly identified as they formed up at the south end of the bridge and Major Munford, the artillery forward observer attached to the brigade HQ group, called down several salvos from the 1st Light Regiment's No.3 Battery.[3] The heavy armoured cars were first across the bridge, spraying fire from their 20mm cannon and machine guns. One lost a wheel to a daisy chain of mines laid on the road surface, but all five passed through the airborne perimeter without drawing fire. The airborne troops were probably waiting for the mines to bring the armoured cars to a halt before firing, but they did not make the same mistake twice. Gräbner's half-tracks and trucks drove into a storm of fire from small-arms and mortars as they came into view over the mid-point of the bridge. This was thickened with PIATs, hand grenades and anti-tank gunfire as they drew abreast of the British-occupied buildings, and the north ramp was quickly blocked by a tangle of burning vehicles. Two half-tracks that tried to avoid the carnage by driving down a narrow slip road were destroyed by 1st Parachute Squadron RE lobbing grenades into their open troop compartments from the upper storey of the Van Limburg Stirium School, which overlooked the bottom of the slip road.

Seeing all this, the vehicles further back in the column paused on the bridge, while the survivors from the knocked-out vehicles sought shelter among the girders of the bridge superstructure. Incredibly, the remaining vehicles then made several more attempts to force a way through the wreckage, each of which was met with the same withering storm of fire and the same result. In all, the attack lasted for somewhere between two and three hours, and by midday the survivors had finally had enough. They backed off and withdrew south across the bridge, leaving an estimated seventy dead, including Gräbner, in and around the wreckage of twelve trucks and half-tracks. They were to extract some revenge for their losses on 19 September when, firing from the brickworks on the south side of the river, they were instrumental in destroying the bulk of the 1st Parachute Battalion in its final attempt to reach the Arnhem road bridge. For now, however, they withdrew to lick their wounds.

British losses in this one-sided action were minimal, and the defeat of Gräbner's force gave the morale of the airborne soldiers a huge boost. The victory was largely illusory, however, not least because Gräbner's attack had been inept in the extreme and succeeded only in practically destroying II SS *Panzerkorps'* single most powerful integral unit for no benefit whatsoever. The victory brought virtually no respite, and in the background the odds were slipping inexorably against the airborne force. Mortar and artillery fire was constant, making movement between buildings extremely hazardous. While the attack was going on, or shortly afterwards, two German field guns were brought up to an area of parkland just north of the bridge ramp, where they could be used in a direct-fire role against the British-occupied buildings. Even more crucially, the first tanks reached the German troops besieging the airborne perimeter in the early evening of 18 September. These were two *Panzer* IVs and six *Panzer* IIIs belonging to *Panzer Ersatz* Regiment Bielefeld, a driver training unit rushed in from Germany. These were immediately assigned to Knaust, whose force was then upgraded to *Kampfgruppe*.

All this was not immediately apparent to the airborne defenders, however. In the early afternoon of 18 September *Kampfgruppe* Brinkmann launched a third attack spearheaded by armoured vehicles – the defenders again claimed these were tanks – under the bridge ramp. The airborne anti-tank guns were again instrumental in repulsing this, with the destruction of at least one vehicle. Behind this, however, German pressure against the eastern edge of the perimeter finally began to yield results, and by the late afternoon the elements of the 3rd Parachute Battalion's C Company and Brigade HQ Defence Platoon had been killed or driven out of the industrial area east of the bridge. To make up for this two more buildings were occupied by elements of B Company, 2nd Parachute Battalion hard up against the east side of the ramp, and as dusk fell another nearby was deliberately set alight to provide illumination. After dark the battle subsided into small-scale skirmishes, as patrols from both sides prowled the streets, although one fairly major effort was foiled at around 03:00 in the morning of 19 September. A German force, apparently intending to attack the Van Limburg Stirium School became disoriented in the darkness and assembled in full view of the airborne soldiers within, chatting casually. The latter picked their moment before showering them with grenades and small-arms fire. At least twenty bodies were counted after daylight.

The first serious German attack on Tuesday 19 September did not commence until late morning, when *Kampfgruppe* Knaust made its debut with yet another attack from the east. This time there were tanks present, three vehicles from the recently arrived *Panzer Ersatz* Regiment Bielefeld, and the execution of the attack marked a significant change in tactics. Instead of barrelling straight into the airborne anti-tank guns or PIATs, the tanks positioned themselves where they could shell the British–held buildings without exposing themselves to counter-fire. Their first target was a house held by elements of A Company, 2nd Parachute Battalion just west of the ramp. The weight of fire obliged the paratroopers to evacuate the building, which was then occupied by German infantry. The attack ceased after Captain Tony Frank stalked and knocked-out one of the tanks, possibly a *Panzer* IV, with a PIAT and prompted the remainder to withdraw. A Company then counter-attacked, recaptured the house and drove off a German riposte. Successful as it was for the British, this action was an ominous portent, showing that not only were the Germans adapting their tactics, but that they had quickly hit on the combination to which the airborne defenders had no effective reply. They merely needed to refine the co-operation between the tanks and their covering infantry.

The German capability to fight in a stand-off manner was increased by the arrival of two Tiger I tanks in the evening of 18 September. These were the first of fourteen belonging to s*chwere Panzer Kompanie* 'Hummel', a *Heer* unit dispatched from Germany in the early hours of that day. The first two were attached to *Kampfgruppe* Brinkmann, and were used to attack from the north at 20:00, moving down the east side of the bridge ramp. This carried them past the Van Limburg Stirium School, which they shot-up in passing, before pumping 88mm shells into the British-held buildings on the east side of the perimeter. The shelling virtually demolished at least two of these, forcing the surviving defenders to evacuate and seek shelter elsewhere. The lead tank then appears to have moved into view of the airborne anti-tank guns covering the approaches under the ramp, presumably while manoeuvring for a better shot. The crew of one gun was wounded by tank machine-gun fire, but others scored at least two hits on the lead Tiger, wounding two of the crew, damaging its gun tube and obliging both to withdraw. The undamaged vehicle was then re-assigned to *Kampfgruppe* Knaust, as were the rest of the Tigers as they arrived.

By nightfall on 19 September, the British situation was growing increasingly precarious. The perimeter had been reduced from eighteen to ten buildings, mostly on the west side of the bridge ramp, and the airborne defenders had lost nineteen dead and over 100 wounded. The original plan had assumed that the latter would be evacuated to St Elizabeth's Hospital, which was to be taken over by 16th Parachute Field Ambulance, but events precluded this expedient. Responsibility for providing medical care thus fell totally on the small Regimental Aid Posts belonging to the 2nd Parachute Battalion and 1st Parachute Brigade HQ, commanded by Captain J.W. Logan RAMC and Captain D. Wright RAMC respectively[4]. The most seriously wounded were gathered in the cellar of the building occupied by Brigade HQ, while the lightly wounded remained with their units manning the perimeter. Food, water and above all ammunition were also running short, and the constant German mortaring, shelling and snipers made movement between buildings hazardous in the extreme. Despite this, airborne soldiers did risk the dangerous move between the buildings, some on orders and some of their own volition. James Sims describes crawling to a backyard standpipe to fetch water for a brew-up in the middle of a furious firefight, and George Lawson, one of Middlebrook's interviewees, was obliged to go begging for ammunition from building to building after a fruitless journey to A Company HQ.[5] While on this dangerous errand Lawson ran into Major Tatham-Warter, the eccentric commander of the 2nd Battalion's A Company who, it will be recalled, had trained his men to respond to bugle calls. Tatham-Warter was prowling the streets wearing his maroon airborne beret and armed with an umbrella, which became his trademark in the desperate struggle around the north bridge ramp. He was seen leading a counter-attack brandishing it at least once, and on another occasion he held it over the 2nd Battalion's *padre*, Father Bernard Egan, to ward off shrapnel.[6]

Sadly, the hard-pressed airborne soldiers needed rather more substantial help than Major Tatham-Warter's umbrella, good for morale though it might have been. In the late morning of Wednesday 20 September, however, radio contact was established with Division HQ and Frost learned officially that they were not going to get it from the remainder of 1st Airborne Division. The only hope of relief was therefore from 30 Corps but it had yet to cross the Waal at Nijmegen. The day had dawned damp and overcast in Arnhem, and brought with it another shift in German tactics. The western side of the airborne perimeter had been left largely alone thus far, in part because the narrow street there made it difficult for armoured vehicles to manoeuvre, and because it was screened by the high wall around the Arnhem prison. Now, however, SS *Panzergrenadier*

Battalion 21 began to press in from that direction. They were
supported by guns firing through holes blasted in the prison wall, and
by the artillery pieces positioned to the north of the bridge ramp,
which had been reinforced with two 88mm flak guns. At the same
time *Kampfgruppen* Brinkmann and Knaust began pushing in from
the north, while their tanks stood off to the east from where they
could fire with impunity without becoming entangled in the rubble
and debris that had begun to choke the streets in places. It was here
that Lieutenant Jack Grayburn from the 2nd Parachute Battalion
earned a posthumous Victoria Cross, the only one awarded at the
bridge. Grayburn twice led parties into the open to remove first the
fuses from German demolition charges attached to the bridge ramp
supports, and then the charges themselves. He was killed by German
machine-gun fire while supervising the second operation.

By early afternoon the relentless German pressure was beginning
to tell. Lieutenant Colonel Frost was wounded at around 13:30, and
Major Gough from the Recce Squadron took command of the
defence. At around the same time the thirty surviving paratroopers
and sappers were finally driven out of the Van Limburg Stirium
School, after large calibre shells systematically removed the roof and
upper storey and set the rest ablaze. Some, including the commander
of the RE contingent, Captain Eric Mackay, escaped and made their
way to other positions in the perimeter. Others, including Major
Lewis from the 3rd Battalion's C Company remained with the many
wounded evacuated from the burning building and were captured.
By this point the Germans had cut the airborne perimeter into small
pockets, and the British airborne soldiers lacked the ammunition or
weapons to interfere with them effectively unless they tried to enter
their buildings. The Germans had worked out a routine for reducing
the British-held buildings, as observed by James Sims. The process
began with a long burst of tracer against the chosen building, which
Sims interpreted as a warning to the occupants to get out, although
it could just as easily have been a fire control order to orient the
attackers on the correct building in the smoke and dust. Whichever,
the tracer was followed by the positioning of a tank a matter of yards
from the chosen building, which then fired shells into it until it

collapsed, after which the German infantry would move in to mop up any survivors.[7]

The near-impotence of the British airborne troops in the face of these tactics meant that it could only be a matter of time before the airborne perimeter was eliminated, and this point was being approached by the afternoon of 20 September. The building containing Hibbert's brigade HQ was under direct fire, which destroyed the radio linking the bridge perimeter and Urquhart's HQ, and set the building ablaze. A two-hour truce was arranged to evacuate the British and German wounded from its cellar. Cut off from the positions still fighting around the bridge ramp, the remaining men stationed in the building broke up into small groups and tried to slip through the German cordon to the main divisional perimeter. All were eventually captured. By early evening the Germans considered it safe to withdraw *Kampfgruppe* Knaust from the fight, to reorganise and rearm in preparation for a push south toward Nijmegen. It was probably its tanks that Sims, who was wounded on the evening of 19 September, saw after being evacuated from the cellar of the brigade HQ building.[8] *Kampfgruppe* Brinkmann was left to root out the remaining British defenders, and to clear a path through the wreckage of Gräbner's vehicles on the north ramp. At around this time an airborne radio operator, probably from Major Munford's artillery observation party, broadcast the last message to come out of the bridge pocket. It closed with the words 'God save the King'.[9]

Even then, some of the airborne soldiers stubbornly refused to yield. After dark Major Tatham-Warter, still carrying his umbrella, organised an effort to re-occupy some positions in the morning, but the sheer number of SS troops in the area denied them the necessary freedom of movement, and frustrated efforts by groups and individuals to slip through the German lines. Isolated clashes continued through the night and into the next day, and the area was not considered fully cleared until the early evening of 21 September. Frost's force had therefore denied II SS *Panzerkorps* access to the Arnhem road bridge for three days, and maintained a presence of sorts for almost a further twenty-four hours. Of the 740 men who arrived at the bridge in the evening of 17 September, approximately eighty-

one were killed or subsequently died of wounds, and the vast majority of the remainder were wounded to some degree or another.
Thirty-seven of the dead were killed in the last twenty-four hours,
an eloquent testimony to the ferocity of the fighting and to the
tenacity displayed by the airborne soldiers in the closing stages of the
battle, when they were materially and physically at their weakest.[10]

Almost all the survivors were taken prisoner, although some individuals did succeed in avoiding capture and others managed to
escape before being shipped back to Germany. Probably the most
famous of the latter was Major Anthony Deane-Drummond, deputy
commander of 1st Airborne's signal detachment. Deane-
Drummond managed to find a way into the bridge perimeter on 19
September, and was captured on 22 September after emerging from
a hiding place near the bridge. Shipped to a temporary holding
centre some miles from Arnhem, he escaped by hiding in a cupboard
for thirteen days before making contact with the Dutch resistance,
who smuggled him to safety. Despite the sinister reputation of the
Waffen SS and the ferocity of the fighting, the vast majority of those
captured were treated correctly, and in some cases very well indeed
given the circumstances; several accounts refer to German troops
sharing food, drink or even cigars with their erstwhile foes.[11]

The performance of Frost's force at the bridge has deservedly
been accorded epic status, but it has to be said that their German
opponents suffered even higher losses and displayed at least as
much application, if not more. This was especially true of
Kampfgruppe Euling and the other elements of 10th SS *Panzer*
Division that defended the Nijmegen Bridge to destruction
against the Guards Armoured Division and the US 505th
Parachute Infantry Regiment. The irony that is usually overlooked
is that Euling's battle was the precise mirror image of Frost's at
Arnhem, with the SS men refusing to yield and being blasted out
of their defensive positions by tanks. The major difference was that
the relative handful of SS survivors were able to withdraw to
friendly lines, whereas any of Frost's men who succeeded in reaching 1st Airborne Division's perimeter at Oosterbeek would have
been merely exchanging the frying pan for the fire.

1ST AIRBORNE AT BAY

THE FORMATION OF THE POCKET AND THE INITIAL FIGHTING
ON THE OOSTERBEEK PERIMETER

The process of forming a divisional pocket centred on Oosterbeek actually began the day before II SS *Panzerkorps* finally succeeded in eliminating Frost's gallant band around the north end of the Arnhem road bridge, part by design but mainly dictated by circumstances. The original Arnhem plan had envisaged the 1st Airlanding Brigade setting up a defence line along the western outskirts of Oosterbeek once the second lift was down. 1st Border successfully withdrew from its defensive positions around LZ X and LZ Z during the evening of 18 September, and by mid-morning the next day a line had been established as planned. The south end was located a few hundred yards north of the Lower Rhine, just east of the village of Westerbouwing, and ran north for a mile along the line of a road through the woods up to the Utrechtsweg, mid-way between the river and the Arnhem-Ede railway line. The 4th Parachute Squadron RE initially manned the stretch from the Utrechtsweg to the railway, reinforced later by a variety of units including the remnants of 1st Border's A Company, the 21st Independent Parachute Company, 9th Field Company RE and a contingent of glider pilots. *Kampfgruppe* von Tettau, largely due to its polyglot nature and variable quality, took time to feel its way east across the abandoned British landing areas and defensive positions, and did not reach the approaches to Oosterbeek until late in the afternoon. By then, thanks to a rather convoluted twist of circumstances, units of the 4th Parachute Brigade were blocking the way to the undefended area north of the Utrechtsweg.

The formation of the eastern perimeter was a far more *ad hoc* affair. On the morning of Tuesday 19 September Lieutenant Colonel W. F. K. Thompson, commanding the 1st Airlanding Light Regiment RA, noted individual stragglers and vehicles fleeing west past his gun positions near the Oosterbeek Church. Some of these were disinclined to stop, so Thompson organised a roadblock and collection point near the church. In the afternoon larger groups began to appear through Oosterbeek Laag railway underpass. These were the organised remnants of the 1st, 3rd and 11th Parachute Battalions and the 2nd South Staffs. Thompson, concerned lest his guns be left unprotected on the front line, went forward to meet them and established a defensive screen across the river road. A request to divisional HQ for reinforcements yielded only two spare officers, Major John Simmons of the South Staffs' HQ Company and the deputy commander of the 11th battalion, Major Dickie Lonsdale. The former was put in charge of the stragglers gathered near the church, and the latter took over the forward screen, which by nightfall numbered just over 400 men, along with several anti-tank guns.

The area north of the river road to the Utrechtsweg and beyond to the railway line was undefended, apart from a troop of anti-tank guns from the 2nd Airlanding Anti-Tank Battery and a handful of South Staffs. These fetched-up at the main crossroads in Oosterbeek after falling back from Arnhem, and by chance were positioned to deal with the only German advance from Arnhem that day. At least two armoured vehicles, possibly assault guns from *Sturmgeschütz* Brigade 280, filtered along the small roads and tracks running parallel to the Utrechtsweg, and then attempted to cross the road running north from the crossroads to the Oosterbeek Hoog railway station. The Airlanding Battery's gunners were warned of their approach by some South Staffs gathered nearer to the Oosterbeek Hoog railway station, and both vehicles were knocked out by a six-pounder, the second after the gun had been manhandled from its original position for a clear shot. That the portion of *Kampfgruppe* Spindler in western Arnhem did not move on Oosterbeek in force appears to have been due to the tenacity of

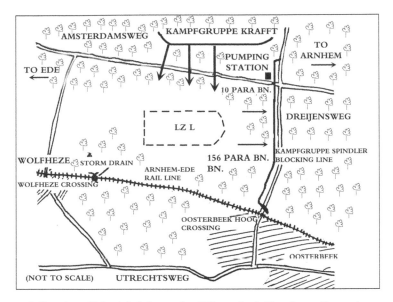

AMSTERDAMSWEG

KAMPFGRUPPE KRAFFT

TO ARNHEM

TO EDE

PUMPING STATION

10 PARA BN.

DREIJENSWEG

LZ L

WOLFHEZE   STORM DRAIN

156 PARA BN.

KAMPFGRUPPE SPINDLER
BLOCKING LINE

ARNHEM-EDE
RAIL LINE   BN.

WOLFHEZE CROSSING

OOSTERBEEK HOOG
CROSSING

OOSTERBEEK

(NOT TO SCALE)   UTRECHTSWEG

4th Parachute Brigade's fight north of Oosterbeek, Tuesday 19 September.

the scattered remnants of 1st Parachute Brigade, whose efforts slowed the process of clearing the area around and west of the St Elizabeth Hospital. The Spindler thus missed a golden opportunity to overrun 1st Airborne Division before it had established a proper defensive perimeter, an oversight for which they were to pay dearly over the next six days.

However, while the eastern side of the congealing Oosterbeek perimeter may have been the most vulnerable, the most severe threat developed to the north. There, it will be remembered, 7th KOSB was guarding LZ Z, which lay between the Arnhem-Ede highway and railway line, for the third glider lift. Half a mile to the east 10th and 156 Parachute Battalions were entangled with *Kampfgruppe* Spindler's northern blocking line, until Urquhart authorised Hackett to withdraw and try again further south in the early afternoon of Tuesday 19 September. The original idea had been for 1st Airlanding Brigade to secure the railway crossing at the Oosterbeek Hoog station. This, however, was a rather unlikely prospect given that the crossing lay at the southern end of the Dreijensweg, and was thus part of the German defence line that had savaged 156 Parachute Battalion. As a result of this and reports from Dutch underground volunteers about the approach of *Kampfgruppe* von Tettau from the west, the decision was taken to use the railway crossing at Wolfheze. This however, lay over two miles to the west, and had been abandoned by 1st Airlanding Brigade in the withdrawal to Oosterbeek. Nonetheless, in the late afternoon 156 Battalion began to withdraw along the north side of the railway line, while the 10th Battalion succeeded in breaking contact from the fight near the pumping station, re-crossed the Arnhem-Ede highway behind a smoke screen and angled south west across LZ Z. As it did so the gliders from the third lift began to land around them.

The third lift should have consisted of Sosabowski's 1st Polish Independent Parachute Brigade, forty-two gliders carrying the Poles' heavy equipment, seven Horsas and a single Hamilcar that had aborted on the previous lifts, and 164 aircraft carrying supplies. However, the parachute lift was cancelled due to poor weather over the launch airfields, which also delayed the glider take off until midday. Forewarned by the previous two lifts, the Germans had re-deployed a large amount of flak to cover the air approaches to Arnhem. These brought down thirteen of the supply aircraft and seven Horsas while still under tow; a further seven Horsas aborted over the UK or the North Sea. Thus only twenty-eight Horsas and the Hamilcar reached the release point shortly before 16:00. Of these, one Horsa crashed short of the LZ after being hit by small-arms fire and several made heavy landings that caused unloading difficulties. Matters were not helped by the presence of the 10th Battalion on the landing zone and a strafing attack by German fighter aircraft that set some of the landed gliders ablaze. It was at this point that German troops appeared in the trees north of the Arnhem-Ede highway.

After withdrawing from the fight against 1st Parachute Brigade on the night of 17–18 September, Battalion Krafft had been sent north to Deelen airfield to rearm and reorganise, where it was reinforced and promoted to *Kampfgruppe*. Sometime after 15:00 on Tuesday 19 September, *Kampfgruppe* Krafft was dispatched south, tasked to secure the line of the Arnhem-Ede highway, where it arrived just as the third lift began to land. Krafft's men promptly opened fire on the landing gliders and then attacked across the road. Their advance overran the north edge of the landing zone, allowing Krafft's men to set fire to several landed machines, although they were not entirely unopposed; 7th KOSB's HQ and D Companies virtually wiped out one of Krafft's companies from their covering positions. This was the exception rather than the rule, however, for the arrival of *Kampfgruppe* Krafft came close to turning 4th Parachute Brigade's re-deployment and the glider landing alike into a rout. In the confusion on the landing zone there were instances of British troops firing on the newly arrived Poles, misled by their unfamiliar language, and almost a full company from the KOSB were taken prisoner after straying too far north in an effort to get clear of the open ground.

By rights the airborne force, caught wrong-footed and totally in the open, should have been destroyed. Fortunately for it, Krafft's force was not large or powerful enough to achieve this alone, and neither does it appear to have pushed as hard as it might have to inflict the maximum amount of damage, despite Krafft's rather self-aggrandising report on the action.[1] Consequently, some airborne elements, mainly on foot, were able to cross the railway embankment, and a number of jeeps escaped through a storm drain under the railway embankment, until it was blocked by vehicles bogged in the churned up soil. The bulk of the retreating force reached the Wolfheze crossing to the west, although this was not achieved entirely without interference. Krafft's men were held back from getting in among the retreating transport by B Company, 7th KOSB and the 10th Battalion's A Company, commanded by Captain Lionel Queripel. Both units fought vicious close-quarter actions in two small areas of woodland that projected north from the railway embankment. The KOSB contingent successfully withdrew across the railway line to Wolfheze after dark, where 4th Parachute Brigade had established

a perimeter. However, German attacks against A Company continued through the night and into the next morning, when the
survivors were finally obliged to attempt a breakout. Captain
Queripel was last seen covering their retreat with hand grenades
and a pistol, and was awarded a posthumous Victoria Cross in
recognition of his selfless action.

Hackett's Brigade HQ and the remains of the 10th and 156
Parachute Battalions spent an undisturbed night in Wolfheze, prior
to moving off for the divisional perimeter at dawn with the 10th
Battalion in the lead. By then, however, troops and tanks from
Kampfgruppe von Tettau had infiltrated into the woods between
Wolfheze and Oosterbeek, and the move turned into a series of
running fights for the withdrawing airborne soldiers. The 10th
Battalion, reduced in the process to sixty men, broke through to
Oosterbeek in the early afternoon of Wednesday 20 September.
Hackett's HQ group and the bulk of 156 Battalion, reduced to
around 150 men in all, became pinned down in a wooded hollow
400 yards short of the Oosterbeek perimeter after a series of
confused clashes in the woods. There they remained for the next
eight hours, until darkness allowed a last ditch charge that carried
the survivors into the divisional perimeter through positions held
by 1st Border south of the Utrechtseweg. The 10th Battalion and
Hackett's party were the last organised elements of 1st Airborne's
organic formations to reach the divisional perimeter. B Company
7th KOSB, accompanied by a small party from 156 Battalion, had
become detached from Hackett in the withdrawal from Wolfheze.
Major Michael Forman, unaware that a divisional perimeter was
being formed at Oosterbeek, struck off south-west through the
woods toward the Lower Rhine in the hope of locating friendly
troops. Shortly thereafter they were surrounded by a much larger
German force and obliged to surrender. Some men from 156
Battalion attempted to evade on their own, but virtually all were
rounded up later.

By the morning of Thursday 21 September what remained of
1st Airborne Division was compressed into a thumb-shaped
perimeter projecting just over two kilometres from the Lower

Rhine, to just short of the Arnhem–Ede railway line. At the base, the perimeter ran for just over a kilometre from the Westerbouwing Heights in the west to the Oosterbeek Church in the east, a few hundred metres north of the riverbank. At its apex it narrowed to around 600 metres, from the north-western corner of Oosterbeek to just short of the Oosterbeek Hoog railway station, and was sheltered to an extent by the railway embankment. Over half the area within the perimeter consisted of wooded parkland or polder, with most of the buildings being concentrated in the centre and north of the Utrechtsweg, which marked the perimeter's east-west centre line. A smaller built-up area was located near the Oosterbeek Church in the south-east corner of the perimeter. Within this pocket were gathered 3,600 men and 2,500 Dutch civilians.[2] Around a third of the airborne soldiers were infantrymen. The rest were a mixed bag of glider pilots, sappers, artillerymen of various types and support troops. Brigadier Hicks commanded the western and northern sides of the perimeter, and Brigadier Hackett was given command of the western sector. Urquhart's divisional HQ remained in the Hartenstein Hotel, which was by now roughly in the centre of the perimeter.

Urquhart has been criticised for not establishing 1st Airborne's perimeter further west, around the north end of the Heveadorp cable ferry.[3] This lay just outside 1st Border's sector of the perimeter and, because metalled roads ran right down to the river on both banks, was the best location for putting a Bailey Bridge or something similar across the Lower Rhine. Securing it would have been in keeping with the second of 1st Airborne Division's specified tasks, which was to '…establish a sufficient bridgehead to enable the follow-up formations of 30 Corps to deploy north of the Lower Rhine'.[4] But the overarching problem was that 1st Airborne did not become aware of the existence of the ferry until it was too late. As we have seen, the 2nd Parachute Battalion was not briefed about it even though it lay only a few hundred yards off its route, and Urquhart was later adamant that it had not figured in the pre-landing briefings either.[5] This scarcely credible oversight highlights the haste and over-confidence with which the Arnhem operation was mounted, for control of the ferry would have allowed 1st Airborne to establish a presence on both sides of the Lower Rhine very shortly after landing.

Precisely when the British became aware of the existence of the Heveadorp ferry is unclear, although at least one Dutch resistance worker had informed them of its presence on 17 September, and Dutch civilians continued to use it until at least the evening of 18 September.[6] It appears to have come to Urquhart's notice after his return to 1st Airborne's HQ in the mid-morning of 19 September. According to Ryan it then became a central part of his planning, although this appears to be putting a rather positive spin on things. Urquhart did dispatch airborne engineers to examine the ferry, and his interest was presumably why 1st Border placed first a platoon and then an entire company on the Westerbouwing Heights, overlooking the north end of the ferry just outside the divisional perimeter.[7] In fact, Urquhart's influence over where the divisional perimeter came to rest was minimal. Only half the western side was formed by design, and that was in keeping with the original plan rather than new orders from Urquhart. The remainder congealed where the remnants of 1st and 4th Parachute Brigades stopped running after their beating in western Arnhem and north of the Arnhem-Ede railway line on 19 and 20 September. Things might have gone differently had Urquhart not been needlessly absent from his HQ for forty hours, but by the time he returned to the helm the initiative had passed very firmly to the Germans, leaving Urquhart with very little room for manoeuvre.

In any case, even if Urquhart could have somehow established his divisional perimeter around the north end of the Heveadorp ferry, it is highly unlikely it could have been held. The terrain there consisted almost exclusively of woods and open polder, and the lightly armed airborne troops simply could not have stood against armour in that kind of terrain. Like Frost's force at the Arnhem road bridge, 1st Airborne was only able to hang on in the Oosterbeek pocket for as long as it did by fighting from buildings turned into strong-points. There were virtually no buildings within the proposed Heveadorp ferry perimeter, and there was insufficient time or indeed manpower to construct field defences. Centring the divisional perimeter there would therefore merely have simplified the task of the German attackers. Circumstances had cast the die, not Urquhart, and 1st Airborne Division would fight for its survival within the Oosterbeek perimeter.

German units began putting the pressure on the still forming British perimeter on Wednesday 20 September. *Kampfgruppe* Spindler began a series of determined attacks against Major Lonsdale's scratch force east of the Oosterbeek Church shortly after first light, and continued throughout the day. The airborne soldiers doggedly obliged the SS to fight for every house and virtually every room, and fought them to a standstill by early evening. In the process one of the South Staffs' anti-tank gun commanders, Lance-Sergeant J.D. Baskeyfield, knocked-out at least three German armoured vehicles at close range. When the crew of his original gun was killed, he crawled to another despite being wounded in the leg, and manned it alone until he too was killed. Baskeyfield was awarded a posthumous Victoria Cross for his courage and dedication. However, the intensity of the fighting so weakened Lonsdale's forward force that it had to withdraw to the main line nearer the Oosterbeek Church in the early evening. Lonsdale, himself suffering from minor wounds in the arm and head, rallied his men in the church and delivered a morale-raising speech from the pulpit while they slept, ate or cleaned their weapons. As well as exhorting his men to make every shot count, the gist of the speech was that the Germans had not been good enough to beat the airborne troops in North Africa, and they were certainly not good enough to do so now. Lonsdale's performance was immortalised in the 1945 film of the battle, *Theirs Is The Glory*, and the door on which he pencilled the speech as a crib is currently displayed in the Hartenstein Hotel Airborne Museum in Oosterbeek.

The heaviest fighting of the day may have taken place on the eastern perimeter, but things were not exactly quiet elsewhere. On the western side 1st Border repelled an attack by infantry supported by *Panzer Kompanie* 224 with its ex-French Char B tanks, some of which appear to have been equipped with flame-throwers.[8] At least two tanks were knocked out, possibly by a seventeen-pounder anti-tank gun, but the Germans nonetheless succeeded in overrunning a detached platoon and penetrated into the perimeter between 1st Border's A and C Companies. They were driven out again, but the effort and the fighting all along the 1st Border sector cost fifteen British dead.[9] In the north the surviving KOSBs, around 270 strong, fought a series of small actions against German infiltrators around the Dreyeroord Hotel, also known as the White House, which stood just south-west of the Oosterbeek Hoog railway crossing. An anti-tank gun attached to the KOSBs also knocked out an armoured vehicle of some kind near the rail crossing.

The German pressure on the divisional perimeter on 20 September was somewhat uneven because the main focus of their attention remained on clearing Frost's force out from the north end of the Arnhem road bridge. Things were changing in the background, however, and the final elimination of Frost's force allowed a reorientation of forces and priorities. Most importantly, German command arrangements were reorganised. Hitherto, II SS *Panzerkorps* had controlled 9th SS *Panzer* Division and its various attachments, while *Kampfgruppe* von Tettau remained subordinate to General Christiansen's *Wehrmachtbefehlshaber Niederlande*, the supreme German HQ in Holland, a cumbersome arrangement that complicated efficient co-ordination. Sometime after 18 September *Heeresgruppe* B placed *Obersturmbannführer* Harzer in charge of all the German forces involved in reducing the Oosterbeek pocket and gave him a direct line to *Heeresgruppe* B HQ. This move also simplified the reinforcement and supply situation considerably, as illustrated by the reaction to complaints by Harzer that his men were suffering casualties due to a shortage of backpack flame-throwers. Not only were supplies of these weapons immediately made available, but a specially trained assault pioneer unit was flown into Deelen airfield by *Luftwaffe* transport aircraft.[10]

During the night of 20–21 September 9th SS *Panzer* Division's four *Kampfgruppen* were reorganised in line with experience gained at the Arnhem road bridge. This involved building assault groups around flame-thrower-equipped pioneer sections, and breaking *Sturmgeschütz* Brigade 280's assault guns into three vehicle sections which were attached to these groups. In addition, Harzer was given a *Heer* artillery regiment and an SS unit with twelve 'Nebelwerfer' multi-tube rocket launchers, and he authorised a rather unconventional but nonetheless effective step to secure additional supplies. The 9th SS *Panzer* Division's intelligence officer translated British instructions for setting out supply drop zones captured at the beginning of the battle, and proceeded to do just that with captured smoke pots and marker panels from 19 September. Thus most of the supply drop that accompanied the third lift gliders on that day fell into German hands, to the tune of 369 tons.[11] Little wonder Harzer later commented that the Oosterbeek battle was the cheapest he had ever fought in material terms. Most accounts of the battle refer to large amounts of British airdropped supplies falling into German hands, with the inference that this was accidental; it was anything but. Suitably reinforced and re-supplied, Harzer ordered a co-ordinated general attack on all sides of what the German troops involved were beginning to call the *Hexenkessel*, or Witch's Cauldron, for 08:00 on Thursday 21 September.

Despite their reorganisation, 9th SS *Panzer's* four *Kampfgruppen* made little progress against the eastern perimeter in a day of ferocious fighting. *Kampfgruppe* Möller's attack down the Utrechtsweg was fought to a standstill by the remnants of the 10th Parachute Battalion. The paratroopers stood up to close-range shelling from assault guns belonging to *Sturmgeschütz* Brigade 280 and then fought for every room and garden with the assaulting SS pioneers and infantrymen. Assault guns that came too close to defended buildings were attacked with Gammon bombs, and one abandoned example was manned briefly by a group of British paratroopers who ran the gauntlet of the bullet-swept road to reach it. Unfortunately they were unable to get the steering mechanism to work, and had to abandon it in turn.[12] The stubborn British resistance limited the German advance to a couple of hundred yards, but at the price of virtually destroying the already severely depleted 10th Battalion. Only a handful of men were still on their feet, all the battalion's officers had been killed or wounded, and Hackett was obliged to withdraw them into the illusory safety of reserve on the night of Friday 22 September. The relatively intact 21st Independent Parachute Company took their place on the perimeter.

Kampfgruppen Harder and von Allwörden made the main German effort against the eastern side of the divisional perimeter, where the remnants of 1st Parachute Brigade and the 2nd South Staffs were gathered under the 1st Airlanding Light Regiment's commander, Lieutenant Colonel Thompson. The German advance was directed down the riverside road toward the Oosterbeek Church, and was half of a concerted effort to cut off the British perimeter from the river. The initial attack was driven off with the assistance of the 1st Airlanding Light Regiment's 75mm pack *howitzers*, sometimes firing over open sights. Their fire was subsequently augmented by the 64th Medium Artillery Regiment, firing from positions near Nijmegen. This was made possible by the establishment of radio contact by the Light Regiment's operators, which was maintained for the rest of the battle and provided the only reliable link with the world outside Oosterbeek.[13] In the late morning Lieutenant Colonel Thompson was wounded by German mortar fire, and command devolved to Major Lonsdale. Another German attack in the afternoon was also stopped, although SS infantry and assault guns succeeded in making some headway into the British perimeter. Major Cain of the South Staffs, once again wielding a PIAT, engaged the German armour until the premature detonation of one of his PIAT bombs temporarily blinded him, after which he was evacuated for treatment at the nearest aid post. He went back to the fighting line when his sight returned, and fought the rest of the battle with metal fragments embedded in his face. Major Cain was subsequently awarded the Victoria Cross, and was the only recipient of that award to survive the battle.

Kampfgruppe von Tettau's part of the attack to pinch the divisional perimeter away from the river made much better progress. The southernmost sector of the perimeter was held by B Company, 1st Border positioned on top of the Westerbouwing Heights around a restaurant of the same name. After a fierce fight a battalion of the Hermann Göring *Ausbildungs* Regiment, a *Luftwaffe* NCO training unit, supported by four Char B tanks from *Panzer Kompanie* 224, overran the B Company positions and pursued the survivors down the slope to the east. This carried them into B Company's rear platoon, which promptly knocked out three of the tanks with a PIAT. However, three counter-attacks organised by Major Tom Armstrong, B Company's commander, failed to dislodge the Germans. The survivors were then amalgamated into a composite force under Major Charles Breese, and established new positions to the east. This withdrawal halved the width of the base of the divisional perimeter, to around 700 metres.

This was a notable achievement, but it was not matched by the remainder of *Kampfgruppe* von Tettau, which failed to make any progress against the western side of the British perimeter. The final German attack took place in the north. At around 16:30 a company-size assault went in against the 7th KOSB positions in the grounds of the White House, near the Oosterbeek Hoog railway crossing. They were driven back out with a bayonet charge led by 7th KOSB's commander, Lieutenant Colonel Robert Payton-Reid. While successful, the action reduced the KOSB contingent to less than 150 effectives, prompting Urquhart to order a small withdrawal to shorten the line. From the German perspective, this withdrawal and the success of the attack on the Westerbouwing Heights were a meagre return for the effort expended. Harzer's men were unaware of the impact on the defenders, however, and this was considerable. As we have seen, the 10th Parachute Battalion was virtually wiped out, and Lonsdale Force, the KOSB and 1st Border all suffered relatively severe losses. The battle of Oosterbeek had become one of attrition, and that was a competition 1st Airborne simply could not win without rapid and substantial reinforcement. This was not to be forthcoming, although as far as the Germans were concerned the arrival of the third parachute lift briefly made such a development seem possible.

THE POLES AND THE ISLAND

THE ARRIVAL OF THE 1ST POLISH INDEPENDENT
PARACHUTE BRIGADE

The third parachute lift was forty-eight hours late, thanks to poor weather over the airfields in England, which had not entirely cleared when the 114 US C-47s carrying the 1st Polish Independent Parachute Brigade took off in the early afternoon of Thursday 21 September. Forty-one aircraft were recalled shortly afterwards when the weather closed in again. The remaining seventy-three C-47s did not receive the recall signal due to a coding mix-up and continued to Arnhem via the southern route over Belgium, where one was damaged by German flak after straying away from the prescribed route; the pilot dispatched his stick of paratroopers over friendly territory before turning back for England. Unsettled by the British landings on 18 and 19 September, *Heeresgruppe* B had tapped into the *Luftwaffe's* early warning system, and the bypassed garrison of Dunkirk on the French Channel coast alerted the German defence to the approach of the US transport formation almost an hour before it approached Arnhem. A flak brigade, equipped with 88mm, 37mm and 20mm anti-aircraft guns, had also been moved into the Arnhem area from the Ruhr on 19 September.[1] Its gunners put up a formidable barrage when the Poles began their run in shortly before 17:00, which was thickened by every German weapon within sight on both banks of the Lower Rhine and a number of *Luftwaffe* fighters. Despite this ferocious reception, only five C-47s were lost, all of which managed to dispatch their sticks of paratroopers.

Slightly over 1,000 Polish paratroopers were delivered on, or near, their designated DZ, which lay to the west of Driel village, just under a mile south of the Lower Rhine. There were few German troops in the immediate area, but the DZ was in full view of *Kampfgruppe* Knaust and SS *Panzer Aufklärungs Abteilung* 9, which were moving south from the recently cleared Arnhem Bridge. They fired on the Poles in the air and called in artillery and mortar fire on their landing area, although Polish casualties were relatively light in the circumstances; five men were killed and twenty-five wounded in the drop or immediately afterwards.[2] It was not until after the Poles had rallied that their commander, Major-General Sosabowski, discovered that over a third of his men had failed to arrive thanks to the weather recall, and he was unable to make radio contact with Urquhart's HQ. Undaunted, the Brigade moved north to the Lower Rhine, one battalion heading for the Heveadorp ferry and the other making for the riverbank opposite the Oosterbeek Church. On reaching the river, Sosabowski made a further unwelcome discovery.

On the morning of September 20 Sosabowski had been informed that the original scheme to drop the Polish Brigade south of the Arnhem Bridge had been scrapped, and that it was to be dropped near Driel and ferried across the Lower Rhine to Oosterbeek instead. As we have seen, Sosabowski was far from happy about the Arnhem operation from the outset, and his disquiet increased when the Driel drop was postponed for a further twenty-four hours, and he was unable to obtain up-to-date information about 1st Airborne Division's situation. Sosabowski suspected that his formation was going to be sacrificed to reinforce failure, and he therefore informed his British liaison officer, Lieutenant Colonel George Stevens, that he would not take off for Driel without an accurate situation report. Stevens returned from 1st Allied Airborne Army HQ at 07:00 on 21 September and informed Sosabowski that the Heveadorp ferry was definitely in British hands.[3] Stevens was relaying the gist of a signal received from Urquhart in the early hours of Thursday 21 September.[4] Urquhart had been communicating with Browning through 21st

Army Group HQ via the GHQ Liaison Regiment, or 'Phantom'
communication team attached to 1st Airborne HQ since at least 19
September. It was through this link that Urquhart had recommended the Driel DZ and ferrying the Poles via the Heveadorp
ferry on 21 September.[5] The latter signal informed Browning that
1st Airborne Division was under pressure from east and west, that
the situation was serious, and that a close perimeter was being
established in Oosterbeek. It ended by stating that 1st Airborne still
controlled the ferry.[6]

This was quite simply not the case. The nearest the British came
to physically holding the ferry was when four airborne engineers
inspected it sometime on Wednesday. Positioning B Company 1st
Border on the Westerbouwing Heights merely allowed them to
overlook the approaches to the ferry, which was hardly controlling
it. Urquhart apparently intended to seize the ferry with this
company when the Poles arrived, but it is difficult to see how he
seriously expected them to succeed, given that 1st Border's
frontage had been under heavy attack by tanks and infantry
throughout 20 September. Neither was this the end of the matter.
A small recce patrol dispatched after dark on 20 September to
check the condition of the ferry found the cable cut and the ferry-
boat missing, and a report to this effect reached Urquhart in the
early morning of 21 September.[7] This development removed the
whole point of putting the Polish Brigade in at Driel at a stroke,
but Urquhart appears to have kept it to himself, even though there
was sufficient time to get word to Sosabowski and cancel the drop.
As a result, when Sosabowski's men rushed to the Lower Rhine
they discovered there was no way of getting across, and the arrival
of a courageous Polish liaison officer from 1st Airborne who swam
the river explained why. After a fruitless search for boats and
attempts to fashion rafts from barn doors, the Poles had no option
but to fall back and establish a defensive perimeter around Driel.

Urquhart was operating under a great deal of pressure at this
point, and he can therefore be forgiven to an extent for playing fast
and loose with the truth in an effort to obtain desperately needed
reinforcements. It was up to the next command level to ascertain

the feasibility of his requests, and direct matters accordingly. This meant Browning, to whom 1st Airborne's communications were being routed. The tone of Urquhart's signal, with its frank admittance that the situation was serious and that 1st Airborne was all but surrounded, should have raised the question of whether it was wise to dispatch more men north of the Lower Rhine. Browning, however, does not appear to have picked up on this, or if he did, he was happy to ignore it and allow the Poles to be dropped into harm's way for no good reason. It is not hard to see why. Browning had staked his military reputation, such as it was, on the success of Market Garden, and by 21 September Market Garden was rapidly coming unstuck. Browning was prepared to grasp at any straw that promised to redress the balance, however flimsy.

In addition, Browning had fought a long battle with Sosabowski to gain control of the 1st Polish Independent Parachute Brigade, and the latter had been a vociferous critic of the Comet and Market Garden plans. Personal animosity may, therefore, have also played a part in the decision to get the Poles involved, and it may also be relevant that Browning was later prominent in an attempt to use Sosabowski as a scapegoat for the failure of Market Garden. Browning's personal motivation to one side, there was little, if any, military justification for dropping the Poles into Driel. Even if the Heveadorp ferry had not been rendered inoperable, it is doubtful whether their lightly armed presence would have made any difference whatsoever to the outcome in Oosterbeek. That the Poles were superfluous is underlined by the fact that the British 43rd Infantry Division arrived in strength at Driel on Friday 22 September. In practical terms therefore, Sosabowski's men merely spent a few fruitless hours wandering the south bank of the Lower Rhine and holed up in Driel before being relieved by far more numerous and better equipped units from 30 Corps. It can thus be argued that at best the dispatch of the Poles to Driel was an example of an increasingly irrelevant plan being allowed to run on regardless. At worst it was the result of desperate flailing by the architect of Market to hold the threadbare scheme together.

British 30 Corps had finally resumed the advance north from Nijmegen into the low-lying area known as the Betuwe, or the Island, in the early afternoon of 21 September. The order to move had been given at 11:00, but the ire of Lieutenant Colonel Tucker and his paratroopers had clearly done nothing to shake the Guards out of their customary torpor. They got as far as Elst, mid-way between Arnhem and Nijmegen, when they ran into a hasty defence organised around six *Panzer* IVs from the 2nd Battalion, SS *Panzer* Regiment 10. These had been ferried across the Pannerden Canal, east of Arnhem, on the night of 19–20 September by the 10th SS *Panzer* Division's pioneer battalion. The destruction of the lead three British tanks brought the advance to a stop, and there the Guards remained, apart from a couple of half-hearted attempts to outflank the German positions. This was an especially poor performance even by the less than dynamic standard set by Guards Armoured to date, which supports the suggestion that the Guardsmen were more concerned with being relieved by 43rd Infantry Division than fighting their way through to Arnhem.[8]

That said, the Germans also appear to have been uncharacteristically tardy in moving across the Arnhem Bridge to reinforce *Brigadeführer* Harmel and his weak screen from the Frundsberg. *Kampfgruppe* Knaust, reinforced with the Tiger Is from *schwere Panzer Kompanie* Hummel and a number of Panthers from the newly arrived 1st Battalion, SS *Panzer* Regiment 10, did not move off for Elst until after midday on 21 September. Knaust's orders were to reinforce the line at Elst, but this changed with the Polish drop. II SS *Panzerkorps'* immediate concern was that the new landing would be directed toward the Arnhem Bridge, and thus cut off the 10th SS *Panzer* Division and the units dispatched south to support it. Knaust was ordered to detach *Kampfgruppe* Brinkmann to attack the Polish landing area at Driel, which it did over the next forty-eight hours, until the new German line was firmly established. Harzer was ordered away from the fight at Oosterbeek to establish a line to seal off the new landing, which began to take shape on the night of 21–22 September, using a variety of units hastily drafted-in from elsewhere in Holland. These included *Kriegsmarine* and *Luftwaffe* infantry, a *Heer* coastal machine-gun battalion and a battalion of Dutch SS. These were used mainly to fill the gap between the Lower Rhine and *Kampfgruppe* Knaust in Elst. The line ran south along the railway line from the Arnhem rail bridge before curving west around Elst and then east to the Pannerden Canal.

Fighting south of the Rhine continued while this line was consolidated, as the lead elements of the British 43rd Infantry Division hooked to the west from Nijmegen. In the early evening of Friday 22 September *schwere Panzer Kompanie* Hummel, unwisely probing west from Elst without infantry, clashed briefly with elements of the 5th Battalion, The Duke of Cornwall's Light Infantry (5th DCLI), part of 214 Infantry Brigade. The British, reasoning that the Tiger Is would have to return by the same route, laid an ambush which knocked out three with PIATs; two more of the fifty-six-ton heavies were abandoned after running off the road and becoming bogged. Later that night *Kampfgruppe* Brinkmann attacked the Polish perimeter at Driel. However, the soggy ground, dykes and ditches hampered the movement of its armoured cars and half-tracks, and the attack also bumped into the British 214 Infantry Brigade just west of Driel. Ascertaining that the interlopers were regular infantry rather than airborne troops, Brinkmann withdrew toward Elst. 214 Brigade launched its own attack on Elst on Saturday 23 September, which continued through the night. Despite all this, however, the line established by Harzer and Harmel held until the end of the battle.

THE LAST ACT

THE REDUCTION AND EVACUATION OF
THE OOSTERBEEK POCKET

On 09:00 on 22 September, the day after the Polish landing, *Kampfgruppe* von Tettau launched another attack along the entire western length of the perimeter, while *Kampfgruppen* von Allwörden and Harder renewed their attack down the riverside road from the east. The former made negligible progress in the woods, while the latter wrested some shattered ruins from Lonsdale Force. This pattern was repeated the next day, when the Germans claimed to have taken almost 100 airborne prisoners of war. The higher relative success of the 9th SS *Panzer* units appears to have been due to their reorganisation in light of experience gained at the Arnhem Bridge. This does not appear to have been passed to *Kampfgruppe* von Tettau, which had to work out new tactics for itself once it came out of the woods and into the north-west outskirts of Oosterbeek.[1]

This contradicts the claim in most accounts that the German preoccupation with stabilising the situation south of the Lower Rhine provided a respite for 1st Airborne in Oosterbeek.[2] Admittedly, some fresh infantry units were redirected to the south, but it is important to note that no units were taken from those ranged around the airborne perimeter. Despite claims to the contrary, the armour used around Elst was already en route well before the Polish drop arrived.[3] The sole exception was the two companies from *schwere Panzer Abteilung* 506 equipped with Tiger II heavy tanks, which arrived by rail from Germany on the night of 23–24 September. One company was sent to Oosterbeek, and the other to Elst. There is no evidence that the arrival of the Poles at Driel prompted any slackening in the effort against Oosterbeek. In fact, it hardened the German resolve to wipe out 1st Airborne as rapidly as possible. The widespread perception of a respite, however fleeting, is therefore false, and springs from the fact that the Oosterbeek perimeter had been compressed to the point where there was simply no longer any space for German attacks to drive the airborne defenders back. The latter were quite literally fighting with their backs to the wall, and the German attackers were obliged to embark on the time-consuming and dangerous process of digging out the airborne defenders room by room, block by block and trench by trench.

The losses incurred by German armour in the final stage at Oosterbeek provide perhaps the clearest illustration that there was no let up in the fighting in the Oosterbeek *Kessel*. By 24 September all of *Panzer Kompanie* 224's Char Bs had been knocked out, as had at least two Panthers attached to Hermann Göring *Ausbildungs* Regiment, and *Sturmgeschütz* Brigade 280 had lost at least four of its assault guns. This toll was largely due to a combination of the relatively high number of anti-tank guns present in the Oosterbeek perimeter, and crew inexperience. Despite high hopes, the arrival of the Tiger II company from *schwere Panzer Abteilung* 506 did little to redress the balance. The road foundations were unable to bear the weight of these sixty-eight-ton monsters in many places, it was difficult to manoeuvre them effectively in the narrow thoroughfares, and the length of their 88mm gun barrels made it difficult even to traverse their turrets in places. In addition, these high-velocity weapons were not especially effective for, unlike the area around the Arnhem road bridge, there was rarely sufficient room for the tanks to stand-off from their target buildings, and their shells frequently passed straight through them without exploding. Neither were they invulnerable despite their thick armour. One Tiger II attached to *Kampfgruppe* von Allwörden was immobilised by an anti-tank gun and then destroyed by fire, apparently after a chance mortar bomb exploded on a fuel tank vent.

However, while such incidents were good for airborne morale, they did nothing to alter the underlying realities. Both sides were stretched by manpower shortages, but the Germans were nonetheless still more capable of replacing losses than their British airborne opponents, and by 24 September the latter's loss rate was rapidly becoming unsustainable. Urquhart had pinned his hopes on reinforcement with the arrival of the Poles, but this was not to be forthcoming for a variety of reasons. As we have seen, the destruction of the Heveadorp ferry prevented Sosabowski's men crossing the Lower Rhine on the night of 21–22 September. Attempts to get reinforcements over the river were made on the three succeeding nights, although the results were disappointing. Fifty-two Poles were ferried across on the night of 22–23 September, using half a dozen two-man rubber dinghies and a larger RAF example, presumably recovered from a crashed aircraft. A further 150 Polish paratroopers crossed the following night, using assault boats provided by the 43rd Infantry Division. The largest contingent, 315 men from the 4th Battalion, The Dorsetshire Regiment, was put over the Lower Rhine in the early hours of Monday 25 September.[4]

This was clearly insufficient to do more than replace casualties on the Oosterbeek perimeter, and that was always assuming that the new arrivals could reach it. This was certainly not the case with the Dorsets, who were unable to reorganise after being delivered at several scattered spots along the north bank of the Lower Rhine. A party of around 200 led by the commander of 4th Dorsets, Lieutenant Colonel Gerald Tilly, briefly made contact with 1st Border, but then became cut off on the Westerbouwing Heights and were obliged to surrender. Most of the rest, congregating in small groups, sought shelter in the woods along the north bank. Thirteen Dorsets were killed in the crossing or after reaching the north bank, and almost all the remainder were taken prisoner by the Germans without contributing anything to the battle. The failure of the effort to get reinforcements into the Oosterbeek pocket was due in part to the prevailing conditions. The Lower Rhine, which was over 200 yards wide opposite Oosterbeek, had an unexpectedly strong current, and all involved were obliged to work in near total darkness to avoid drawing German fire. Despite this, the latter were aware that something was afoot, and they set up machine guns on fixed lines to sweep back and forth over the river, and at the slightest hint of activity plastered the crossing area with everything they had, including *Nebelwerfer* rockets.

Moreover, until the lead elements of 30 Corps reached Driel, there was simply not enough bridging or river crossing equipment, or the expertise to use what little there was. It was hardly practical for the Poles, who were expecting to use the Heveadorp ferry in any case, to bring boats or bridging equipment. Nor was such equipment available to 1st Airborne Division, although its engineers did at least make the effort by producing the lash-up from rubber dinghies and signal wire employed on the night of 22–23 September. About a dozen assault boats became available with the arrival of the 43rd Infantry Division at Driel, but there were no trained engineers available to man them. This put the Poles in the same position as the US 504th Parachute Infantry at Nijmegen, but without the benefit of daylight. It is therefore hardly surprising that they were only able to get a handful of men over the river. More substantial numbers of assault boats with trained crews only became available for use on the night of Sunday 24 September, forty-eight hours after the lead elements of the 43rd Division reached the south bank of the Lower Rhine.

The underlying reason for the failure of the reinforcement effort was the same as that which had dogged operation Garden from the outset; a near total lack of urgency and a consequent lack of basic forward planning. The course of events at Driel from Friday 23 September provides a prime example of this. Three scout cars from the Household Cavalry reached the Polish positions in the early morning, and Sosabowski used their radio to send a situation report to 30 Corps HQ. In the afternoon Lieutenant Colonel Mackenzie, 1st Airborne's Chief-of-Staff, arrived at Sosabowski's HQ. Dispatched by Urquhart to stress the gravity of the situation in Oosterbeek, Mackenzie had crossed the Lower Rhine in daylight in a rubber dinghy, accompanied by the Division's CRE,

Lieutenant Colonel Edmund Myers, who was to assist in organising the ferry effort. Mackenzie also used the scout car radio to pass
a detailed report on the situation in Oosterbeek to 30 Corps HQ,
which is presumably why two DUKWs loaded with supplies
accompanied the lead elements of 214 Infantry Brigade. These two
potentially invaluable vehicles became irretrievably bogged after
they were driven down to the riverbank despite warnings from the
Polish engineers who had surveyed the area. It is unclear why they
were not directed down the metalled road running down to the
Heveadorp ferry.

It is, therefore, clear that the 43rd Infantry Division had been
acquainted with the situation by the time it dispatched elements of
214 Infantry Brigade and then the whole of 130 Infantry Brigade
to Driel. Given this, it would be reasonable to assume that these
formations and their constituent units would have been prepared
to hasten the dispatch of reinforcements across the Lower Rhine.
This was not the case, however, for the Poles had to beg 130
Brigade for the use of the dozen available assault boats, which were
not immediately available despite the lesson of Nijmegen. When
they did arrive at around midnight several hours of valuable darkness had been wasted, and this was compounded by the additional
time necessary to manhandle the boats across the 500 yards of
boggy ground and ditches to the riverbank. It was thus around
03:00 before the Poles were able to begin ferrying troops, only a
couple of hours before dawn. In effect, therefore, poor preparation
by 130 Brigade wasted the best part of a night. It is difficult to
avoid the impression that the 43rd Infantry Division considered its
task to be complete on reaching the Lower Rhine, and that what
was going on across the water in Oosterbeek was not really its
affair. This was a remarkably similar attitude to that displayed by
the Guards Armoured after crossing the Nijmegen road bridge,
and it came straight from the top.

On Saturday 23 September Mackenzie and Myers managed to
reach Nijmegen and talked to Horrocks and Browning at 30
Corps HQ, and visited the 43rd Division's HQ on the way back to
Driel. Both men noted a distinct lack of urgency all round, and

were convinced that the officers they spoke to thought they were exaggerating their case, a point Mackenzie made to Urquhart when he returned to Oosterbeek that night.[5] Perhaps the clearest illustration of the depth of this failure to comprehend the plight of 1st Airborne comes from a radio exchange between Urquhart and the commander of the 43rd Division, Major-General Ivor Thomas, on Sunday 24 September. When Urquhart mentioned the toll that the constant German mortaring and shelling was having on the beleaguered defenders in Oosterbeek, Thomas demanded to know why 1st Airborne simply did not shell and mortar them back. This incredibly naïve response prompted Urquhart to enquire heatedly how his men were expected to do any such thing while sheltering in holes in the ground with no ammunition.[6] Thomas's comment displayed a breathtaking and inexcusable lack of insight into the reality of what was happening in Oosterbeek, given the information Urquhart had been passing out via the radio and personal courier. It also displays a similar level of ignorance of the likely capabilities of an airborne formation after fighting alone and virtually unsupported for almost a full week rather than the forty-eight hours it had been briefed for.

It is also significant that there was no overt discussion of how to proceed until Sunday 24 September, almost a full forty-eight hours after elements of the 43rd Division had reached the Lower Rhine at Driel. This was a meeting attended by Horrocks, Browning, Thomas and Sosabowski at 43rd Division's HQ at Valburg. It would appear that the reports emanating from Oosterbeek had been noted higher up the chain of command. Just after 20:00 on Saturday 23 September British 2nd Army HQ, 30 Corps' parent formation, authorised the evacuation of 1st Airborne across the Lower Rhine if the local commanders thought it necessary. Interestingly, this information was not passed to Mackenzie before he returned to Oosterbeek.[7] Nor did it figure in the Valburg meeting, which appears to have been convened solely to inform Sosabowski that it had already been decided that only two battalions were to be put across the Lower Rhine that night. The meeting grew acrimonious when Sosabowski was brusquely informed by Thomas, nominally an equal rather than a superior, that he was to lose one of his battalions, and Horrocks was obliged to restore order by pulling rank on the hapless Sosabowski. Thomas then added insult to injury by issuing orders to the Polish brigade through the British liaison officer even though Sosabowski was standing next to him. Nor was the Polish commander informed that the decision had been taken to evacuate the Oosterbeek pocket, with only the time to be decided. This was communicated to Urquhart via two sealed letters entrusted to Lieutenant Colonel Myers, 1st Airborne's CRE, and an officer from the Dorsets. Both men were assigned to the Sunday night crossing.

Although Sosabowski strongly disagreed with it, the decision to evacuate was the correct one. The question arises over the length of time it took for 30 Corps to reach it, or at least overtly to acknowledge it. There should have been a high-level effort to obtain a clear and objective view of the overall situation immediately the 43rd Division reached the 1st Polish Independent and the Lower Rhine. The first priority should have been to ascertain the precise situation at Oosterbeek, although this should have been abundantly clear from the communications Urquhart had managed to get out. The person to do this should have been Browning, if only because he was doing nothing else and because he was, after all, Urquhart's immediate superior. Even the most superficial examination would have shown that 1st Airborne's only option was evacuation, and as rapidly as possible. Unfortunately for 1st Airborne and the Poles, Browning appears to have decided that the arrival of 30 Corps absolved him of any responsibility toward them, and he turned his attention to securing quarters befitting his status in Nijmegen.

The second priority should have been to ascertain whether or not 30 Corps was capable of mounting a major cross-river effort in support of 1st Airborne. The realistic outcome of such an investigation had to be that it was not, for three reasons. First, there was simply insufficient equipment immediately available, as the sorry saga of the attempts to get reinforcements across the Lower Rhine clearly showed. Second, it was not clear that there were enough troops available to establish a sufficiently strong lodgement on the north bank of the Rhine even if the necessary equipment had been available. There was no prospect of getting tanks across, and it is difficult to see how unsupported infantry from the 43rd Division would have fared any better than 1st Airborne against the combined strength of *Kampfgruppen* von Tettau and Spindler. Third, there was no realistic prospect of bringing up more boats, DUKWs or indeed bridging equipment in the time available because of the congestion in, and continuing threat against, the airborne corridor. It should be remembered that Veghel was under heavy German pressure at the point when the 43rd Division reached the Rhine, and that the corridor was cut between Veghel and St Oedenrode on the night of 24–25 September, and remained cut for twenty-four hours.

Given all this, the decision to withdraw 1st Airborne across the Lower Rhine could, and should, have been taken by Saturday 23 September and the authorisation from 2nd Army HQ in the late evening of that day suggests that this was in fact the case. The problem was that no-one bothered to inform Urquhart, Sosabowski or the Dorsets, which meant that many men were killed and wounded in pointless attempts to reinforce an acknowledged failure. The standard justification for this, at least as far as the Dorsets are concerned, was the need for extra troops to cover the evacuation; no-one at 30 Corps HQ appears to have been overly worried about Polish casualties. This argument, however, misses the point that there were simply not enough boats to get sufficient troops across the Rhine to make a difference in the time available. It is therefore difficult to avoid the conclusion that Horrocks, Browning and Thomas kept the evacuation decision to themselves for thirty-six hours while they went through the motions to avoid being blamed for the failure of Market Garden. This suggestion is supported by discrepancies between Horrocks's and Thomas's recollection of events,[8] and the shameful subsequent attempt to place the blame on Sosabowski, which began with his treatment at the Valburg meeting. More seriously, the delay cost lives on both sides of the Lower Rhine, and saw the 4th Dorsets virtually wiped out for no practical benefit whatsoever.

Urquhart received the sealed letter authorising him to withdraw from Oosterbeek from Mackenzie at just after 06:00 on Monday 25 September. Urquhart radioed Thomas two hours later, informing him that the evacuation was to commence that night. Two and a half hours after that he convened a conference at the Hartenstein Hotel, and set his staff to drawing up the necessary arrangements. In the meantime, 1st Airborne had to hold off the latest round of German attacks, and especially the renewed effort to cut the divisional perimeter away from the Lower Rhine along the riverside road. A morning attack was only halted just short of the Oosterbeek Church with the assistance of the 64th Medium Artillery Regiment, but the attack was renewed with the support of *schwere Panzer Abteilung* 506's Tiger II tanks once the barrage ceased. It was during this afternoon fighting that the single Tiger II knocked out in Oosterbeek was destroyed. Despite this, the hard-pressed Lonsdale Force was unable to stop *Kampfgruppen* von Allwörden and Harder overrunning the 1st Airlanding Light Regiment's command post and several of its gun pits. One of the remaining 75mm pack howitzers, firing over open sights, succeeded in blasting the German troops out of one of the newly occupied buildings near the Oosterbeek Church, but the situation on the riverside road had reached a critical point. The German attack narrowed the base of the divisional perimeter to 600 yards, and left Lonsdale Force clinging to the western edge of the old village. The decision to evacuate the Oosterbeek pocket had clearly come in the nick of time.

Urquhart's evacuation plan was inspired by a promotion exam question about Gallipoli, and envisaged a concentric withdrawal towards the river. These were to be covered by every available gun in the 30 Corps area, which were to fire concentrations and shift back into the perimeter in time with the withdrawals. The complex fire plan took 1st Airborne's artillery staff six hours to complete and encode for transmission. The airborne troops were to be guided away from their positions in small groups by men from the Glider Pilot Regiment, to a rendezvous near the Oosterbeek Church. A white tape laid by airborne engineers marked the route from there to the pick-up point on the river-bank, and embarkation was controlled by a number of specially selected officers. On the perimeter what surplus equipment existed was surreptitiously destroyed, and all ranks were instructed to shave. Last-minute preparations included securing weapons and equipment to prevent tell-tale rattling, wrapping metal-shod ammunition boots in scraps of material salvaged from derelict houses, and a final application of burnt cork or something similar to faces for night camouflage. Walking wounded were permitted to join the evacuation, but non-ambulatory casualties were to remain behind with the medical staff. Airborne gunners were instructed to bring the sights and breech-blocks from their various pieces for disposal in the Rhine.

The barrage was to begin at 20:50, and initially prompted a strong response from the Germans. The most northerly airborne positions began their withdrawal ten minutes after the friendly bombardment commenced. Strong wind and steady rain concealed their movements, the men holding onto the webbing or tailpiece of the Dennison smock of the man in front in the dark-ness like gas casualties from the First World War. Unlike so much at Arnhem, the evacuation ran largely like clockwork, although some men did become disoriented in the wind-lashed, rainy darkness and clashed with German outposts, sometimes with fatal results. The last positions were abandoned by 02:30 on the morning of 26 September, although some brave souls remained at their posts as the perimeter silently collapsed inward around them. 1st Airborne Provost Company maintained a full guard on the German POWs incarcerated in the tennis court at the Hartenstein Hotel until 01:30, after which a single volunteer took over and remained until dawn; he evaded capture and later made it to Allied lines and safety. A sadly unknown radio operator continued to man the sets at Division headquarters as a disinformation measure until signing off at 03:30. Once at the riverbank, the airborne soldiers formed orderly and impressively silent queues up to 150 yards long, with the wounded being ushered to the front. Thanks to this impressive discipline the Germans assumed that the activity they did detect was another small-scale reinforcement effort. Consequently, while they swept the river itself with machine-gun and light cannon fire, most of the artillery was directed at predicted routes and forming-up points well to the south of the river rather than either bank.

The ferry operation began on schedule at 22:00, by which time a considerable number of airborne soldiers were already queuing patiently. 260 (Wessex) Field Company RE provided sixteen assault boats, and the 23rd Canadian Field Company, Royal Canadian Engineers contributed twenty-one storm boats, larger, metal-hulled affairs powered by petrol engines. The engines suffered frequent breakdowns as water penetrated their electrical systems, but the Canadian sappers repeatedly managed to effect running repairs, usually accompanied by outbursts of spectacularly foul language. Even so, the storm boats carried the majority of the evacuees to the south bank, making a total of 150 individual crossings. By dawn, there were only two storm boats left, the rest having succumbed to damage inflicted by repeated rough grounding and German fire. Five Canadians and an unknown number of their airborne passengers were killed by German fire, or drowned after their overloaded craft overturned in the fast running black water.

It is unclear precisely when Urquhart found a place on a south-bound boat, although he appears to have merely taken his place in the queue rather than playing a part in the evacuation of his men. Neither did he play a part in guiding them away from the south bank to the reception centre set up by the 43rd Division, making his way to 43rd Division HQ instead. While his aide tried to extract transport from Thomas's less than helpful staff, a jeep driven by Browning's ADC arrived to carry him to the Advanced Airborne Corps HQ in Nijmegen. On arrival, Urquhart was offered the chance to clean up but, to his credit, insisted on seeing Browning as he was. He was then kept waiting for almost half an hour until Browning appeared, attired in his usual immaculate Guards fashion. Urquhart informed Browning that the evacuation of 1st Airborne was all but complete, and apologised for failing to carry out his mission. Browning magnanimously responded by telling Urquhart he had done all he could, offered him a drink and advised him to get some rest before disappearing, presumably back to his bed.

As Browning was the senior British airborne officer in Holland and fully aware of 1st Airborne's withdrawal, it is extraordinary that he did not go forward to meet Urquhart and the airborne evacuees. That he chose to remain in his comfortable HQ instead speaks volumes about his leadership, and strongly suggests that he did not fully appreciate that there was more to military leadership than playing politics and displaying the immaculate turnout maintained by his batman. The usual excuse for Browning's absence is that operational control of 1st Airborne had passed to 30 Corps, but this did not, and should not, have precluded him from at least acting as an observer, an action that would have done no harm to the survivors' morale. Indeed, given his senior airborne status, it could be argued that this was his duty. In the event, his behaviour suggests that, like Guards Armoured and the 43rd Division, Browning had somehow decided that whatever was happening at Oosterbeek and on the Lower Rhine was not really his affair. This would certainly explain why Browning did not visit Sosabowski at Driel either. It is difficult to interpret this reticence as other than part of a deliberate strategy to deflect blame for the failure of Market Garden, a charge supported by his involvement in the subsequent and shameful British attempt to foist the responsibility onto Sosabowski. There is something extremely distasteful in the spectacle of Browning sleeping comfortably between clean sheets while his men were struggling and dying in the rain a few short miles to the north. Donkeys leading lions from the comfort of opulent *châteaux* were less prevalent in the First World War than popular perception might suggest, but it certainly appears that the spirit was alive and well in Nijmegen in September 1944.

Back on the Lower Rhine, the Germans became aware that something was afoot as dawn approached and belatedly redirected their fire at the tenuous ferry link and the landing points on both banks. The last multi-boat crossing commenced at around 05:00,

when it was sufficiently light for the Germans to see them. A
Canadian storm boat made the very last crossing in full daylight
half an hour later, and almost every man was wounded in the
process. Sadly a large number of men – estimates vary between 150
and 300 – were left behind. Many of these unfortunates were
glider pilots or men from 1st Border and the South Staffs, who had
been the last to leave their positions, and were still waiting on the
north bank. A large group from D Company 1st Border never even
got the order to pull out. Almost all these men were taken prisoner. Nonetheless, a total of 2,398 men had been plucked to safety
against the odds. As well as men from 1st Airborne, this figure
included 160 Poles, seventy-five Dorsets, several shot down RAF
aircrew and a single, elderly Dutch Jew who had acted as a guide
for his erstwhile airborne liberators. The price had been high. An
estimated 258 Allied soldiers had been killed in the last twenty-
four hours of the Oosterbeek pocket, the second highest daily
death toll of the entire Arnhem battle. This sacrifice was not in
vain, for it prevented the Germans realising that a withdrawal was
under way, until *Kampfgruppe* von Tettau began its scheduled attack
at dawn, and found itself faced only by empty positions, abandoned airborne wounded and Dutch civilians. Thus the battle of
Arnhem ended with the virtual destruction of the 1st Airborne
Division, almost nine days after its first elements landed near
Wolfheze.

THE AFTERMATH
AND REFLECTIONS

With the end of the battle came the reckoning. In all, 1st Airborne Division took just under 12,000 men into Arnhem. By Monday 25 September 1,485 of them were dead, and 6,500 had been captured; approximately a third of the latter were wounded. Air losses in support of 1st Airborne were similarly heavy. The RAF lost sixty-eight aircraft shot down, and in all 474 aircrew were killed, including seventy-nine army dispatchers and twenty-seven USAAF personnel.[1] Incomplete records make it difficult to provide a precise figure for German losses, but estimates suggest the units fighting at Arnhem suffered between 2,565 and 5,175 casualties, and between 6,315 and 8,925 for Market Garden in total.[2] Neither was the cost restricted to the combatants. An estimated 453 Dutch civilians were killed across the Market Garden battlefield, and their ordeal did not end with the Driel evacuation. On 23 September 1944 the Germans ordered around 100,000 Dutch civilians out of a zone north of the Lower Rhine, which they then systematically plundered for materials for their new defences. Civilian rations were also significantly decreased, resulting in the death of 18,000 Dutch civilians in the 'Hunger Winter' of 1944–45.[3] Little wonder then that Prince Bernhard of the Netherlands responded to Montgomery's subsequent claim that Market Garden was ninety per-cent successful with the bitter observation that his country could ill afford another Montgomery success.[4]

The evacuation of the Oosterbeek pocket was the end of the battle for the majority of the 1st Airborne Division, but the fighting did not cease elsewhere. The US 82nd and 101st Airborne Divisions were still embroiled in the struggle to keep the airborne corridor open despite the presence of 30 Corps. That both US divisions remained in the front-line in Holland for several weeks after 1st Airborne was evacuated across the Lower Rhine is frequently overlooked. The 82nd Airborne was not withdrawn until 11 November 1944, after fifty-six days in continuous action, during which it suffered a total of 3,400 casualties; the 101st Airborne was not withdrawn until almost the end of November, and suffered 3,792 casualties.[5] These casualty figures, it should be noted, are at least as severe as those suffered by 1st Airborne if the prisoner of war figure is excluded from the latter's tally. In addition, the 2nd Battalion, 506th Parachute Infantry Regiment was instrumental in rescuing 138 men from 1st Airborne who had evaded capture with the assistance of courageous Dutch civilians. This group, led by Lieutenant Colonel Dobie and including Major Tatham-Warter, Major Deane-Drummond, the injured Brigadier Lathbury and several Allied aircrew, were ferried across the river on the night of 22–23 October.[6] A second large-scale rescue was aborted after running into a German patrol and losing two killed, but most of these men, including Brigadier Hackett and other individual evaders, were smuggled out later by the Dutch resistance.

Two of the bridges around which the battle had focused did not long outlast the official end of Market Garden. *Kriegsmarine* combat swimmers succeeded in damaging the Nijmegen road bridge and dropped a complete span of the adjacent railway bridge on the night of 28–29 September, and the Arnhem road bridge was destroyed by aircraft from the USAAF's 344th Bombardment Group just over a week later. This trapped the bulk of the German force between the Waal and the Lower Rhine, and prompted von Tettau to establish a bridgehead on the south bank of the Lower Rhine two kilometres downstream from the Heveadorp ferry on 1 October. In a mirror image of events at Driel, a force commanded by *Hauptsturmführer* Heinrich Oelkers succeeded in getting across, and held out for ten days under near-constant artillery and mortar fire and attacks from the 4th Dorsets and then units from the 101st Airborne. The German force was finally evacuated on 10 October, with Oelkers being the last man out on a riddled inflatable dinghy.[7]

While all this was going on the British high command, and Browning in particular, were busily engaged in trying to shift the blame for the failure of Market Garden onto the 1st Polish Independent Parachute Brigade and Sosabowski. As we have seen, Browning stood by while the Polish commander was humiliated and his brigade dismembered by Thomas at Valburg. On 26 September Sosabowski was summoned to Browning's Nijmegen HQ and his brigade was assigned to protect a section of the airborne corridor to the south with immediate effect. Thus the Poles moved straight from Driel to the vicinity of Neerloon and began to construct field positions, while the other survivors from 1st Airborne Division were resting prior to returning to the UK.

This, however, was only the beginning. On 17 October, in a letter to CIGS Alan Brooke, Montgomery criticised the Polish brigade for an unwillingness to take risks, complained that it had performed extremely poorly at Driel and demanded Sosabowski be removed from his command.[8] This was followed by a written report on Sosabowski's performance from Browning to the Deputy CIGS, Lieutenant-General Sir Ronald Weeks, on 20 November. This claimed that Sosabowski had been incapable of grasping the urgency of the situation at Driel, that he had been needlessly argumentative and unwilling to obey orders, and cited Horrocks and Thomas as witnesses to these and other misdemeanours. It ended by recommending that Sosabowski be removed from command of the 1st Polish Independent Parachute Brigade because of his temperament and inability to co-operate.[9] Interestingly, this dissatisfaction with the Poles and their commander did not prevent Browning from accepting the Order of Polonia Restituta on 18 November, for his assistance in the establishment of the Polish Parachute Brigade, a process in which he played a marginal role at best. The British pressure finally became intolerable, and the Polish president in exile relieved

Sosabowski of his command on 9 December 1944. Some of his
soldiers staged a hunger strike in protest.

There was not a shred of truth in any of this, which was a blatant
and shameful attempt to conceal the British incompetence that
sealed the fate of Market Garden. Quite what Montgomery based
his judgements on is unclear, given that he never went near Driel.
The fact that the Polish brigade lost a quarter of its strength,
including ninety-two dead, gives the lie to his allegations. It is also
unclear how Horrocks and Thomas were qualified to comment on
Sosabowski's competence, given that they only met him on the day
of the Valburg conference. Quite simply, Sosabowski was pilloried
for no other reason than being an obstacle to Browning's ambi-
tions. He repeatedly rebuffed Browning's attempts to gain control
over his brigade, he publicly and repeatedly pointed out the flaws
in the Comet and Market Garden plans, and, most unforgivable of
all, events proved him to be absolutely right on all counts. The
scapegoating of Sosabowski and his men was a spiteful, unwar-
ranted and unforgivable slur on a competent and conscientious
commander whose only crime was to refuse to play the Whitehall
game to Browning's satisfaction, and upon a courageous body of
men whose only failing was an inability to walk on water.

In the event, it appears that the powers that be were not taken in
by Browning's shameful attempt to shift his culpability onto
Sosabowski and his men. He lost his deputy command of the 1st
Allied Airborne Army to the infinitely more competent Gale, and
he never held an operational command again, although the pill was
sweetened in typical British fashion when he was invested with the
Companion of the Order of the Bath at Buckingham Palace.
Before 1944 was out he had been dispatched to Burma to act as
Chief-of-Staff to the Supreme Commander, South-East Asia
Command, Lord Louis Mountbatten, a far more appropriate
employment for his political talents. In 1946 he was sidelined to
the War Office, where he served as Military Secretary, and two
years later he was quietly removed from the active list and made
Controller and Treasurer to Princess Elizabeth's Household, a posi-
tion he held until retirement in 1952. Operation Market, far from

being the capstone of Browning's career and guarantee of his place in the airborne canon as he had hoped, effectively marked the end of it.

This leaves the matter of apportioning responsibility for the defeat of the 1st Airborne Division at Arnhem. The battle of Arnhem has been described as a tragedy of errors, which is a fair enough description, but a more accurate one would be a succession of needless errors. While a few were admittedly unavoidable, none was fatal in itself, and any tragedy lay in their sheer number and the failure to address the ones that mattered. Consequently, the lion's share of responsibility has to go to the airmen involved, whose decisions significantly tilted the odds against the airborne soldiers before they left the UK. The refusal of Williams and Brereton to countenance two lifts into Arnhem on the first day was a serious and needless error, for it meant that 1st Airborne's delivery was to be spread over three days. This highlights the pitfall of placing a member of one service with limited understanding of the realities of the other in overall control in a joint-service venture. Without effective checks and balances, narrow service interests will almost inevitably be placed ahead of the greater operational good, which is precisely what happened in this instance. The same problem underlay the infinitely more serious RAF insistence that 1st Airborne was delivered to the distant landing zones near Wolfheze. This compounded the effects of delivering 1st Airborne over a three-day period, it flew in the face of all airborne experience, and the professional opinion of the airborne soldiers involved. The location of the landing zones was thus the single most important factor in the failure at Arnhem. The Arnhem portion of Market Garden failed not because 30 Corps did not reach the town within the allotted time, although that was an avoidable failure in its own right. It failed because the bulk of 1st Airborne's first lift did not manage to reach the Arnhem road bridge at all, and the major reason for this was the distance between the landing areas and that bridge.

There was absolutely no reason why the Arnhem Bridge could not have been seized by a glider *coup-de-main*, and the first lift delivered south of it as, incidentally, the RAF planners always intended to do with the third lift. Frost and his scratch force of just over a battalion held the north end of the bridge for three days. Putting the entire first lift south of the bridge would have avoided the problems that ultimately doomed Frost. A full brigade would have been able to establish a more effective perimeter north of the bridge on ground of the airborne troops' choosing, rather than having to occupy whatever was in reach. Placing the second brigade in a perimeter to the south, backing onto the river and enclosing the landing area would have provided a much tighter and more defensible divisional area. This would have concentrated 1st Airborne's fighting power in a single location, rather than scattering it ineffectually between Wolfheze and the Arnhem Bridge, as ultimately happened. It would also have provided a much more compact and identifiable target for subsequent lifts and resupply drops. The crux of the problem was the nonsensical British arrangement that gave the RAF untrammelled control over the air side of airborne planning. This permitted the desk-bound RAF planners *carte blanche* to draw up and impose their plans upon the airborne soldiers without reference to operational or tactical realities, or even common sense.

This point leads us to the second in line, who was Browning, and not merely because he wilfully approved a seriously flawed RAF plan despite the misgivings of his subordinate airborne commanders. Browning's culpability for the failure at Arnhem is the most extensive of any individual concerned. He personally ensured that 1st Airborne Division was saddled with a totally inexperienced commander even though a highly experienced candidate was already in place. He deliberately suppressed vital intelligence about the scale and, more crucially, the calibre of likely German opposition in the Arnhem area. He weakened the already overstretched first lift into Wolfheze by needlessly diverting thirty-two badly needed Horsa gliders. His interference with the 82nd Airborne's operational planning and on the ground, with his insistence that the Nijmegen bridges be ignored in favour of the Groesbeek Heights, came close to losing the bridges altogether.

Finally, he made no effort even to contact 1st Airborne once across the Nijmegen bridges, and washed his hands of the matter altogether once it became apparent that Garden had failed at Arnhem. Were the story of Arnhem an Alistair Maclean novel, Browning would have to have been the German spy in the Allied Command, for it would be difficult to add to this list if one were deliberately trying to sabotage the operation. Unfortunately there was nothing so dramatic, for Browning's main motivation was pure self-interest. There is thus some justice in the fact that the failure of Operation Market, to which he contributed so much, marked the effective end of his military career.

Next comes 30 Corps, and in particular the Guards Armoured Division. This formation operated in a strictly business as usual manner, and was either unwilling, or unable, to modify its operating procedures despite the attempts of the Corps commander, Horrocks, to stress the need for haste. Stiff resistance was blamed for the slow rate of progress, but the German side of the story clearly shows that this was much exaggerated, and the real reason appears to have been a simple lack of urgency. Guards Armoured was late in jumping off from the Neerpelt Bridgehead, it was extremely prompt in ceasing operations at the onset of darkness and equally tardy in resuming the advance for the first four days of Market Garden. On no occasion when it was advancing into German-held territory did the Guards Armoured move off before midday, each time wasting several hours of priceless daylight. This pushed the Market Garden schedule further and further behind, and the inexplicable failure to advance north of the Nijmegen road bridge for over twelve hours squandered the last and single best opportunity to reach the beleaguered defenders at the Arnhem Bridge. The irony of this is that these long stops caused Guards Armoured more casualties in the long run, for they invariably allowed the Germans to reorganise their thinly stretched defences in time for the next leisurely Guards advance. The tribal nature of the British regimental system played a clear part in the Guards' inflexibility and underpinned their palpable lack of urgency. It is interesting to speculate whether the Guards

Armoured would have moved faster had the 1st Guards Airborne Division been fighting in Arnhem. It is also sobering to ponder on whether Guards Armoured could have secured Nijmegen at all without the assistance and sacrifice of Gavin's far more aggressively minded paratroopers.

That said, the British 43rd Infantry Division exhibited the same lack of urgency, by wasting the entire night of 20–21 September and part of the next day bivouacked near Grave when additional infantry were desperately needed in the fight for and advance across the Nijmegen bridges. Poor to non-existent forward planning was also a feature of 30 Corps' performance, as shown by the fact that it does not appear to have occurred to anyone to have the corps and divisional allotment of assault boats on hand until US and Polish airborne commanders asked for them. This was an amazing oversight for formations advancing across multiple water-courses, and supports the suggestion that for some unfathomable reason Guards Armoured and the 43rd Division did not really consider what was happening north of the Waal and Lower Rhine to be their affair. The problem appears to have lain with Lieutenant-General Horrocks who, seemingly because of illness, failed to keep a close enough grip on his subordinate commanders Adair and Thomas.

Third, 1st Airborne Division itself was not totally blameless. In the vital opening phase of the battle, the 1st Airborne Reconnaissance Squadron and parts of the 1st Parachute Brigade displayed a lack of urgency comparable to that of 30 Corps. At the top, Urquhart made a series of avoidable errors in the opening stages of the battle that compounded the considerable handicap blithely handed down by the RAF planners by effectively leaving the Division leaderless for the first forty hours of the battle. These started with his initial decision to leave his HQ near Wolfheze, which is usually justified by reference to the radio difficulties experienced at Arnhem. However, even if the radios had for once operated as advertised, there is no guarantee that Urquhart would not have gone forward to see what was happening in any case. Even with properly functioning communications, it is arguable whether or not Urquhart could have exerted much control over the situation as it developed after the advance from Wolfheze.

This was because 1st Parachute Brigade's plan for the advance to Arnhem was poorly thought out and in effect consisted merely of turning the brigade's three battalions loose in the same general direction, and with two distinct objectives. This needlessly dispersed the brigade's combat power precisely when it needed it most, in the first clashes with the still forming German defence. A rapid, sustained and concentrated advance was the one tactic that might have overcome the handicap of the ridiculously distant landing zones and permitted the 1st Parachute Brigade to take and hold the Arnhem road bridge in sufficient strength to hold it until relieved. The error of trying to do too much with too little was also repeated at the battalion level. The 2nd Parachute Battalion, which was tasked to secure the Arnhem railway, pontoon and road bridges as well as the main German HQ in Arnhem, provides the clearest example of this. The 1st Parachute Brigade ultimately paid the price for squandering so much training time earlier in the year. More formation-level training in the run up to the Normandy invasion should have ironed out this tendency before it caused the harm it did on the ground at Arnhem.

This leaves the question of whether Market Garden could have worked. In the wider sense, it is doubtful whether the operation would have led to the grand strategic success Montgomery had in mind, if only because Eisenhower was unlikely to have been willing, or able, to allot the necessary resources. In the narrow sense, however, it is clear that Market Garden could have achieved all its objectives, if only because despite all the errors, needless and otherwise, it was such a close run thing. Despite itself, 30 Corps still came agonisingly close to reaching the Arnhem road bridge while Frost's men were still holding out. Had the German defence of the Nijmegen bridges been less stubborn, and had the Guards Armoured behaved with anything like the urgency the situation merited, the link up could have been achieved before midnight on 20 September, only twenty-four hours late. The margin between success and failure was that narrow.

BIBLIOGRAPHY

UNPUBLISHED SOURCES

Stone, William J., *The English Silver Summer*. Unpublished personal account. Mr Stone
    served in Holland with Battery B, 321st Glider Field Artillery Battalion, 101st
    Airborne Division
Public Record Office Files
AIR 20/2333 16th SS *Panzer* Grenadier & Reserve Battalion Report
AIR 37/775 1944: Subsidiary Airborne Operations to Further Operation OVERLORD
AIR 37/776 1944: 1st Allied Airborne Army: Formation and Employment
AIR 37/1214 1944: Report on Operation MARKET GARDEN: Allied Airborne
    Operations in Holland
AIR 37/1249 1944: Operation MARKET GARDEN
WO 171/393 1st Airborne Division War Diary
WO 171/589 1st Airlanding Brigade War Diary
WO 171/592 1st Parachute Brigade War Diary
WO 171/594 4th Parachute Brigade War Diary
WO 205/313 Operation MARKET GARDEN Part 1
WO 205/693 Operation MARKET GARDEN: Reports and Instructions

PUBLISHED SOURCES

Anderson, Dudley, *Three Cheers for the Next Man to Die* (London: Hale, 1983)
Baynes, John, *Urquhart of Arnhem: The Life of Major-General R.E. Urquhart, CB, DSO*
    (London: Brassey's, 1993)
Blair, Clay, *Ridgeway's Paratroopers: The American Airborne in World War II* (New York: The
    Dial Press, 1985)
Burgett, Donald R., *The Road to Arnhem: A Screaming Eagle in Holland* (Novato
    [California]: Presidio Press, 1999)
Chatterton, Brigadier George, DSO OBE *The Wings of Pegasus: The Story of the Glider
    Pilot Regiment* (Nashville: The Battery Press, 1982)
Cholewczynski, George F., *Poles Apart: The Polish Airborne at the Battle of Arnhem*
    (London: Greenhill Books, 1993)
Curtis, Reg, *Churchill's Volunteer: A Parachute Corporal's Story* (London: Avon Books, 1994)
D'Este, Carlo, *Decision In Normandy: The Unwritten Story of Montgomery and the Allied
    Campaign* (London: Collins, 1983)
Devlin, Gerard, *Paratrooper! The Saga of US Army and Marine Parachute and Glider Combat
    Troops During World War II* (New York: St. Martin's Press, 1979)

Dover, Major Victor MC, *The Sky Generals* (London: Cassell, 1981)

Ellis, John, *The Sharp End: The Fighting Man in World War II* (London: Pimlico, 1993)

Fairley, John, *Remember Arnhem: The Story of the 1st Airborne Reconnaissance Squadron at Arnhem* (Bearsden: Peaton Press, 1978)

Farrar-Hockley, Brigadier Anthony, *Airborne Carpet: Operation Market Garden* (London: Macdonald, 1969)

Foley, John, *Mailed Fist* (London: Panther Books, 1957)

Frost, Major-General John, CB, DSO, MC *A Drop Too Many* (London: Sphere, 1983)

Garlinski, Jozef, *Poland, SOE and the Allies* (London: Allen & Unwin, 1969)

Gavin, James M. *On To Berlin: Battles of an Airborne Commander, 1943-1946* (London: Leo Cooper, 1979)

Golden, Lewis OBE, *Echoes From Arnhem* (London: Kimber, 1984)

Harclerode, Peter, *Arnhem: A Tragedy of Errors* (London: Caxton, 2000)

Harvey, A.D., *Arnhem* (London: Cassell, 2001)

Hibbert, Christopher, *Arnhem* (Moreton-in-Marsh [Glos.]: Windrush Press, 1998)

Kershaw, Robert J., *It Never Snows In September: The German View of MARKET-GARDEN and The Battle of Arnhem, September 1944* (Marlborough: The Crowood Press, 1990)

Kent, Ron, *First In! Parachute Pathfinder Company. A History of the 21st Independent* (London: Batsford, 1979)

Lamb, Richard, *Montgomery in Europe 1943-1945: Success or Failure?* (London: Buchan & Enright, 1983)

Mawson, Stuart, *Arnhem Doctor* (Staplehurst: Spellmount, 2000)

McKee, Alexander, *The Race for the Rhine Bridges* (Dorset: Dorset Press, 2001)

Middlebrook, Martin, *Arnhem 1944: The Airborne Battle* (London: Viking, 1994)

Millar, George, *The Bruneval Raid: Flashpoint of the Radar War* (London: The Bodley Head, 1974)

Morris, Eric, *Circles of Hell: The War in Italy 1943-1945* (London: Hutchinson, 1993)

Otway, Lieutenant Colonel T.B.H., DSO, *Airborne Forces* (London: Imperial War Museum, 1990)

Packe, Michael, *Winged Stallion: Fighting and Training with the First Airborne* (London: Secker & Warburg, 1948)

Powell, Geoffrey, *The Devil's Birthday: The Bridges to Arnhem, 1944* (London: Leo Cooper, 1992)

Quarterly Army List – January 1940

Rapport, Leonard and Arthur Northwood Jr., *Rendezvous With Destiny: A History of the 101st Airborne Division* (Fort Campbell Kentucky: 101st Airborne Division Association, 1948)

Rottman, Gordon, *US Army Airborne 1940-90* (London: Osprey, 1990)

Ryan, Cornelius, *A Bridge Too Far* (London: Hodder & Stoughton, 1977)

Saunders, Hilary St. George, *The Red Beret: The Story of the Parachute Regiment at War 1940-1945* (London: Michael Joseph, 1950)

Sims, James, *Arnhem Spearhead: A Private Soldier's Story* (London: Imperial War Museum, 1978)

Stainforth, Peter, *Wings of the Wind* (London: Grafton Books, 1988)

Sosabowski, Stanislaw, *Freely I Served* (London: Kimber, 1960)

Terraine, John, *Right of the Line: The Royal Air Force in the European War 1939-1945* (London: Sceptre, 1988)

Thompson, Julian, *Ready For Anything: The Parachute Regiment at War 1940-1982* (London: Weidenfeld & Nicolson, 1989)

Tout, Ken, *Tank! 40 Hours of Battle, August 1944* (London: Sphere, 1986)

Turnbull, Jack & John Hamblett, *The Pegasus Patrol* (Marple: 1994)

Urquhart, Major-General R.E., CB DSO *Arnhem* (London: Cassell, 1958)

Waddy, John, *A Tour of the Arnhem Battlefields* (London: Leo Cooper, 1999)

White, Peter, *With the Jocks: A Soldier's Struggle for Europe 1944-45* (Stroud: Sutton Publishing, 2001)

Wright, Lawrence, *The Wooden Sword: The Untold Story of the Gliders in World War II* (London: Elek, 1967)

Zwarts, Marcel, *German Armoured Units at Arnhem, September 1944* (Hong Kong: Concord Publications, 2001)

GLOSSARY

AA:	anti-aircraft		for CLS, from 6 October 1940
Abteilung:	battalion		
ADC:	aide-de-camp	CLS:	Central Landing School
Airlanded:	British term for units landed by powered aircraft		– original title of the British parachute training school at RAF Ringway
Airlanding:	British term for glider units	CRE:	Commander Royal Engineers
AT:	anti-tank		
Aufklärungs:	reconnaissance, literally 'enlightenment'	Despatcher:	aircraft crewman charged with supervising para- chute or supply drops; jumpmaster in US parl- ance
C-47:	militarised version of the Douglas DC-3 airliner, standard US military trans- port aircraft during WW2		
		DZ:	Drop Zone, for para- chute landings
CIGS:	Chief of the Imperial General Staff	*Fallschirmjäger*:	paratrooper, literally 'parachute hunter'
CLE:	Central Landing Establishment – new title	*Festung*:	fortress

Flak:	anti-aircraft fire; abbreviation of German *FLugzeugAbwehrKanone*
GSO:	General Staff Officer
Hamilcar:	large British glider, capable of lifting a maximum load of 7.8 tons. Possible loads were a single Tetrarch light tank, two Universal carriers, or a 17-pounder AT gun with prime mover
Heeresgruppe:	Army Group
Horsa:	Standard British troop-carrying glider. Capable of carrying twenty-nine passengers plus two pilots, or a variety of heavy equipment including the jeep with or without trailer and various artillery pieces
Heer:	army
Jumpmaster:	see Despatcher
Kampfgruppe:	Battlegroup
KOSB:	King's Own Scottish Borderers
Kriegsmarine:	German navy
Luftwaffe:	German air force from 1933
LZ:	Landing Zone, for gliders or powered aircraft
Oberkommando der Wehrmacht:	Armed Forces High Command
Panzer:	tank or armoured vehicle
Panzerjäger:	literally 'tankhunter', usually applied to self-propelled anti-tank vehicles & units
PIAT:	Projector, Infantry, Anti-Tank. British spring and recoil operated hand-held bomb thrower, with hollow charge projectile.
PTS:	Parachute Training School
RA:	Royal Artillery
RAF:	Royal Air Force
RAOC:	Royal Army Ordnance Corps
RASC:	Royal Army Service Corps
RE:	Royal Engineers
REME:	Royal Electrical and Mechanical Engineers
RTR:	Royal Tank Regiment
Serial:	group of transport aircraft or glider tugs within a larger formation. Usually all the aircraft carrying a specified unit or team for a task
SHAEF:	Supreme Headquarters Allied Expeditionary Force
Stick:	group of parachutists scheduled to exit the aircraft during one run over the DZ; usually the whole complement except on restricted DZs requiring two or more runs
Sturmgeschütz:	assault gun
USAAF:	United States Army Air Force
Waco CG4:	Standard US glider, capable of carrying fifteen passengers. Called the Hadrian in British parlance
Waffen SS:	military arm of the Nazi para-military political organisation

APPENDIX

Waffen SS Ranks with nearest British equivalent:

Oberstgruppenführer	General	*Sturmscharführer*	Warrant Officer
Obergruppenführer	Lieutenant-		1st Class
	General	*Stabsscharführer/*	
Gruppenführer	Major-General	*Hauptscharführer*	Warrant Officer
Brigadeführer	Brigadier		2nd Class
Oberführer	no direct	*Oberscharführer*	Colour/Staff
	equivalent		Sergeant
Standartenführer	Colonel	*Scharführer*	Sergeant
Obersturmbannführer	Lieutenant-	*Unterscharführer*	no equivalent
	Colonel	*Rottenführer*	Corporal
Sturmbannführer	Major	*Sturrmann/*	
Hauptsturmführer	Captain	*SS-Obersaut*	Lance Corporal
Obersturmführer	Lieutenant	*SS-Oberschütze*	no equivalent
Untersturmführer	Second Lieutenant	*SS-Mann*	Private

NOTES

INTRODUCTION

1. figures from Martin Middlebrook, *Arnhem: The Airborne Battle*, p. 439
2. figures from Clay Blair, *Ridgeway's Paratroopers*, p. 349
3. see Middlebrook, pp. 447-448

CHAPTER ONE

1. there was no link here with David Stirling's later unit of the same name; the new title merely reflected the Battalion's proposed function
2. see *The Quarterly Army List –1940 January*

3. see Major Victor Dover, MC, *The Sky Generals*, p.86
4. see Major-General John Frost CB, DSO, MC, *A Drop Too Many* (London: Sphere, 1983), pp.38–39
5. see George Millar, *The Bruneval Raid*, p.26
6. see Lieutenant Colonel T.B.H. Otway DSO, *Airborne Forces* (London: Imperial War Museum, 1990), p.61
7. see Blair, op. cit., p.64
8. see James M. Gavin, *On To Berlin*, p.83
9. see Major-General R.E. Urquhart, CB, DSO, *Arnhem*, p.15
10. see Blair, pp.34–35
11. see Otway, p.62

12. see Brigadier George Chatterton
    DSO OBE, *The Wings of Pegasus*,
    pp.40–42
13. see Eric Morris, *Circles of Hell*, p.58
14. figures cited from Otway, p.125.
    Morris claims there were 126 C-47s;
    see Morris, p.87
15. see Julian Thompson, *Ready For
    Anything*, p.78

CHAPTER TWO

1. This line was repeated as late as 1994;
   see Middlebrook, op. cit., p.21
2. see for example Urquhart, op. cit.,
   p.13
3. see Stanislaw Sosabowski CBE,
   Freely I Served, p.118
4. see Thompson, op. cit., p.89
5. see for example Middlebrook,
   pp.21–22; and Baynes, *Urquhart of
   Arnhem*, p.72
6. see Baynes, pp.72–73
7. see Middlebrook, p.22
8. see PRO *WO 171/592*, 1st Parachute
   Brigade War Diary; *WO 171/594*,
   4th Parachute Brigade War Diary;
   and *WO 171/589*, 1st Airlanding
   Brigade War Diary
9. see for example Sir Mark Henniker,
   An Image of War (London: Leo Cooper,
   1987); cited in Baynes, p.73; and
   Christopher Hibbert, *Arnhem*, p.30
10. see Baynes, p.73
11. ibid., pp.49–50

CHAPTER THREE

1. the memo was written by the
   Brigade's new Brigade Major, Major
   John Fitch; see PRO *WO 171/592*,
   1st Parachute Brigade War Diary

2. see PRO *WO 171/592*, 1st Parachute
   Brigade War Diary
3. see Saunders, *The Red Beret*, p.224
4. see PRO *WO 171/594*, 4th
   Parachute Brigade War Diary
5. see James Sims, *Arnhem Spearhead*
   (London, Imperial War Museum,
   1978), pp.22–25
6. see Frost, op. cit., p.195; and
   Middlebrook, op. cit., p.25
7. see Saunders, p.223; and Frost, p.195
8. see Urquhart, op. cit., p.12
9. see Saunders, pp. 223–224; Frost,
   pp.196–197; and Sims, pp.22–23
10. see Sims, p.23
11. The Polsten was a lightweight, maga-
    zine-fed 20mm automatic cannon
    issued to British glider units. The
    weapon was also issued to infantry
    battalion support companies in the
    52nd (Lowland) Division when that
    formation was redesignated an
    'Airportable' formation in the summer
    of 1944. For an account of the Polsten
    being used in action by elements of
    the latter formation, see Peter White,
    With the Jocks, pp.xiii, 23–26
12. for a participant account, see Dudley
    Anderson, *Three Cheers for the Next
    Man to Die*
13. see Urquhart, p.56

CHAPTER FOUR

1. see George F. Cholewczynski, *Poles
   Apart*, p.47
2. details from interview with
   Lieutenant Colonel Jan Jozef Lorys,
   on 16 June 1998
3. see Cholewczynski, p.47
4. see William F. Buckingham, *The
   Establishment and Initial Development
   of a British Airborne Force, June 1940-*

January 1942 (Ph.D. Thesis, University of Glasgow, 2001), pp.241–257

5. see Jozef Garlinski, *Poland, SOE and the Allies*, p.39

6. see Sosabowski, pp.90–92

7. ibid., p.97

8. for details of the obstacles, see PRO *AIR 39/7*, doc. 78A, report 'Parachute Training School – Polish', from CLE to 70 Group & ACC, dated 27/07/1941

9. see Sosabowski, pp.96–97

10. see Dover, op. cit., pp.144–145

CHAPTER FIVE

1. for details of the kit bag and the Eureka/Rebecca equipment see Otway, Appendix 'D', pp.405–406, and Appendix 'E', pp.410–411

2. see PRO *WO 171/592*, 1st Parachute Brigade War Diary; and PRO *WO 171/594*, 4 Parachute Brigade War Diary

3. for a detailed account of the thinking behind the establishment of the 1 Allied Airborne Army, see Otway, pp.201–206

4. for details, see Blair, op. cit., pp.298–299

5. see Urquhart, op. cit., p.18

6. see Middlebrook, op. cit., p.6; and Geoffrey Powell, *The Devil's Birthday*, p.16

7. the order is reproduced in Urquhart, Appendix II, pp.211–218

8. see Otway, p.214

CHAPTER SIX

1. see Sosabowski, op. cit., p.140

2. the cook analogy is cited in Peter Harclerode, *Arnhem: A Tragedy of Errors*, p.54

3. see Urquhart, op. cit., p.17; and Middlebrook, op. cit., p.8

4. for a detailed discussion of events in this period, see Carlo d'Este, *Decision in Normandy*, pp.467–475

5. for details of the directive and Eisenhower's reaction, see A.D. Harvey, *Arnhem*, pp.26–30. Interestingly, Powell interprets Eisenhower's ambiguous response as giving Montgomery the go-ahead for his grand scheme; see Powell, op. cit., p.26

6. see for example the television documentary *Great Battles of World War II: Arnhem*, broadcast on UK Channel 5 TV on 23 August 2001

7. see Hibbert, op. cit., p.50

8. for a detailed account from the Dutch perspective, see Cornelius Ryan, *A Bridge Too Far*, pp.23–35

9. for details, see Robert J. Kershaw, *It Never Snows in September*, pp.25–28

10. see Ryan, p.93; Powell, op. cit., p.29; and Middlebrook, p.11

11. see Ryan, pp.93–94

12. see Powell, pp.29–30

13. see Urquhart, p.4; and Ryan, pp.93–94

14. see Ryan, p.94; and Harvey, front cover

15. Urquhart's biographer also casts doubt on whether Browning expressed any such reservation, and suggests the bridge too far comment came from Montgomery; see Baynes, op. cit., p.87

16. see A.D. Harvey, *Arnhem*, p.34

17. see PRO *WO 171/393*, 1 Airborne Division War Diary, '1 Airborne Division Planning Intelligence Summary No. 1'

18. see Powell, p.39; and Blair, op. cit.,
     p.320

CHAPTER SEVEN

1.   see Urquhart, op. cit., pp.1–4
2.   quoted in Powell, op. cit., p.30
3.   the 475 (332 RAF and 143 USAAF)
     figure is taken from Middlebrook,
     op. cit., p.75; the remainder from
     Powell, p.35
4.   see Gavin, op. cit., p.150
5.   see Operation Order 'Comet', RAF
     No.38 Group; cited in Powell, p.36
6.   see Ryan, op. cit., pp.199–200
7.   see Harclerode, op. cit., pp.51–52
8.   Middlebrook claims that Gale
     confided his view to the Curator of
     the Airborne Forces Museum, Major
     Geoffrey Norton, in the early 1970s,
     with the proviso that it was not to be
     revealed while any of those involved
     were alive. Norton passed the infor-
     mation on to Middlebrook by a letter
     to a third party on 4 March 1992; see
     Middlebrook, footnote 5, p.18
9.   see Harvey, op. cit., p.45
10. see for example Powell, p.35
11. see for example Harclerode, p.49
12. see Urquhart, p.6
13. see Powell, p.39; and Middlebrook,
     p.114
14. see for example Harvey, pp.43, 45
15. see Kershaw, op. cit., p.43
16. see Urquhart, p.18
17. see Middlebrook, p.165
18. see Powell, p.118
19. figures cited in Middlebrook, p.76
20. ibid., pp.63–64
21. see John Fairley, *Remember Arnhem*,
     pp.26–27
22. see PRO *WO 171/393*, 1 Airborne
     Division War Diary, '1 Airborne

     Division Planning Intelligence
     Summary No.1'
23. see Powell, p.64

CHAPTER EIGHT

1.   in some accounts Gräbner's fore-
     name is given as Paul

CHAPTER NINE

1.   This is an extract from a longer
     account entitled 'The English Silver
     Summer' kindly provided by Mr
     Stone via by personal communica-
     tion on 30 July 2000. I am indebted
     to Mr Stone for permission to
     include his account in this work
2.   see Powell, op. cit., p.51
3.   timings from Ryan, op. cit., p.170;
     and Gavin, op. cit., p.153
4.   details from Powell, pp.51–52
5.   see Ryan, pp.90–191
6.   this section is based on Rapport and
     Northwood, *Rendezvous With Destiny*,
     pp.265–287; and Blair, op. cit., p.331.
     For a vivid participant account of the
     506 Regiment's assault on the flak
     guns at Son see Donald Burgett, *The
     Road to Arnhem*, pp.35–43
7.   see Gavin, p.149
8.   ibid., p.153
9.   see ibid., pp.161–163; and Kershaw,
     op. cit., p.101
10. see Kershaw, pp.43–45
11. see Powell, p.82
12. see Alexander McKee, *The Race for the
     Rhine Bridges*, pp.119–127. I am
     indebted to Mr Colin Williams of the
     TankNet Military Discussion Forum
     for bringing this information to my
     attention

13. see for example John Ellis, *The Sharp End*, p.126
14. see for example John Foley, *Mailed Fist*, pp.17–18
15. see Ken Tout, *Tank!*, p.210
16. I am indebted to Mr Robert Field of the TankNet Military Discussion Forum for bringing this to my attention. The information appears in Tim Saunders, *Hell's Highway (Battleground Europe Series)* (London: Leo Cooper, 2001)

CHAPTER TEN

1. see Middlebrook, op. cit., p.85
2. see Ryan, op. cit., p.180
3. see Urquhart, op. cit., Appendix III, table 'Market Glider Allotment by Lifts', p.219
4. timings all cited in Middlebrook, pp.96–107
5. timings from Kershaw, op. cit., p.73
6. ibid., p.75
7. see Fairley, op. cit., p.41
8. ibid., pp.26–27
9. this was Lieutenant Colonel David Dobie, commanding the 1 Parachute Battalion: see Middlebrook, p.138
10. see Louis Golden, *Echoes From Arnhem*, pp.146–147
11. see Dover, op. cit., p.135

CHAPTER ELEVEN

1. Major Peter Waddy from the 3rd Parachute Battalion should not be confused with Major John Waddy, commanding B Company, 156 Parachute Battalion, 4th Parachute Brigade

2. see interview in the television documentary series *'Great Battles of World War II – Arnhem'*, broadcast on Channel 5 television, 25 August 2001
3. see Middlebrook, op. cit., p.145
4. see Jack Turnbull and John Hamblett, *The Pegasus Patrol*, pp.69–82 figures cited in Middlebrook, pp.287–288

CHAPTER TWELVE

1. see Harclerode, op. cit., p.110
2. see Kershaw, op. cit., p.89
3. ibid., p.115
4. ibid., pp.145–147; and Rapport and Northwood, op. cit., pp.314–318
5. see Rapport and Northwood, pp.360–361 see Kershaw, pp.279–280

CHAPTER THIRTEEN

1. see Kershaw, op. cit., pp.121–122
2. ibid., p.123
3. see Ryan, op. cit., pp.222–223
4. see Blair, op. cit., p.341; for Gavin's version, see Gavin, op. cit., p.175
5. see Powell, op. cit., p.133
6. see Ryan, p.406
7. ibid., p.408
8. see Kershaw, pp.211–214
9. see Ryan, pp.421–422; and Gavin, pp.181–182
10. see Ryan, p.423
11. see Powell, p.163
12. ibid., p.183

CHAPTER FOURTEEN

1. see Kershaw, op. cit., pp.108–111

CHAPTER FIFTEEN

1. Major Powell is the author of *The Devil's Birthday*

CHAPTER SIXTEEN

1. see *AIR 20/2333* 16 SS *Panzer Grenadier & Reserve Battalion Report*. Excerpts are cited in Kershaw, op. cit., p.125
2. see Sims, op. cit., p.57; Kershaw, p. 134; and Marcel Zwarts, *German Armoured Units at Arnhem*, p.50
3. see Middlebrook, op. cit., p.292
4. ibid., p. 288. I am indebted to Mr Niall Cherry for pointing out my ambiguous wording in the original edition.
5. see Sims, p.60; and Middlebrook, p.306
6. see Ryan, op. cit. pp.382–386
7. see Sims, p.74
8. ibid., p.84
9. see Powell, op. cit., p.165
10. figures cited in Middlebrook, p.321
11. see for example Sims, pp.86–87; and Middlebrook, pp.320–321

CHAPTER SEVENTEEN

1. excerpts from this are reproduced in Kershaw, op. cit., pp.205–209
2. figures cited in Middlebrook, op. cit., p.339
3. see for example Hibbert, op. cit., p.140; and Middlebrook, p.340
4. quoted from Otway, op. cit., p.262
5. see Ryan, op. cit., p.253
6. ibid., pp.286, 334–335
7. ibid., p.442
8. see Zwarts, op. cit., p.66

9. figure cited in Middlebrook, p.331
10. it is unclear when these assault pioneers arrived at Deelen, but it might have been on the night of 20–21 September; see Kershaw, p.228
11. ibid., pp.228, 230–232
12. Participants on both sides noted this incident. See Middlebrook, p.344; and Kershaw, pp.239–240
13. see Powell, op. cit., p.170; and Baynes, op. cit. p.126

CHAPTER EIGHTEEN

1. see Kershaw, op. cit., pp.228–230
2. figures cited in Middlebrook, op. cit., p.404
3. see Sosabowski, op. cit., pp.156–158
4. a copy of this signal is held in the Polish Institute and Sikorski Museum, London: see Middlebrook, p.403
5. see Powell, op. cit., p.112; and Ryan, op. cit, pp.388–389
6. the signal is reproduced in full in Ryan, p.444
7. it was found later by Dutch civilians near the demolished railway bridge. The cable was apparently cut by artillery fire rather than by design; see ibid., p.444
8. see Harvey, op. cit., p.126

CHAPTER NINETEEN

1. see Kershaw, op. cit., p.275
2. see for example ibid., p.243; Middlebrook, op. cit., p.352; and Powell, op. cit., p.178
3. see for example Powell, p.178
4. all figs cited in Middlebrook, pp.410, 411, 420

5. see Powell, p.203; and Ryan, op. cit.,
    pp.482–483
6. see Baynes, op. cit., p.142
7. see Powell, p.206
8. ibid., pp.213–214

CHAPTER TWENTY

1. figures cited in Middlebrook, op.
    cit., pp.435–441
2. see Kershaw, op. cit., pp.339–340; and

Ryan, op. cit., p.539
3. see Powell, op. cit., p.229
4. cited in Ryan, p.537
5. figures from Blair, op. cit., p.349
6. see Rapport and Northwood, op.
    cit., pp.400–401; and Middlebrook,
    p.438
7. see Kershaw, pp.316–320
8. see Richard Lamb, *Montgomery in
    Europe*, p.251
9. the report is reproduced in full in
    Cholewczynski, op. cit., pp.312–313

LIST OF ILLUSTRATIONS

15. British and US airborne medics tend wounded. National Archive, USA. Tempus Archive.
16. British M4 Sherman. National Archive, USA.
17. 75mm Pack Howitzer National Archive, USA. Tempus Archive.
18. Men from 1st Airborne Division recovering small-arms ammunition. National Archive, USA. Tempus Archive.
19. Vehicles from 30 Corps crossing the Nijmegen road bridge. National Archive, USA. Tempus Archive.
20. Vehicles from 30 Corps crossing the Nijmegen road bridge. National Archive, USA. Tempus Archive.
21. Street-fighting in the Oosterbeek Cauldron. National Archive, USA. Tempus Archive.
22. Three members of the British army's Film and Photographic Section. National Archive, USA.

Tempus Archive.

MAPS

p.24   1st Parachute Brigade's attack on the Primasole Bridge. Author illustration.
p.81   Operation Market Garden, route and objectives. By kind permission of the Imperial War Museum..
p.88   British 1st Airborne Division's landing zones and objectives. By kind permission of the Imperial War Museum.
p.109   US 101st Airborne Division's landing zones and objectives. Author illustration.
p.115   US 82nd Airborne Division's landing zones and objectives. Author illustration.
p.179   1st Parachute Brigade's attack into Arnhem. Author illustration.
p.197   4th Parachute Brigade's fight north of Oosterbeek. Author illustration.

GENERAL INDEX

MILITARY INDEX

Other Units

319th Glider Field Artillery Battalion 155
320th Glider Field Artillery Battalion 155
321st Field Artillery Battalion 11, 104
376th Parachute Artillery Regiment 112
456th Parachute Field Artillery Battalion 155

UNITED STATES ARMY AIR FORCE

8th Air Force 107
9th Air Force 63, 107
9th Troop Carrier Command 33, 38, 78, 80,
  82, 87
344th Bombardment Group 228
52nd Troop Carrier Wing 38, 40, 79, 106
53rd Troop Carrier Wing 106

ABOUT THE AUTHOR

WILLIAM BUCKINGHAM completed his PhD on the establishment and initial development of a British airborne force. His other books include *D-Day: The First 72 Hours*. He lives in Bishopbriggs near Glasgow.

Praise for *D-Day: The First 72 Hours*

'A compelling narrative... Buckingham offers an alternative view to the usual concentration on the horror of the American landings on Omaha Beach'

The Observer

Lightning Source UK Ltd.
Milton Keynes UK
UKOW06f0832260216

269159UK00007B/109/P